Praise for *Overwhelmed &*

"There are many aha moments in this enlightening boo[k]... work/life balance and time-management strategies that have resulted in our doing more with less for far too long. With a combination of insight, honesty, spirit, and humor, Christine Arylo helps us see and release behaviors that aren't working, and embrace wiser choices. An empowering and smart guidebook for any woman who wants to focus her life on what matters and live in greater harmony and with a sense of purpose."
— **Bobbi Silten**, Managing Director of the Shared Value Initiative and former EVP of Global Talent & Sustainability for Gap Inc.

"For more than three decades, we've been talking about how overwhelmed women are, yet nothing really changes. Finally, here is a manual for women to show us how to design our most productive and purposeful lives in ways that actually lead to our wholeness and wellness. *Overwhelmed & Over It* offers women the wisdom to return to the feminine so they can find their innate power to create a sustainable life plan that inspires what they truly want from life. This book is a powerful and transformational blueprint for change!"
— **Kristine Carlson**, *New York Times* bestselling author of *Don't Sweat the Small Stuff for Women*

"In this very accessible book, Christine Arylo has given us a true gift. Affirming wisdom over information, she illuminates a path to liberation not just from burnout itself, but from the structures, beliefs, and paradigms that create and drive it. Embracing the power of self-transformation as the ultimate driver of social and systemic change and interweaving yogic science, feminine wisdom, and corporate know-how, Arylo provides a *whole-being* approach that goes beyond typical self-care directives."
— **Leisl M. Bryant**, PhD, ABPP, board-certified psychologist

"As an executive who spent too many years overworking and overdoing, I've changed how I view and live my life by following the grounded guidance Christine Arylo teaches. I am now designing my life to fit my deeper goals and natural flow. Her breakthrough approach to overwhelm and to living and working differently has not only transformed my life but has also positively impacted the lives of those around me, from my family to my team at work. Christine shows us the way to live a plentiful and fulfilling life without the stress and burnout that are endemic in the world today."
— **Barbara Fagan-Smith**, CEO, ROI Communication and Living ROI

"As I read this book, I felt as though I had a wise mentor guiding me down the path to a richer, fuller, and more authentic life. Now, when I find myself feeling as though I'm bearing the weight of my organization, teams, or family, the principles and practices in this book are my support bolster to do things differently. I'm eternally

grateful for Christine's profound and practical life guidance and leadership wisdom. Her fierce and compassionate voice called me home to my heart."
— **Cheryl Ann Shartle**, Vice President of Human Resources, Columbiana Foods, Inc.

"This book speaks to the truth we need women and girls to know and trust: that their power as leaders, mothers, partners, and humans comes from their compassionate, courageous, and wise hearts. Christine melds her deep wisdom, visionary structures, and practices into a graceful process to help us discover our unique part, path, and power — just in time. I'm gifting this brilliant book to every woman I treasure in my life!" — **Laura Berland**, Executive Director, Center for Compassionate Leadership

"Both practical and mystical, Christine guides the future of the feminine with a clear voice and a devoted heart. Give this book to your women friends, and give it to yourself. As a woman who has always worked outside the 'systems' as an artist, an entrepreneur, and a community leader, I still find myself in situations where what I am doing, even though I love it, is not sustainable. This book offers a solution I can work with." — **Shiloh Sophia**, founder of MUSEA: Intentional Creativity®

"Liberated, energized, and filled with hope! That's how I felt after reading *Overwhelmed & Over It*. Blending feminine, yogic, and earth wisdom and down-to-earth practices for daily life, this gem offers women an enlightened path for how to work, live, and manifest." — **Renée Peterson Trudeau**, speaker and author of *The Mother's Guide to Self-Renewal* and *Nurturing the Soul of Your Family*

"For years women have been striving and driving with so much effort to create greatness in their lives and the world. Yet instead of feeling successful and supported, too often we are left feeling like we don't have enough, aren't doing enough, and need to keep doing and making more. Christine Arylo has really nailed it here by giving us the 'how' to *finally* step out of these generational suffering and self-sacrificing patterns so we can realize a life that reflects our true dreams and desires. A must-read!"
— **Julie Murphy**, CFP, founder of JMC Wealth Management, wealth adviser, and author of *Awaken Your Wealth*

"Christine Arylo offers a path for women to show up as powerful forces in their lives and the world, without having to sacrifice their wellness, wholeness, and relationships to make a difference or achieve success. This is a guidebook for creating sustainable success — first for ourselves and then for our world — that is full of deep feminine wisdom, fierce truth, and practical superpowers. An essential, enlightening, and empowering read for women globally." — **Nilima Bhat**, coauthor of *Shakti Leadership* and founder-director of the Shakti Fellowship

Overwhelmed & Over It

Overwhelmed & Over It

Embrace Your Power to Stay CENTERED & SUSTAINED in a Chaotic World

CHRISTINE ARYLO

New World Library
Novato, California

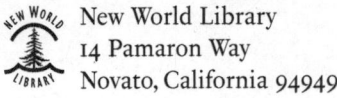
New World Library
14 Pamaron Way
Novato, California 94949

Copyright © 2020 by Christine Arylo

All rights reserved. This book may not be reproduced in whole or in part, stored in a retrieval system, or transmitted in any form or by any means — electronic, mechanical, or other — without written permission from the publisher, except by a reviewer, who may quote brief passages in a review.

Illustrations by Katherine Torrini
Text design by Tona Pearce Myers

Library of Congress Cataloging-in-Publication Data

Names: Arylo, Christine, date, author.
Title: Overwhelmed and over it : embrace your power to stay centered and sustained in a chaotic world / Christine Arylo.
Description: Novato, California : New World Library, [2020] | Includes bibliographical references. | Summary: "A former corporate executive examines why many working women feel exhausted and overwhelmed as they try to balance the competing demands of career and family. The author diagnoses the roots of the problem and proposes pragmatic methods to integrate work, relationships, health, and spirituality into a harmonious whole."
 -- Provided by publisher.
Identifiers: LCCN 2020025618 (print) | LCCN 2020025619 (ebook) | ISBN 9781608686773 (paperback) | ISBN 9781608686780 (epub)
Subjects: LCSH: Work-life balance. | Work and family. | Women--Job stress. | Self-realization in women.
Classification: LCC HD4904.25 .A758 2020 (print) | LCC HD4904.25 (ebook) | DDC 650.1082--dc23
LC record available at https://lccn.loc.gov/2020025618
LC ebook record available at https://lccn.loc.gov/2020025619

First printing, October 2020
ISBN 978-1-60868-677-3
Ebook ISBN 978-1-60868-678-0
Printed in Canada on 100% postconsumer-waste recycled paper

New World Library is proud to be a Gold Certified Environmentally Responsible Publisher. Publisher certification awarded by Green Press Initiative.

10   9   8   7   6   5   4   3   2   1

*For Bonnie: may your spirit and light continue
to open hearts through the words written in these pages.*

*For all women who've felt the burden of too much with too little:
may we find the courage, power, and wisdom to create
a different way, for ourselves and the generations to come.*

*For the planet and her people: may we be free,
may we know peace, may we trust that choosing
the path of harmony will always lead us to a better world.*

Contents

Preface	*It's Not Your Fault You Feel Overwhelmed and Overstretched*		xi
Introduction	*Awaken Your Fierce Feminine Heart and Take a Stand for Yourself*		1

Part One: LIBERATE YOUR SUCCESS

Chapter 1	RELEASE:	Do, Be, and Have It All	
	EMBRACE:	Choose What's Right for You	25
Chapter 2	RELEASE:	Maintain Work/Life Balance	
	EMBRACE:	Cultivate Harmony	43
Daring Act of Liberation #1: Give Your Life a Harmony Adjustment			58

Part Two: LIBERATE YOUR LIFE FORCE

Chapter 3	RELEASE:	Drain Your Energy, Get Sick or Burn Out, Then Refill	
	EMBRACE:	Cultivate and Retain Your Life Force, Daily	69
Chapter 4	RELEASE:	Start the Day Harried and Hacked	
	EMBRACE:	Start the Day Connected and Protected	91
Chapter 5	RELEASE:	Manage Stress	
	EMBRACE:	Release Stress	107
Daring Act of Liberation #2: Bookend Your Days			122

Part Three: LIBERATE YOUR HEART

Chapter 6	RELEASE:	It's Better to Give *Than* Receive	
	EMBRACE:	It's Better to Give *And* Receive	131
Chapter 7	RELEASE:	Work Hard to Succeed	
	EMBRACE:	Work Wise to Thrive	145
Chapter 8	RELEASE:	Do It on My Own	
	EMBRACE:	Receive Support and Sisterhood	165

Daring Act of Liberation #3: Get Your Giving and Receiving into Harmony — 183

Part Four: LIBERATE YOUR TIME

Chapter 9	RELEASE:	Make and Find More Time	
	EMBRACE:	Create and Claim Space	197
Chapter 10	RELEASE:	Make It All Happen Now	
	EMBRACE:	Focus on What Matters	220
Chapter 11	RELEASE:	Push. Force. Strive.	
	EMBRACE:	Pause. Flow. Pace.	244

Daring Act of Liberation #4: Reset Your Weekly Rhythm — 265

Part Five: LIBERATE YOUR POWER

Chapter 12	RELEASE:	Take It All On	
	EMBRACE:	Stay Focused on My Part	277

Daring Act of Liberation #5: Embrace Your Power to Release the Pressure — 292

Conclusion	*Welcome to the Sisterhood of Wise Women Choosing to Do It Differently*	301
Appendix 1	*Self-Sustainability Stand Summary*	307
Appendix 2	*Gather Your People: Use This Book to Create Real Connection, Conversation, and Change*	311
Acknowledgments		313
Notes		317
About the Author		322
Ways to Connect and Go Deeper		324

Preface

It's Not Your Fault You Feel Overwhelmed and Overstretched

Stretched beyond capacity. Struggling to get it all done. Sacrificing yourself to take care of everything and everyone else. Not just for a moment or a season but as a consistent cycle you cannot seem to free yourself from. Sound familiar?

Welcome to the sisterhood of women who have become so strong and self-sufficient that we've come to accept the frenzied, overfilled, fast pace at which we work and live as "normal." We do what we must in order to survive and succeed. And because you and I are so darn capable, we pull it off — for a time. But then there comes the moment when the pressure and pace are too much, even for women like us. We crash down or lash out. Like a keg pumped with pressure, spout flowing out for far too long, we have run dry. We are tapped. Burned-out. Nothing more to give but with so much more still to do, and no one else but us to do it.

Perhaps you have found yourself in a stream of spontaneous tears that won't stop flowing? In the throes of what I have come to call the "Superwoman Sob." My first Superwoman Sob erupted in a hotel bathroom one tar-melting hot August afternoon in Texas. If you had been there, you would have found me sitting on the toilet-seat lid, my face cupped in my hands, bent over with tears streaming down my face and pangs of despair pulsing through my heart.

I had been working tirelessly to promote my first book. After four years of writing it, and thirty-three years of living it, I had a burning desire to get this labor of love into the world. In one way, I had reached some significant milestones. I had left the safety of a consistent corporate paycheck to follow my passion and purpose. I was a published author. I had achieved success. But at a cost.

I was straddling two jobs to pay for it all — the work I loved as a writer, transformational coach, and speaker that was not yet enough to support me, and the work as a consultant, which was paying my bills and funding the book tour. After four months of keeping up the pace of working ten-plus hours a day; draining my savings to keep it all going; and juggling a marriage, a mortgage, and my own health, I was depleted. And even worse, I felt defeated. I was not having the impact I desired. Being on television looks glamorous, but the reality was that flying from city to city to spend five minutes talking about celebrity breakups was not changing lives or leading to the deeper conversations I believed we needed to be having as women. It all felt empty, and so did I.

I wasn't being nourished by working this way, nor was I being sustained financially. I believed if I just worked *harder*, I could make it all happen, and something would change.

There is often a tipping point or a triggering moment that sets off our Superwoman Sobs. What have been some of yours? Can you recall the tipping points that opened the floodgates of emotion and tears, heard or silent? For me, it was a loving photo sent via text from my life partner, Noah. He was standing with our Siberian husky at our home in California in a garden overflowing with sunflowers we had planted together earlier that spring. A dream we had achieved together. As I looked at the photo, I saw the home and partnership that truly nourished me staring back at me. So much love and beauty and support *there*, yet I was trapped in an unimpressive air-conditioned hotel room, surrounded by parking lots, 1,700 miles from home, alone, feeling completely bankrupt inside.

Like a brick of self-honesty, it hit me. I realized that I was the one who had created this unsustainable, busy, overworking reality in which, in order to achieve professional success, financial stability, and my mission to empower and support women and girls, I had to sacrifice my needs as a human and desires as a woman. So there on the toilet seat, I just let the tears flow, during my first, but not my last, Superwoman Sob.

Maybe you can relate? While the details may differ, recall the times when the pressure was too much, even for you. And know you are not alone. If honest, most of us would admit our bodies are bone-tired, our minds frazzled, our spirits weary, and our hearts heavy. We feel unsupported, stretched too thin, and like we're not getting what we need, not because we are weak or doing something wrong but because the pressure and expectations are too much. Our strategy has been to work harder and do more just to keep up. We've even come to accept anxiety, hormonal imbalances, whacked-out thyroids, depression, chronic fatigue, burnout, and exhaustion as normal, just what happens. And we are setting up our children and the generations to come for the same unsustainable, unhealthy racetrack reality.

The real travesty is that we *know* this, yet with all the talk about women's empowerment, we don't stand up, speak up, and say:

> *"This way of working isn't working.*
> *And it has to change now!"*

Instead, as the tears subside and the pressure releases, our minds calm, and we allow ourselves to play out fantasies of how, just maybe, we could create a less stressful reality. We consider quitting our jobs and moving to where the cost of living is less. We imagine vacating our lives to take a month off and head to a beach or foreign country to unplug. We let all kinds of options, which we will never do, run through our minds just to escape the reality that comes rushing in: *I can't run away from my life. This is my life. And there is no one to take care of all this stuff except me.*

So, we sigh deeply and promise to do a better job at "finding balance." We shake off our Superwoman Sob and charge back into this unsustainable reality, just to repeat the overwhelm, burnout, and self-sacrificing patterns all over again.

We women have become so resilient that we've become too tolerant.

We do our best to make healthy choices. We earnestly attempt re-generating activities like meditating, going to yoga classes, cleansing, or taking technology-free weekends. But the reality is that many of us are just holding on, treading water, praying we don't sink and go under.

I want you to know that it's not for lack of "information" that you haven't been able to find the solutions to the overwhelm you feel. The truth is, you *know* a lot: Get good sleep. Eat well. Exercise. Limit sugar and screen time. Practice mindfulness.

You don't need more lists of information; what we all need is access to deeper wisdom, the kind that has the power to lead us to lasting personal and social transformation. We need the space to connect more deeply with ourselves to discern what is right and true. And we need connection with other conscious women to give us the courage and clarity to do things differently. Which is why instead of filling your head with more tips, life hacks, and surface-level fixes that add to an already-full to-do list and just give you enough oomph to keep your head above water, I want to get real with you. I want to share with you, heart-to-heart, the wisdom it's taken me over a decade to discover:

> *It's not your fault you feel so stretched and overwhelmed.*
> *The systems you work and live in were built for burnout.*
>
> *It's not for lack of desire, intelligence, or effort*
> *that you struggle to create supportive realities*

in which you feel both successful and sustained.
How you've been trained and expected to work, lead,
and succeed is not the way women —
or humans in general — naturally operate and create best.

You haven't been given the wisdom or superpowers
you need to thrive in intense and changing times.
Repeat. It's not your fault.

When I share this with a room full of women, I often feel like the doors are going to swing open from the pressure-release gale that comes from each woman freeing herself from the self-judgment. You can feel the energy in the room lighten as each woman starts to see how she's not the only one striving to meet unrealistic goals, timelines, and markers of success, or the unattainable nirvana of work/life balance. Now I share that same truth with you.

Exhale with me now.
Really, just try it.

Exhale all that pressure you have been carrying around like a twenty-five-pound sack of judgment against yourself. The guilt, expectations, obligations, criticisms, comparisons, and ideals of what you should have done, accomplished, or figured out by now. All the ways in which you deem you are not measuring up, keeping up, or doing enough. The cause of the shoulder knots, jaw clenching, anxiety, mental fogginess, depression, despair, and exhaustion. It's heavy!

Here's what I want you to know right now. You are not making this up. You are not being too sensitive. You are not whining. You haven't done anything wrong. And the answer is not to keep pushing and working harder or doing and giving more. Drop the sack of self-judgment by saying to yourself:

"It's not my fault."

And then imagine this. Instead of feeling like it's all up to you and you are the only one who hasn't figured out how to manage and balance it all, imagine standing in a room of thousands of women who feel just like you. Overworked, overwhelmed, and over it. And then consider embracing this: if you truly want to thrive, then you have to do this differently. The current norms for how we work and operate as a society are not something you want to lean into.

While it's not your fault your current reality is what it is, you are the only one with the power to change it.

Overwhelmed & Over It is a call and an invitation to you and women around the world to liberate ourselves from the self-sacrifice and burnout, first. Then, by tapping into our feminine wisdom and our power of influence, we make shifts happen in the systems we work, lead, and live in, together. We:

1. Stop tolerating this way of working and living as *normal* and *acceptable*.
2. Stop trying *to cure the symptoms*, and instead get to *the root of the systems* that keep us trapped in the burnout cycle and overwhelm.
3. Start putting *wellness*, *sustainability*, *wholeness*, and *real wealth* at the core of our own lives, not as an afterthought but as a requirement for how our jobs, roles, organizations, and lifestyles are designed.
4. Start *asking courageous questions* and *questioning* what does not feel right or good, unleashing our feminine wisdom to speak and challenge the status quo.
5. Wield our power as women to *birth and design* new ways of working, relating, and living that support and sustain people and the planet.

To liberate means "to free (a group or individual) from social or economic constraints or discrimination, especially arising from traditional role expectations or bias." I love the power embedded in the energy of the word *liberate*. You and I can consciously apply this power to free ourselves, individually and collectively, of the insanity that has become normality in our current culture. I believe with all my heart that together we can achieve powerful results in our lifetimes, for our children and the causes and concerns that matter most to us, but only if we first create realities and ways of working and living that sustain us.

Just as Wonder Woman had her golden lasso and superpowers, you and I need access to more powerful wisdom, practices, and tools in order to maintain a centered presence amid the swirl of the world and be the leaders we were born to be at this time. Leadership is not a position given or attained — it's a choice one embraces — and it starts with how you show up and make choices within all aspects of your life. If we join together collectively to conjure up the clarity, confidence, and courage to do things differently within our own lives first and then within our families and the organizations and communities where we live and work, that would be enough to change this world.

We are that powerful.

You are that powerful.

I am glad we have found each other.

I look forward to this journey with you.

Welcome to the sisterhood of wise women,

choosing to do it differently.

Introduction

Awaken Your Fierce Feminine Heart and Take a Stand for Yourself

The first step in changing what's not working for you is *awareness* — becoming conscious of what you are currently blind to. You simply cannot change what you cannot see. But when you do see what was previously hidden, you gain the power to change it.

When you can see both the *systemically created* and the *self-generated* roots of overwhelm, burnout, and self-sacrifice, you become empowered to make changes not previously available to you. In this book we will open up your eyes to both.

The *systemically created* roots are tied to the *collective and cultural systems* for how we work, educate, relate, and operate, as a society and within our families, communities, and organizations. Ignorant that we could do things differently, we ignore our inner knowing by not questioning what doesn't feel good or right inside. We accept things as normal, as just "how it is." As you read on, you'll see that what we've deemed *normal* for how we work, live, and succeed as a collective world is anything but *natural*.

The *self-generated roots* stem from what I think of as your personal "internal operating system." Similar to how a computer has an operating system that runs its programs and drives its functionality, you have your own version of a motherboard chock-full of programs that drive your emotions, thoughts, and choices. Your internal operating system drives how you design your life, how you approach your work, and how you define and experience success. It dictates how you give and receive in relationships, relate to money, and operate in the face of all the demands and within the diverse realms of your life. The problem is, the programs within you are much more like blueprints for burnout than imprints for self-sustainability and real success.

7 Roots of Overwhelm, Burnout, and Self-Sacrifice

What follows are seven of the root causes at the core of the burnout cycles, self-sacrificing choices, and unsustainable realities women like us haven't been able to free ourselves from — yet. Read each with the intention of increasing both your *systemic awareness* and your *self-awareness*. Consider how each has affected your life. Then we'll illuminate where to find the power to start making changes.

Root 1: The systems we work and live in were built for burnout, not to support us to thrive.

Designed during an era when profit and productivity were king, our current systems lack human sustainability and wellness at their core. Which is why no matter how hard you personally try to maintain sustainability and wellness, you can't.

Take a closer look at the current business, financial, educational, health-care, and government systems and consider the consciousness of the culture and the people when these systems were designed. Created to fuel an industrial revolution and ignite an information age that exploded us into this age of technology, the core intention was not about supporting and sustaining women, families, humanity, or the planet. These systems were designed with a focus on maximizing productivity and profit; minting workers to manufacture more stuff; and training leaders to grow bigger and faster so they could succeed in a world rooted in competition, domination, accumulation, and consumption. Humans were and still are referred to as "resources."

And in the current collective consciousness, resources are things to be utilized and monetized for short-term gains, not nurtured and protected for long-term sustainability.

Now that may sound sinister. And while you and I both know there have been sinister acts that have exploited people and planet, I don't think there was a clandestine meeting headed up by a Dr. Evil–like dude with the agenda to dominate humans for personal gain. If we look back, we can see both the positive and negative impact of what the former consciousness created — infrastructure, transportation, technology, and advancement in medicine and science. We can't really know if we could have evolved differently as a society. Maybe the pace at which all this growth occurred, and the choices made, was how it had to happen to bring us to where we stand now. Maybe not. We'll never know.

But if you look at the present state of humanity and the planet, and into the future — really look — this knowing becomes crystal clear: *the consciousness that got us here cannot take us to what we need now*. A society and market system that values domination, accumulation, and consumption, where the measures of success are rooted in profit and productivity instead of people and planet, is just not sustainable. "Grow, grow, go, go, more, more, faster, faster" is causing us all — and the planet — to burn out just in order to keep up. And things need to change, now. We need to do things differently.

Now do not go into overwhelm as I start to peel the film off how big a systemic issue we have. Or start feeling like, *Oh great, more I have to do! How am I going to change that? I can barely manage my life now.* I don't want you to take this on or do anything right now. I just want you to become more *aware*.

Root 2: We accept the ways we work and live as how things have to be. But humans made the systems, which means we have the power to change them.

Clarissa Pinkola Estés, PhD, author of *Women Who Run with the Wolves*, refers to our collective systems as the *overculture*: "the dominant and often power-mad culture we try to navigate without being crushed or over-assimilated into." Sound familiar?

The truth is, women didn't create the current systems. *We acclimated* to survive within them, because we had to. In the 1970s and '80s, when women entered the workforce in full force, we became men in black suits, warriors armoring up, ceiling breakers, and fighters. We put on shoulder pads and bow ties to look like men. We became tough on the outside to play with the boys. We suppressed our feminine presence. We stepped on and over our sisters to succeed in the patriarchal hierarchy. These were acts of survival.

We didn't have the mass of women in positions of authority or influence even a decade ago or the consciousness to do things differently. We had to play by the rules that were set for us. As a result, we have come to accept how we work and live as "normal," even if intuitively we know it's unhealthy and unnecessary. Here are just a few examples that point to how insane our way of working and living has become:

- For doctors in residence, laws require working a *maximum* of eighty hours a week, with no shift exceeding twenty-eight hours. Awake for twenty-eight hours? That's like working thirteen hours a day, six days a week, for four years. For the people in charge of our physical health, and lives! Is this even humane or safe?
- Forty-one percent of teachers leave the profession in the first five years, citing burnout stemming from the volume of work, lack of enough time to do the work, and inadequate resources. I would add "and insufficient financial compensation." The people responsible for educating our children — those we give birth to and love — are some of the most underresourced, undersupported, and underpaid. What does that say about what we value as a society?
- Think it's better to work for yourself? Seventy-two percent of entrepreneurs report mental health concerns, and

entrepreneurs are thirty percent more likely to experience depression than the general public.
- Maybe just get a job with less responsibility or that's mentally less taxing? Employees in packing and shipping facilities for some large internet-based retailers have been forced to wear bracelets around their wrists to monitor their productivity, driving some to pee in bottles so they don't get docked for time going to the bathroom. Really.

We could spend the rest of the book talking about how the policies of government and the organizations we work for still do not support women, or the reality of families, but I think you get the picture. But here's just one more point that really drives home just how not supportive our systems are. Of the 193 countries in the United Nations, 185 have national paid-leave laws. Those that don't are Papua New Guinea, Suriname, a few small South Pacific island states — and the United States. The United States is the only high-income country that doesn't provide paid maternity leave, nationally. While other countries do better in this area, I think it's safe to say that the unsustainability we are experiencing is global.

This is just the tip of a long list of the insanity we've come to accept, results of an overculture that just keeps moving faster, in the name of "progress." The pressure coming from this overculture is real — housing prices skyrocketing, the cost of living increasing by double digits, exorbitant tuition for private education just to give our kids a better future. This all makes it so we must work more and earn more money, just to keep afloat. No wonder we don't have the energy to question why our society and world is working this way.

We've been assimilating for so long that, like goldfish living in a fishbowl, we don't realize we aren't living free. Lost in the frenzy of trying to survive, we forget that other worlds — oceans of possibility — outside the fishbowl exist. And then one day, we go belly-up from all the stress and self-sacrifice. And you know what happens? We get flushed down the toilet and replaced by another fish that looks just like us and moves into our plastic castle, and the overculture continues without us. And for what, really?

We do not have to live and work this way. Humans made every nonnatural system on the planet. Think about all the systems — the financial and consumer markets, education, corporations, government, health care, agriculture, religious institutions, and so on. These are all *human designed*. Which means humans — of which you, and I, are one — have the power to design and create something new. Just take that in. We can vision and create the new systems and ways of working and living.

Now, here's the empowering wisdom that honestly keeps me motivated to continue showing up and waking up. Systemic change can only start in one place, within yourself. Which, as it turns out, is where you have 100 percent of the control and power. If every woman knew this and embraced her power of systemic transformation through self-transformation, we'd bring about a tidal wave of awakening that would catalyze and change things in potent ways.

Root 3: Your personal "internal operating system" is programmed to work hard, take it all on, and sacrifice your personal needs. Even if you want to change, your internal wiring is set against it.

Let's be honest. Even if someone said you could stop working so hard or doing so much tomorrow, you would just find another way to exhaust yourself and fill up your schedule. It has been imprinted into you.

You would go find another fishbowl or create one of your own. I see this often with women who change jobs and organizations or who start their own gig, thinking it's their ticket to sanity. But in reality, it's the same game, different name. They just design another way of working and living that enslaves and exhausts them. Maybe the prison cell is prettier, is bigger, or has more amenities, but they still get trapped in the same crazy pace and race.

Why? Because if you do not elevate the consciousness within you, the reality on the outside cannot change.

Your internal operating system is deeply affected by the environments you grew up in; were educated within; and work, live, and interact in now. Which means you've got a boatload of programming for self-sacrifice and overwhelm, such as:

> "I have to work hard to succeed."
> "Taking care of my needs is selfish."
> "If I don't do it, no one else will."
> "I can't rest until all the work is done."

These internal programs are not just *beliefs* in your mind; they are deeply ingrained *imprints* in your being and body. This is why even if you really want to change, you resist. These imprints are embedded into your emotional, physical, and energetic bodies and your mind. Which is why you cannot mentally think, plan, strategize, or hack your way out of burnout and self-sacrifice. These imprints form your thoughts, feelings, and cellular-body memories. They drive you to unconsciously make choices that cause you to take on too much, work too hard, and give too much — which, as it turns out, your human body was not built for.

Root 4: Your nervous system has not been conditioned to handle the amount of information coming at you, nor the accelerating pace and intensity of today's world, so you keep short-circuiting.

The yogis predicted we would come to this period when the human body would not be prepared to handle the technological advances, the onslaught of information, and the increased input and resulting pace of life. They warned that the effects of technology would create living and working environments that our nervous and glandular systems were not strong enough to cope with, sending us into emotional, mental, and physical overwhelm. In a lecture in 1995, before the advent of addictive technology like social media and handheld smartphones, Yogi Bhajan, PhD, who brought Kundalini yoga (which I practice and teach) to the West, shared:

> This new pressure on the mind has only just begun. We are sensing the first ripples of a vast tidal wave of pressure on humanity....
>
> The massive overload of information we will all be subjected to destroys the balance of the mind and creates conditions of unimaginable disorientation....
>
> At first people will try to deal with this gap with increased electronic technology. We will attempt to use more sophisticated devices, software, even special intelligent helpers to sort the flood of information....
>
> We do not need new choices. We are flooded with choices. We need an elevated capacity to make choices. We do not need more information. We need the wisdom to use all the information.

Just as the earth can't handle the pace at which we are sucking out its resources, we can't handle the pace at which we are expected to operate. This doesn't make us weak. It makes us human.

You and I are not machines. We are human beings. We would be foolish to keep leading our lives and running our organizations and families believing that the amount of information and stimulation is not having a harmful impact on us all — adults and children — in ways we don't see and have not been trained to deal with. We need to wake up and really look at what technology is doing to our brains and bodies. We need to stop blindly accepting the acceleration and integration of technology as inherently healthy and good for people and the planet. We'd be plain ignorant to keep trying to manage the symptoms of the information and technology overwhelm with the same old strategies.

Root 5: The solutions and strategies we've been taught to deal with overwhelm, stress, and burnout are insufficient. We haven't been taught the wisdom or tools we need to thrive in these intense times.

You wouldn't expect a ten-year-old computer to handle the speed and volume required to operate in the current technological reality. It would keep crashing, no matter how many times you rebooted it. If you keep trying to apply the same old equations for success and approaches to self-care and stress management, you will keep crashing, too.

Our traditional job and educational training, as well as the plethora of well-meaning self-care tips, has given us surface strategies to cope, not the wisdom to rise out of the overculture or to cultivate the resilience needed to thrive. The conventional solutions help you *manage* your work and life so you can survive. But they do not possess the power to *elevate* you into a different consciousness from which you can achieve your goals and dreams without burning out. We need new equations, strategies, and focuses that have our sustainability and a much healthier, more harmonious definition of success at the core.

Root 6: We've come to value and embody the distorted qualities of strength and definitions of success perpetuated by the overculture, and discount and dismiss our innate feminine wisdom and power.

As women who have had to assimilate into societal systems, we have taken on some of the traits valued in this domination- and accumulation-driven culture that go against our nature as women. Like racehorses bred to be achievers, we've been conditioned to drive, compete, and push. Bred to prize productivity over pausing and action over contemplation, we've learned to value *doing* over *being* and trust logic and scientific fact over our intuitive knowing. Which is why even if you want to slow down or do manage to create space to rest, you feel guilty, lazy, or like you should be doing something. Did you ever wonder why you feel more comfortable telling someone who asks how you are doing, "I have been so busy!" than "I have been resting"?

We've been trained to work like an arrow pointed straight up — set for exponential growth — to climb ladders and maximize profit, which never seems to get us to a destination where we can rest and receive. Working this linear way is not your first instinct or first nature. It's a learned behavior and a distorted way of thinking and succeeding.

Women work best in ebbs and flows, in cycles, like the natural world. Like a spiral, where things naturally grow over time and the momentum of the organic growth creates the energy, versus us having to expend all our effort pushing. Did you ever consider that if Mother Nature has survived and thrived for billions of years, it might be wiser to emulate her, rather than the human-made market system, with respect to how we work; think about success; and go about designing our lives, systems, and world?

Until we elevate our internal value systems as women; embrace our *feminine* wisdom and power; and begin to value pausing as much as productivity, spaciousness over being busy, and our intuition as much as the intellect, we won't break free from this learned behavior that makes us work unnaturally, and harder.

Root 7: The reasons we sacrifice and sabotage ourselves are rooted in our hearts — where the feelings and fears we'd rather not experience live.

We are fine with *talking* about the overwhelm, burnout, and pressure. We'll participate in a conversation about work/life balance or listen to a litany of mindfulness tips. But to go where real change happens? No way! Go into our hearts, where the unconscious fears — of everything falling apart, not having enough, not being needed or valued — have become imprints within our internal operating systems silently running our choices, thoughts, and emotions? Heck, we don't want to admit to ourselves that we even have these fears! We'd rather stay where we can be in control. We hide in our minds, skim the surface, and make small changes to get by.

But if those routes worked, you wouldn't be here with me now, looking for something different, and deeper.

Your heart, much more than your head, drives your choices about how you give your time, energy, care, and resources. The thoughts in your mind follow the feelings in your heart. While understanding brain science and mindfulness is valuable, if you don't possess the awareness of how your *heart* functions — emotionally, intuitively, and spiritually — and the deeper imprints driving you, then your choices are much more likely to come from your weaknesses, wounds, and fears than your innate strength and wisdom.

We just don't link what's happening in our hearts to the busyness, burnout, and pressure we experience in our daily lives. And until we do, nothing can really change.

Embrace the Power of Your Fierce Feminine Heart

As I started to wake up and see the root reasons underneath the burnout, anxiety, pressure, dis-ease, and self-judgment we feel, something inside me ignited. Some deep, primal part turned on. Like a fierce mountain lion protecting her young, I wanted to stand up and roar for all of us, "This is *not* okay with me! We cannot keep sacrificing ourselves for profit, productivity, or other people's well-being. There has to be a different way."

I've come to call this part that awakens within a woman our "fierce feminine heart." It's the part of you that empowers you to speak up and take a stand when things don't feel right, even if everyone else seems to be going along with the status quo. It's the courageous and curious part that calls you to seek a different way. It's the wise part that will lead you to find the path. It's the part full of the perseverance and commitment you need to keep going on the days you'd rather not get out of bed. It's the fuel that keeps your inner faith lit that something more is possible.

Your heart is your power center. The path to liberating yourself out of the ways of working and living that lead to burnout and self-sacrifice is through your heart, not your head. Liberation is an act of love; freedom always emanates from the heart. Think of any significant elevation in consciousness in human history — women's right to vote, civil rights, the independence of colonized countries. The catalyst always rises up through the human heart. Revolutionary change takes courage, compassion, and commitment to do things differently. Your personal liberation and elevation will be no different.

When my fierce feminine heart woke up to the root reasons why I kept getting trapped in these unsustainable realities, I knew I *had* to go deeper. For two decades, I had tried emulating and applying the models for leadership, productivity, happiness, and success I had been taught — first in my career working for others and then as a social-impact entrepreneur. Filled with passion to make a difference, and perspectives from a top-business-school MBA, I worked *hard* to pursue success and security and make a meaningful difference.

Then somewhere in my thirties, I saw the cycle of endless striving and giving I was stuck in, which drove me to continually sacrifice my needs and wellness for a project, goal, vision, greater good, person, team, [fill in the blank]. I finally saw what I'd previously been blind to — the models for success and how to structure our lives, organizations, and societies were not created by or for women. Nor were they created to support sustainability — mine, yours, the planet's, or humanity's overall. Something within me told me if I kept working and managing my life, career, business, and family this way, I was going to get sick.

Awakened to the reality that I had been imprinted with such an unsustainable model for success, I turned my focus to finding a different way that could empower us to be successful in achieving our goals — personally and professionally — in a manner that sustains us on all levels: physically, mentally, emotionally, spiritually, financially, and relationally. A new reality for success — one that by its nature cultivates wholeness and wellness.

This led me down a path of deep study and experimentation in what's known as a "wisdom tradition" — specifically, in yogic science, sacred feminine, and indigenous earth teachings, none of which had been talked about in my traditional education or on-the-job training.

In fact, as I learned more *wisdom*, I began to suspect that perhaps there was a reason for the exclusion of this deeper knowledge.

The more I embraced and embodied the "new" perspectives and practices that were really thousands of years old, the more I became empowered to make conscious, wise choices, for myself, others, and the organizations I worked with and created. I became more courageous in speaking up for what didn't seem right for me, other people, or the planet. I became freer to design a life and a path to professional and personal success that worked for me, even when it defied conventional wisdom and flew in the face of what everyone else was doing.

In the process of my exploration, I found I had a gift for translating deep wisdom into practical "superpowers" for truly succeeding and thriving in these intense, changing times. Not as a mental construct or spiritual ideal but as an embodied reality. I've come to embrace this power as how my intellectual-MBA self and my intuitive-mystic self come together to find and create new ways of working and leading that empower us as women to create whole lives, in which we can both *achieve* what matters to us and *receive* what we need. I've been teaching and sharing this practical wisdom around the world for many years — and most importantly, I live it myself.

I am committed to showing you how to access a deeper well of wisdom within you that really does have the power to liberate you out of overwhelm. I promise I won't just give you more "to-dos." I will teach you how to take what you learn through this book and create a structure, rhythm, and way of working and living that just straight-up supports and sustains you.

I also promise I will do my best not to overwhelm you! Which I know is a possibility whenever we choose to make changes within already-full lives. The parts within you that want the change are gung ho. But the parts that resist like to convince you that you don't have time, are too busy, or will get back to this later when life settles down — which never happens. I've designed this book to be an experience that will stretch you in such a way that you feel *supported* and *sustained*, just like we want you to feel in your everyday life.

How to Work with This Book So It Supports You vs. Overwhelms You

This entire book is about empowering you to make different *choices* in how you work, create, operate, relate, and approach and design both your day-to-day life and your big life goals. As you make different choices — not just in what you do but also in how you feel, show up, and interact on the inside — your reality and relationships (to your work, people, health, money, home...*everything*) shift.

Think of this like an upgrade to your personal internal operating system — mind, body, spirit, *and* heart. We are elevating the blueprint within you that affects your impulses, emotions, and thoughts, which in turn drive your actions and choices, which determine the reality of your life, work, relationships, health, wealth — everything. Remember, this is more than a set of *beliefs*; these are *imprints* that exist in your emotional, physical, and energetic bodies and your mind. To make lasting change, you have to work on the mental, emotional, physical, and spiritual realms — all four, which we will.

Set Your Expectations for Success – How Transformation Happens

Too often I see people fail at making the changes they desire, because they buy into the overculture's promises of quick fixes and seven-step panaceas, which may give a short respite or boost of elation but, like most crash diets, eventually revert back to old programming, and they stay stuck. The truth is that lasting personal transformation and elevation is a path, a practice, and a choice in how you live. Change happens in small increments that lead to bigger changes, *over time*, often following these four stages:

Stage 1: Awareness. You see what you were blind to before — habits, beliefs, patterns, relationships, and ways of working that don't serve you.

Stage 2: Reflection. You still choose to self-sabotage or self-sacrifice, but you can look back as an observer, seeing the impact and how you could have chosen differently.

Stage 3: Change in the moment. You possess the inner strength to change your behavior, thoughts, actions, and choices so that instead of habitually reacting, you consciously respond. Your imprints and neural pathways begin to break as you choose self-empowerment and sustainability over self-sacrifice and sabotage. As you continue to make the harmonious, healthy choice, you begin to trust this new way, and the elevated imprint takes root, in body, mind, spirit, and heart.

Stage 4: Integration. The elevated program is installed! How you relate to your work, others, and yourself is different. The choices for how you design your overall life and live your daily life are different. You are freer and more empowered — centered, calm, and clear — within yourself, which your external reality reflects.

The Structure

Over years of research and experimentation, I've homed in on twelve specific imprints at the root of the burnout, self-sacrifice, and overwhelm. In each chapter we will work with one, illuminating the way of working that is *so* not working, so you can consciously *release* it. Then we flow in the practical wisdom to give you a new way of working, relating, creating, and operating, so you can *embrace* a different reality, one that sustains and supports you.

Think of each chapter as an elevation of your self-awareness and systemic awareness, in which you choose to release one way of being, succeeding, and living, and embrace a different way, one that supports you to create a reality that has sustainability and wellness at the core. This empowers you to ultimately make different choices that are aligned; true and right for you; and supportive of what you desire to create for yourself, those you love and lead, and the world.

To make the wisdom personal and practical, I've woven self-awareness *inquiries* throughout each chapter for you, titled "Know Yourself." These are questions and self-assessments whose intention is to help you reveal and feel deeper truths about yourself and the reality around you that perhaps you've sensed but didn't have words to articulate. You'll also learn and experiment with simple but mighty *practices* I call "harmonizing practices." Like hitting a PAUSE button on the swirl, when you feel the onset of the overwhelm or self-sacrifice, these give you the internal power to elevate out of the fray and reactive mode, to reharmonize on the inside, so you can make a self-supportive, self-sustaining choice.

As we go along I will also share with you what I call "self-sustainability stands" and "self-sustainability principles" — easy-to-remember statements that will support you to make choices that sustain you and to create the realities you desire, rather than sacrifice, drain, and distract you from what matters most. You'll also notice "glyphs" in each chapter, which illustrate the wisdom teachings and self-sustainability principles. I often use this powerful tool of visual thinking in my teaching, trainings, and writing, because it combines image, symbol, metaphor, and words to expand our thinking and consciousness beyond our mental conceptions and embedded imprints. The glyphs in this book were created in collaboration with visual-thinking illustrator Katherine Torrini, whom I often work with to teach and apply this wisdom for individuals and organizations.

The last thing to know about the structure is that I've grouped these twelve program upgrades into five sections to help us focus so this liberation feels enlivening and doable in your daily life and empowers you to take action, now. At the end of each section, I will walk you through a *process* that takes all the self-awareness and systemic awareness you've gained through the section and moves you into supportive action to make structural shifts — in how you relate to your life, work, and others — that sustain you. I call these "daring acts of liberation," because doesn't it just sound more fun to embark on a daring act versus doing a process?

Tips to Support You to Receive the Most from This Experience

1. Engage with one section at a time. Apply what you are learning and revealing to your daily life and life choices. I encourage you to take in the perspectives I share, answer the self-awareness inquiries in the chapters, pause to take the daring acts of liberation at the end of each section, and try the practices in your life. Don't feel like you have to read and get through the book like a race. Choose a time span that feels focused and fluid — read a chapter every week or two and experiment in your life. Focus on completing a section each month.

2. Approach this not as another "to-do" but as a guide to, and support structure for, a new way to go about your life, work, and relationships. If you add this to your already-full life as more to do, you will stall before you get started. If you embrace this as a supportive structure — a place that lives outside the chaos and swirl, one you can come home to, like a well where you access deeper realms of wisdom and power — you'll stay committed. And feel nourished by the process. Embrace the book as a permission slip, giving you the juice to create devoted space for yourself in your mornings, evenings, or weekends.

3. Embrace this experience as something you are giving *yourself*. Be clear about *why* this matters to you. If you are connected to the deeper reasons why are you choosing to embark on this journey now, you will be way more likely to keep coming back to this book. Take a moment right here with me now to ask and answer these three inquiries (use the sentence starters to tune in to what's true for you):

- *Why did I pick up this book?*
  I picked this book up because...

- *Why does focusing on myself and taking a deeper look within, now, matter to me?*
  Taking a deeper look at myself and my life now matters because...

- *What's the cost if I just keep doing what I've been doing?*
  If I don't make a change...

4. Create a "wisdom journal" for this process to access deeper insight. A wisdom journal is where you write your thoughts and reflections as you answer the self-awareness inquiries, record wisdom that strikes a chord, and do the daring acts of liberation. If you are not a "journal" person, what would take this book beyond just a mental exercise? Do that. When you write in your handwriting and see your words with your eyes, change happens differently in your brain, heart, psyche, and body — the power of visual thinking. I created a wisdom journal as a companion for this book with all the inquiries and processes in one place. Go to www.OverwhelmedAndOverIt.com to learn more.

5. Ask for and receive support and sisterhood. Share that you are reading this book with one other person. Invite her to join you. Gather a group of friends and do this journey together. At the end of this book, there's more information on how to gather other women for real conversation and connection, as well as how to connect with other women within our community. If accountability supports you, at any time you can take my online program that leads you through these stages. And lastly, I created a book readers' kit with some templates, videos, and meditations to support you. You'll find it all at www.OverwhelmedAndOverIt.com.

Get Curious about Your Burnout Imprints

To begin opening up your self-awareness, let's complete this section by looking at common burnout imprints, some of which are likely embedded in your internal operating system. Illuminating them will help you to see how the overwhelm you feel is linked to your current choices, thoughts, and habits. What follows is a series of typical choices that lead to burnout and self-sacrifice.

On a scale of 1 to 10, rate the frequency and consistency of this behavior in your life today or in the recent past, with 1 being *never or rarely occurs*; with 5 being *true and occurring sometimes, often in times of stress or stretch*; and 10 being *true most of the time — it's how you normally operate*. Remember, this is only for you. It's about getting to know more about how you operate; it's not a test you pass or fail. So be honest. Don't think too much about your rating — go with your first instinct.

Behavior	Rate 1-10
1. I say yes to projects and people when I don't have the time, energy, or money to give.	
2. I work harder and longer than needed.	
3. I take on other people's feelings and problems or make it my job to fix them or better things for them.	
4. I try to figure out every last detail so nothing is left to chance.	
5. I try to do too much at one time and then feel scattered, fragmented, and overwhelmed.	
6. I overstretch my financial resources and then feel like I don't have what I need.	
7. I run my inner batteries and body down.	
8. I try to do it all, and feel like I am the only one who can do it.	
9. I feel like I have to keep track of everything or it will all fall apart.	
10. I try to do too much in one day.	
11. I want things to happen faster than they do, so I push myself and others, getting impatient and frustrated.	
12. I compare myself to others and then judge myself for not doing more, not being further ahead, or not being more successful.	

Behavior	Rate 1-10
13. I check my email or go online in the mornings before I brush my teeth, pee, or connect to myself and my body.	
14. I start a second day of work in the evenings after I get home.	
15. I let other people's needs and desires usurp my own.	
16. I react to other people's emotions, stress, and drama and get pulled into their swirl.	
17. I get so busy with work or taking care of others that I don't cultivate deeper connections with other women.	
18. I watch things that are emotionally dramatic, email, or surf the internet in the hour before I go to bed.	
19. I feel anxious when I slow down or create space to relax.	
20. I feel like I am being lazy and nonproductive if I am not doing something.	
21. I have a hard time slowing down my mind when I go to sleep.	
22. I feel guilty when I say no to a request or a need at work or from my family and friends, so I say yes even when I know I don't have the time or bandwidth.	

Know Yourself
What are my burnout imprints?

Circle or highlight two to four behaviors that reflect how you are currently operating or that you default to during times of stress or stretch (anything you rated over a 7). Don't freak out if you have more than four; just choose up to four that feel relevant now or that you desire to change. Write these in your wisdom journal as "My Current Burnout Imprints." Then begin to notice when you make these choices in your daily life. For now, just become more *aware*.

Let's dive into the first realm of liberation, choosing to redefine success by making choices that lead to harmony.

PART ONE

Liberate Your Success

*Wise women embrace their power
to define success and design lives
that put their wellness and
wholeness at the core.*

Chapter 1

RELEASE: **Do, Be, and Have It All**

EMBRACE: **Choose What's Right for You**

Success isn't a status you attain, a prescribed path you take,
or an image you model your life after.
Success is having the courage and clarity to choose
what's aligned and true for you.

Before the last rise of the feminist and human-potential movements in the mid-twentieth century, words like *self-esteem* and *self-empowerment* were not part of the everyday lexicon. It wasn't until the 1980s that the esteem and empowerment of girls and women really began getting woven into our educational systems and cultural consciousness. This was a good upgrade that has imprinted us and generations of girls since with the belief:

"You can do and be anything."

This is the equation for success we've been working toward. We get educated to get good jobs. Then work hard to get ahead, achieve our goals, and make money so we can buy houses and create stability for ourselves and our families. Then we work harder to get bigger jobs and buy bigger houses, which results in us needing to make more money to pay for and maintain the "successful" lifestyles we create. In the United States this is called the American Dream. I call it the "escalator to death." We are imprinted to keep accumulating more, trying to get ahead, one day hoping we'll get "there." The escalator keeps you following the person ahead of you, without question, like cattle on a conveyor belt, blindly focused on getting to the "next thing" — job, title, degree, house, salary, relationship status, or other financial or life milestone. Even if you do "make it" to the top floors and achieve career or financial "success," your heart weighs heavy and your body breaks down due to what you've had to sacrifice in your relationships and personal wellness and happiness.

Somewhere along the way, the well-meaning message of self-esteem and self-empowerment got distorted and warped into:

"You can do, be, and have it all."

"Do, be, and have it *all*" became the formula for what success looks and feels like. As a result, we learned to value and gauge our own success and self-worth based on the external measures set by the overculture, which (as I explained in the introduction) just keeps moving faster and demanding more. The overculture has defined what "all" looks like for us. "All" in this world is rooted in value and market systems based on accumulation and consumption, on profitability and productivity, not the health and wealth or sustainability of people and the planet as a whole interconnected system. These expectations and ideals — which we and others take on — are sometimes conscious and apparent but are often unconsciously imprinted by the well-meaning people who parent, mentor, and guide us, who have also been imprinted by this distorted overculture.

No wonder so many smart and motivated women like you — who desire to make a difference, achieve their dreams and goals, and experience a whole life — are not only physically tired but emotionally burned-out. No matter how hard we work or try or how much we give, we rarely feel like we have done enough or have enough to sustain ourselves and our families. "All" is an unattainable and unsustainable standard you can never meet. "All" is a setup for self-judgment and stress if you fail to meet the ideals or you deviate from what is deemed the successful and smart path. And it's only getting worse for the young women in the generations coming up behind us.

The number of people on antidepressants rose by 65 percent in the past fifteen years. It's estimated that one person in every eight over the age of twelve recently used an antidepressant — the age of twelve! Antianxiety meds are used by women at almost twice the rate seen among men. And college deans are describing incoming freshmen as "crispies" — so burned-out by the pressures of high school that they get to college unable to engage in the work. Burned-out in high school!

"Do, be, and have it all" was never meant to be the model or message to follow to achieve success and happiness.

As I began to see just how much damage this programming of "do, be, and have it all" was creating, my fierce feminine heart wanted answers. I wanted to understand *why* we received the message "You can do, be, and have it all." Why had this become the directive and definition for being an empowered, successful woman? Something seemed wrong, out of whack. I sensed that before I could help other women, and myself, create different models for success, I needed to find out the real story of how we got here.

This quest to understand led me to talk with women who had been at the forefront of the rise of the women's movement in the 1960s and '70s. Losing the threads of knowledge and experience between generations of women is one of the root reasons why we lose our power to effect *lasting* social and generational change. The wisdom and stories shared through our voices and hearts as women, across generations, are where our secret feminine superpower lies. When we connect the past to the present to the future, we gain insight that would be difficult to find on our own. By keeping the threads of wisdom strong, we can more easily see where to focus our energy. Building on the momentum, we can make change more swiftly, with less struggle.

One of the most illuminating threads came from a serendipitous private conversation I found myself in with Gloria Steinem one fall afternoon in San Francisco. Yes, that Gloria, founder of *Ms.* magazine and committed voice for women's rights for multiple decades. How it all happened is a story for another day and chapter. What I want to share with you now is the wisdom I received that makes how we got here crystal clear. Then we can focus on what's needed now to create ways of working, relating, and succeeding that truly have our best interests at heart.

You can do and be anything, *and you have to make choices.*

You and I were never meant to achieve success by striving to do, be, and have it all, or by trying to fit into fixed ideas about the "path of success." We were meant to believe within our very core that we could do anything we committed ourselves to. That we could be anything that our hearts compelled us to be. But with the wisdom and understanding that we had to make *choices* along the way. Choices that were aligned and in harmony with our unique lives, souls' paths, gifts, and dreams. Not choices based on conforming to or fitting into the images or following the path set by a society, our parents, or anyone else.

The way I see it is that you and I got a well-meaning Post-it note that had been torn in half. We never received the full memo — the part about *choices*, which changes everything. And which is the foundation for everything this book stands for. The truth is, while you and I can do and be anything that we commit to and that aligns with our souls' paths, we cannot do everything at the same time — unless we are okay with compromising our physical, mental, and emotional health; the quality of our relationships; or our hearts' desires for the lives we want to live. Had we received the full memo, we'd have grown up knowing that there is not *one* path to success. We'd have been supported to explore, vary our experiences, and follow our unique path, instead of feeling pressured to have our entire path planned and figured out. We'd have gained the inner strength and faith to embrace uncertainty, take risks, and trust that we — and our paths — are always unfolding, instead of fearing that if we deviated from the norm, we'd be committing career suicide, face financial destitution, or be kicked out of the tribe. We'd have been taught in school and from our parents how to make wise choices, ones that reflected our hearts and souls.

Now, brace your fierce feminine heart, because there's more. Not receiving the wisdom, training, or education we needed to make soul-aligned, supportive choices, rooted in our personal truth, innate wisdom, and internal self-worth, was no accident. It's not your fault that you may have pressured yourself to fit into an image of success or that you may have chosen to follow prescribed paths of success, professionally or personally, over what was right for you. For decades, women have been acclimating to systems that refused to significantly change and acknowledge the reality of what's needed for us to thrive, not just survive, in today's world.

The systems have not sufficiently changed to support women in the workforce, so we just kept doing *more*! Because we had to.

As women gained more rights to make choices about their careers, bodies, and lives, the systems didn't shift to support the expansion of these possibilities and responsibilities. Microchanges, maybe; some significant shifts, yes; but sweeping societal changes — no. If the systems could have spoken back then, it's kind of like they said, "Okay, ladies, go ahead and have your rights, see yourself as equal, get educated, and have careers. But we, the educational, health-care, financial, familial, governmental, and corporate institutions, are not going to make the changes in how *we* work that are really needed in order to support this new constellation of your lives, families, and responsibilities. You are going to just have to do more."

There were not enough women or conscious male allies in places and positions of power and authority to significantly change the systems to support women in the workforce. So, women had to suck it up and play the game that the "go, go, give, give, more, more" systems demanded. And they did. Brave women fought their way up the ladder, did it all, and sucked it up to blaze the trail. Women just added on to already-full plates alongside motherhood, being good wives and daughters, taking part in the community, and staying healthy and thin — we just did *more*. Because we had to.

Those of us in the generations after followed the path to success laid out for us. Some of us stayed on that path and got good at the game. Some left because we didn't like the game. Some chose to never play the game. Some of us were even told we couldn't hack the game because we couldn't handle the pressure. Whatever *your* choice has been, we have all been playing the *wrong game*!

Just take all that in for a moment.

Choices. Do more, or opt out. Meet the unrealistic expectations required for success, or get left behind. Embrace the overculture's ideals for success — about what you should be able to accomplish, achieve, and manage — and the expectations for who you should be and become. Even if they don't sustain your wholeness or needs as a human, or align with your unique desires and path.

And then exhale. Because the time of operating this way — striving to do, be, and have it all or fit into a prescribed path for personal or professional success; taking on more and more because you feel like you have no choice (and maybe you *didn't*); judging yourself for stepping off "the" prescribed path; accepting the current systems as how things "are" and acquiescing to their demands — can be over.

Self-Sustainability Stand
from the Fierce Feminine Heart

If the fierce feminine heart had written the full message, I think she would have said something like this:

Yes, go into the world, dear one!
You can do and be anything,
And remember, you must make choices.

Stop pushing yourself to do and be more.
Stop trying to fit into anyone else's definition of success.
Choose what's right for you, even if that means doing things differently.

Try speaking this message in the first person, from your fierce feminine heart, out loud, as a liberating stand for yourself.

I can do and be anything.
And I also need to make choices.
I refuse to just keep doing more.
I release trying to do, be, and have it all.
I embrace my power to make choices that are right for me.

Now here is where things start to get juicy! If you remember you are always free to exercise *choice*, you can embrace and embody the power of your fierce feminine heart and wisdom to redefine success and create new realities, ones that honor your wellness, wholeness, and innate worth. I can't promise it will be easy — but I can promise the challenge will be much more empowering, enlightening, and enlivening than staying stuck in the status quo, a comfort zone, or the current dynamic.

We have the power to create new realities through our choices, which means we have the power to redefine success and the systems that say what it is.

I want to pause here with you to acknowledge all the ways you have felt like you were not at full choice within your life — times you didn't have the support, resources, or consciousness you would have needed in order to feel at liberty to choose. I imagine that all women, to differing degrees, have stood here. Wherever the pressure was coming from — a job or relationship, finances, health, or someone's expectations exerting their power over you — we have all made choices that compromised our truth, needs, worth, and desires.

Some of us conformed to a prescribed path of success that may have made us look successful on paper or to the outside but left us feeling bankrupt on the inside. Others of us opted for the logical or safe path, choosing to override our passions or deeper heart knowing, and as a result sacrificed our dreams and squashed our souls' expression through our professional and personal choices. Many of us have made choices to keep taking on more — job responsibilities, financial obligations, caring for others, community service — without making a corresponding choice to receive more support, redesign our lives, or reset our expectations, and we buckled under the burden. This happened. This has been, and in many cases is, our shared reality.

But today, at this time on the planet, that reality must shift. Collectively, we have the power to redefine success. It all starts with our choices — the big ones and the day-to-day ones — where you and I have complete control: how we choose to see and feel about who we are, and how we choose to live.

Take a look at the left side of the glyph on the next page — that's the imprint we've been running just to keep up or get ahead, or take care of everything and everyone. We each have our own versions of this, in which our unconscious fears and the imprints from the "do, be, and have more" overculture drive us to sell ourselves out, make ourselves sick, and strive to find success and security. We don't trust that it's safe to hit the PAUSE button, stopping the forward movement or intense pace so we can consider different possibilities, and find the path that's right for us. The overculture imprints have made many a woman afraid to deviate from the norm, to pause her growth in one area in order to focus on another, or to slow down in any way. Fearing we would fail, fall behind, fall short, be left out, become irrelevant, lose financial security, and more, we've all made choices to stay captive in fishbowls versus following our wise, fierce feminine hearts to lead us to oceans of new possibility.

No need to feel bad; we've all done it. Even among those of us who have deviated from the norm, I have yet to meet a woman who is *fully* free from this imprint — but we need to be. Today, at this time on the planet, we are each being challenged to let go of our current comfort zones, to follow our true path even more, to *elevate* versus escalate — because it's time for the world to wake up and do things differently. And for this we'll need access to and trust in the deep well of courage, clarity, and confidence we were born with.

Take a closer look at the left side of the image, and you'll see the seed of innate self-worth and self-trust that was planted in the younger you before any overculture or family imprinting took over. What would become possible if you dared to embrace that seed of innate knowing, trust, and value within you, and you chose to move yourself over to the right side of the glyph, where you choose what is right for you, now in your life, without apology? You don't have to burn down your current life or announce anything to anyone. You start by making a conscious choice to go deeper within — to truly know yourself at a heart and soul level, today. You take action to deepen your capacity to trust yourself, and connect with the wise woman within you. You embrace your power to redefine success by daring to make choices that are right for you, one choice at a time.

If you make this shift within, you'll find yourself wielding one of the most awesome superpowers you have as a woman — *Harmonic Defiance*. In part 5, we'll dive into this, but for now, here's a brief description. Harmonic Defiance is your power to change the way things are done in the world, and within your organizations, family, and communities, by the radical and daring choice to live your life, run your businesses and teams, relate to your jobs, raise your family, create your wealth, and sustain your health differently, in harmony. Everything we do together will support you to live your life more from this empowered and elevated place.

I'm excited about sharing this way of living with you — which I call the "feminine wisdom way" — because I know the power it possesses. Individually and collectively, we are rewriting the definitions and re-creating what success can look like. We are creating new realities, a new world, rooted in images, myth, stories, and symbols that reflect our inherent worth and innate power and wisdom as women.

By the end of this book, my intention is that you activate the wisdom, superpowers, and practices needed to embody your power to make the choices that are right and true for you, now and in the years ahead. And as a result, create a reality for yourself and those you love and lead that is rooted in sustainability, wholeness, wellness, and harmony. I believe with all my heart that when women prosper, the planet prospers. And when women and the planet prosper, all life thrives.

I have to be up-front with you about what living this way means. This is not a mental construct or a pie-in-the-sky Pollyanna pipe dream. It is what self-empowerment really is. It's an embodied reality requiring courage on your part to do things differently with respect to how you structure your daily life — how you work and give your energy, time, focus, and more — and design your overall life. It will ask you to step out of your habitual patterns and comfort zone to create new patterns, perspectives, and possibilities. And it will require you to access and trust the fierce feminine heart within you that dares to make choices that go beyond the status quo and conventional wisdom — as well as your current comfort zone — in order to stay true to a deeper, sustaining wisdom. The good news is that you have already made more choices from this place within you than you know, because you have a feminine superpower.

The courage and clarity to make choices that are right for you come from the deep, feminine wisdom within you willing to shake up the status quo to stay true to herself.

Within the awakened heart of every woman — yours included — is a superpower called "Crazy Wisdom." This superpower gives you the courage and clarity you need to make choices that are right and true for you, even if they differ from what everyone else is doing, defy logic, and fly in the face of the way things have always been done. Crazy Wisdom isn't reckless; it is rooted in the deep intuitive place within you that knows what is right, real, and aligned for you.

The Feminine Superpower of Crazy Wisdom Is...

The willingness to explore, trust, speak, and act from your deep heart wisdom over conventional wisdom or outside intelligence even if it seems crazy, irrational, improbable, or irresponsible or stretches you outside your comfort zone.

While you may not be familiar with the phrase *Crazy Wisdom*, I can assure you that you have it, and that you've used it before. Crazy Wisdom is not always rational, but when you hear it or receive it, you know its truth because it lands in your body. You feel it in your heart or belly, you hear it like a voice that rings through you, and you innately know it's true even if you can't explain it. This is because this inner knowing is your innate, intuitive feminine wisdom, which isn't here to just be logical or rational, play along, or follow the status quo. It's here to guide the way to choices that support life, expand possibility, and care for and nurture both you and the whole.

Our feminine wisdom comes from our hearts and then informs our heads. It is fierce, compassionate, courageous, and straight-up wise. This is the same kind of wisdom for which women have been called emotional, hysterical, and unrealistic, and even been locked up and persecuted. Because, as it turns out, Crazy Wisdom is crazy powerful. And those who want the status quo to stay that way don't want our Crazy Wisdom unleashed. Because that is where our power resides.

By intentionally reclaiming the word *crazy* and the power of our feminine wisdom, we can stop needing to justify, prove, or rationalize what we know, see, feel, and sense as intuitive beings who are also incredibly intelligent. "Crazy" has been used like a weapon to dismantle a woman's power, discount her ideas, and make her doubt herself, with retorts like "Don't be crazy; you can't..." We even do it to ourselves. Have you ever heard yourself or another woman say, "I know this is going to sound crazy, but..." or "Don't think I am crazy, but..."?

By reclaiming "crazy," we stop being afraid of being called crazy or being seen as irrational and emotional. The truth is, the overculture will try to brand you crazy when you dare to do things differently or speak up and out from your feminine wisdom. But when you embrace your Crazy Wisdom as powerful, others stop having power over you. So, what if instead of couching or discounting your innate knowing, you embraced your deep feminine wisdom, without apology or explanation, even when, *especially* when, she has radical, non-normal, reality-breaking, soul-awakening, system-challenging, heart-invoking — crazy — things to say?

If we gave our fierce feminine hearts the microphone and let the Crazy Wisdom stream, here's what we might hear:

Women, you have the wisdom within you to birth new realities, possibilities, definitions of success, and ways of working and living. No one is coming to save you or this world — you are the ones with the power within to do things differently. Take a stand and liberate yourself first from what isn't right, aligned, and in harmony.

Be "M.A.D.D." enough to **m**ake **a** **d**ifferent **d**ecision in how you design your life; define success; and lead and show up for your families, teams, organizations, businesses, and community.

Embrace your deeper intuitive feminine wisdom and trust it to guide you in your choices, big and small. Unleash your superpower of Crazy Wisdom when you need to step outside the status quo, defy logic, or do things in ways that stretch you. Remember the many women who have walked before you who dared to do things differently and, as a result, changed this world for the better. You are that powerful, too.

Crazy Wisdom gives you the superpower to break through the overculture mentality, illuminate the truth, and see a different way. You are going to need your Crazy Wisdom to stay awake, aware, and centered in this chaotic world so you can make the choices that keep you true to your path. One of the biggest challenges we will face ahead is not trusting our intuitive wisdom when it arises. Like with all superpowers, to access the full power of your Crazy Wisdom, you must learn about it, experience it, practice it, and cultivate the strength and trust to use it. Developing your ability to receive intuitive guidance, listen to and decipher the wisdom, and trust yourself enough to take action is a lifelong practice.

Whether you are just beginning to reconnect with your innate feminine wisdom or you've been developing this relationship for years, I invite you to choose to embrace your connection more deeply now. Your feminine wisdom knows how to navigate your path and can lead you to possibilities your mind cannot imagine but your heart knows are your truth. There's so much to share and teach about this. I believe remembering and revaluing our intuition is so essential that I founded a feminine-wisdom school, the Feminine Wisdom Way, where you can learn more (www.FeminineWisdomWay.com). For now, let's start strengthening your connection by finding evidence of how your intuitive Crazy Wisdom has served you in the past. When you see and acknowledge the results of following your intuition to step outside the norm, and stay true to yourself, you strengthen your trust in your own knowing.

Know Yourself
When have I trusted my Crazy Wisdom and embraced my power to choose differently?

Recall a time in your personal or professional life when you did tune in to your feminine wisdom and took action, even if that meant doing things differently than others.

Ask: *When have I...*

- *Made a choice in my education, career, business, or life design that was different from everyone else around me, because it felt right inside?*
  You embraced staying true to your path.
- *Said no to just piling on more, to sacrificing my wellness and relationships, even if that meant disappointing another or not staying on the fast track to "success"?*
  You embraced self-sustainability and redefined success with your personal well-being at the core.
- *Chosen to consciously redesign how I was working and living to support and sustain me, my family, or my organization?*
  You embraced the need to make changes, even if they challenged your sense of self or security.

When you remember these instances, while things may not have worked out the way you thought, you are still here standing, right? Look back now and see how something held and guided you through the process. Look back and consider this: isn't a life lived true to the self, in ways that feel meaningful and sustainable, always worth the challenge? If you and I were sitting together, having a wise-woman heart-to-heart, what stories would you share with me about how your Crazy Wisdom guided you to step outside the status quo to stay true to yourself? How have you trusted and allowed your fierce feminine heart to take the lead, even if your logical mind could not see a clear path? I love sharing Crazy Wisdom stories when I gather women together; it always fills us up with so much courage and clarity. I'd like to share one of my own with you.

> I was twenty-nine, contemplating my next career step. Something within me caused me to take a pause (which I know now was my feminine wisdom, but then I had no idea I even had this superpower) to consider if the "track to success" I was on was one I really wanted to follow. It led me to take a good look at the executives of the marketing consulting firm I worked for, which was an innovative, passionate, privately held company led by leaders I believe did care about the people. As I paused, this is what I saw.
>
> The women, especially, looked tired. I can still see the dark circles under their eyes. Many were single, desiring a relationship but without the space for one. Others were in relationships that were strained because they had little time for nurturing their intimate connection.
>
> It was like my inner wise woman from the future reached back in that moment to show me I had a choice. And I saw the potential paths so clearly. I knew I could climb to the top and succeed if I wanted. But my feminine wisdom said, *Just because you* could, *doesn't mean you* should! Wisdom

illuminator — *boom!* The truth was, I was working sixty to eighty hours a week, spending my creative life force and utilizing my intelligence to market things to people that weren't good for them and that they didn't need. I didn't want to sacrifice my health or relationships and keep giving my life force to something that was not meaningful or making people's lives better.

My Crazy Wisdom led me to leave my "cool" job in the industry everyone was clamoring to get into to take a nonsexy job in an industry with no glamour or clamor. What I didn't know at the time was that the nonsexy job would become my life-sustaining one as I worked full-time, got my MBA at night (which was 80 percent paid for by my new company), and went through the unanticipated and life-altering ending of my engagement. During which the dot-com bust blew up all the cool jobs and speculative financial incentives. But I stayed sustained because I followed my Crazy Wisdom, rooted in my feminine wisdom, who knew what I could not possibly see. Thank god I trusted.

My experience of following my inner wise woman to do a career pivot cemented a lifelong practice of redefining success for myself, trusting my feminine wisdom to guide me, and doing things differently. Eventually it led me to what I'm doing now, here with you — creating new ways to achieve, succeed, lead, live, and make a difference that support how women naturally work best.

Which brings me to getting curious about what *your* fierce feminine heart and her Crazy Wisdom is trying to show you. I imagine it's this part of you that caused you to pick up this book. So let's invite her into our wise-woman heart-to-heart and see what she has to say. Give your fierce feminine heart the microphone, and let her — *your* — personal truth and wisdom stream. No one's watching or listening, so let her speak — no holding back.

Know Yourself

What is my Crazy Wisdom whispering to (or screaming at) me about what's not working and what changes it's time to make?

If you let your Crazy Wisdom guide your choices, as you have before, what wisdom would she speak to you?

- *What is not working for me anymore? What am I tolerating?*
- *What feels like it's just too much to keep holding or doing? What reality or relationship – with a person, community, or organization – is unsustainable?*
- *What choices and changes am I being called to make?*
- *What have I been resisting changing? What scares me about making these shifts?*
- *What does my inner wisdom know is true?*

What trips women up, what I see keeping them from trusting that deeper knowing within and unleashing its power to pioneer the way forward, is that they mistakenly think they have to have all the answers or a plan all figured out. Not true. You don't need to know the "how"; in fact, you really can't — no one can. That's not how the world works today. We need to know how to work with uncertainty, not fear it. We are most powerful when we embrace the mystery as part of the process of how we create, unfold, and evolve. We receive the most support from the Universe when we can allow synchronicity and expanded possibility to arise. Much like on any adventure, yes, it's wise to have an intention or destination. But really you can see only the next few steps ahead. You can expect things will come up that you couldn't have planned. This is where the power of your feminine wisdom will show up for you every time, if you are connected and listening.

Harmonizing Practice
Embrace What You Know and What's Still in the Mystery

When you lack clarity about how to move forward on your path, take a pause and tune in. Speak or write out what you know and what you don't. Then ask your feminine wisdom for the next step.

1. *What I know is…*
2. *What is still in the mystery is…*
3. *A simple but mighty step I can take next is…*

Use this book as a catalyst to step into the choices your heart and soul are calling for. Invite your inner wise woman to guide the way; she knows how to take the wisdom I'll share throughout this book and put it into practical action. She's the part of you ready to re-create and redesign your life, relationships, and work and redefine what success is for you now, at this time in your life. Which is exactly where we're headed next.

Chapter 2

RELEASE: **Maintain Work/Life Balance**

EMBRACE: **Cultivate Harmony**

Wise women don't focus on finding balance in busy lives. We cultivate harmony within dynamic lives, so we can experience whole lives.

Work/life balance has become like a marker of nirvanic success all of us overwhelmed women strive for yet never seem to reach. It's not for lack of trying, focus, or diligence that we fail. The truth is, we've been missing that there's a fundamental flaw inherent in work/life balance as a goal for personal and professional success:

Work/life balance is the wrong equation.

For more than fifty years we've been trying to make the work/life balance equation work within our modern lives. If it was the right solution, we'd all be basking in inner peace already. We need a new way to think about organizing our lives that goes beyond trying to manage, balance, and hold it all, a way in which we are enabled to *flow* within it all. A way to design *whole* lives, in which we are supported to express ourselves fully, make a meaningful impact, be financially sustained, feel healthy and vibrant, show up for those we love and lead, go for and achieve our dreams, *and* breathe.

Try this exercise with me. Instead of thinking of work/life balance as a personal goal to be achieved or an organizational initiative to implement, look at it as the formula you've been trying to manage and organize your life by.

Work/Life Balance
Work over life.
Work divided by life.

Now look at the glyph below to see what running the program of work/life balance looks like on you. Remember that a glyph, if you pause to take it in, can lead you to wisdom and awareness you didn't have language or thought for previously.

Work/Life Balance

← WORK —— LIFE →

Work/life balance is what is called a "duality reality," which by its nature creates tension between two forces. In duality realities — think *Democrat/Republican*, *rich/poor*, *good/evil* — the two forces are engaged in a tug-of-war, pulling for energy, attention, and resources (notice the arrows). Duality realities cause people to feel like they have to choose one side or the other. In this case, you must choose between work and everything else in your life.

Which is why when it comes to balancing work and life, you often feel torn, split, and constantly tugged on. Work is pulling at life. Life is pulling at work. And you get caught in the middle. This is why when you are at work, you feel guilty for not being with your family. Or you feel frustrated that you "don't have the time" to do what you love or to take care of what needs attention in every other place in your life besides work.

Notice, also, how this linear configuration forces you to fit your whole life into two parts — work and life. Which means that everything other than your work must fit under the category of "life." Think about that for a moment. How do you feel about stuffing everything other than what you do for work — family, friends, health, wealth, fun, community, creative expression, sleep, wellness, dreams, home, and so on — into one lump under the category of "life"? No wonder you feel like you don't have enough time or space. Isn't your life as a whole much more than two parts? And if it's not, wouldn't you rather it be?

Work/life balance as a design for organizing your life splits you apart at the seams, as you try to hold these two forces together.

Take a good look again at the woman standing in the middle of work and life who is clearly stretched, stressed, and struggling. That's you, me, and every woman who, even while wearing heels and a skirt, has done her best to survive and thrive in this dualistic paradigm. And many times, we do appear as if we've pulled it off. But damn if we aren't tired and don't have rope burns. No wonder our shoulders are in knots; look at all that tension. And that perspiration you see coming off her brow, is that sweat or the tears of our silent Superwoman Sobs?

When I look at this glyph and let myself viscerally feel the reality of trying to operate this way, all I want to do is let go of it all. *Poof!* I'd love to let it all float away like balloons so I can get out of the suit, put on my yoga pants, go for a walk, breathe, and get a latte! How about you?

Are you willing to release the ropes? Believe you could do it differently? You don't need to know *how* just yet. The first liberating step is to admit to yourself: *Work/life balance is bullshit. And trying to succeed within this duality reality as a life design isn't working.* Then we can press the LIBERATE button and flow in feminine wisdom.

> **Wise women focus on cultivating harmony within dynamic lives so they can feel balanced and centered among the diverse demands and desires of a whole life.**

Our lives are dynamic, not static. Diverse, not divisible into two parts. Cyclical, not linear. Which is why we need a new *constellation* — a configuration — for how to think about, organize, interact with, meet, and design the interconnected parts of our lives. A design that honestly reflects the diverse demands we face and things we care for. A model that supports each of us to create a *whole* life — instead of forcing us to sacrifice parts of ourselves and our personal desires and needs. A new shape that can hold all the parts together, so we don't have to. A picture says it all.

Look at the woman on the right side of this glyph, the one

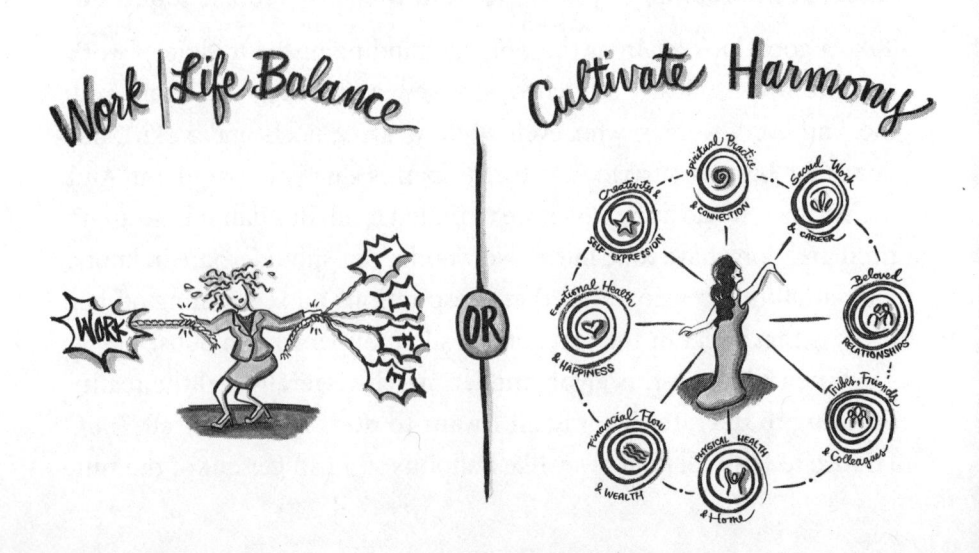

standing within the circle. Imagine her as you. You have chosen to let go of the ropes, and step into the center of your life. As a result, all the parts can now move around you. See yourself like a conductor directing a symphony orchestra. Just like an orchestra has a variety of sections — strings, winds, percussions, and so forth — each with a part to play, so too does your life have a variety of parts. These parts are represented by each of the eight spirals.

Your role is not to balance all the parts or keep all the parts moving. Your sustainable success comes from focusing on your power to *cultivate harmony* between all the parts. Slow down here with me. We're not just changing up some words. We are giving you a powerful upgrade to how you approach the diverse demands and desires of your full life — so you can create a whole life, with space to achieve, succeed, take care of what matters, and breathe. But first, we need to get you aware and clear on the power of harmony and balance so you know how to work with and wield both.

Balance vs. Harmony

Harmony is one of those words that sounds nice, like *self-care*, but doesn't really land in a practical, "how does that help me in my current overwhelming reality?" kind of way. We toss around the word *balance* not really understanding where balance can help and where it actually creates distress and unrealistic expectations. We've been using the wrong tool for the wrong challenge. Keep reading.

> BALANCE: a state of equilibrium. [*Equilibrium* is a state of rest due to the equal action of opposing forces (like a scale). It is also the state of mental and emotional balance.]

> *Balanced is something you want to feel on the inside, so you can stay centered and focused within your dynamic life.*

Balance is not the equation you want to use to organize all the demands and desires of your life on the outside. We've already established that your life isn't like a set of scales with two sides that can stay in equilibrium. Instead, like the woman standing at the center of her life, feeling graceful, focused, and calm within (hence the opera gown), you want to *feel* emotionally, mentally, and physically balanced. The inner balanced state makes you more effective, no matter what swirls around you, empowering you to interface with what's needed in the moment. Balanced and centered on the inside, you become responsive versus reactive, so you make choices that sustain and support you.

> HARMONY: a consistent, orderly, pleasing arrangement of parts that creates congruity, where all parts come together, fit in, and flow.
>
> *Harmony is something you cultivate — foster and tend — to design your overall life, to interact with the diverse parts and needs, and to create a supportive, sustainable reality.*

Harmony by its nature supports many parts to play together in such a way that the whole creates a congruent flow. A rhythm and way of working, living, achieving, and taking care of what matters to you that feels coherent, and consistently fluid — sometimes intense, sometimes slow, sometimes energizingly active, always sustainable. Same with your life. When the parts are played together with direction and consciousness, you move through your life with more flow, and they all work together, versus feeling like you have to choose between one thing or another.

Shifting your focus from work/life balance to making choices — big life ones and small day-to-day ones — that cultivate harmony can transform the very foundation of how you live and interact with the parts and pace of your life. I'm not suggesting you will never feel overwhelmed or stretched or never go through an intense time again. All good symphonies have variation of intensity, and all good conductors are conditioned and trained for it. Same with you. We'll spend the rest of this chapter and section sharing how to make this practical and actionable for you.

Living a whole life is a choice you make and a stand you take.

Choosing to live and create a whole life in this current overculture is a radical act, one that requires you to consciously, courageously, and consistently make choices that support the whole to thrive — including, at times, taking a fierce stand to no longer accept anything *less* than a whole life. When you were working in the duality reality of work/life balance, creating a whole life was, well, pretty impossible, at least in any kind of sustainable way for you. Choosing to cultivate harmony by standing at the center of your life, as the conductor, in relationship to all the parts, opens up the *potential* for creating a whole life and a greater possibility of *feeling* in harmony, even during times of intensity.

Look at the glyph below for creating a whole, harmonized life,

The Harmony Wheel

- Spiritual Practice & Connection
- Sacred Work & Career
- Beloved Relationships
- Tribes, Friends & Colleagues
- Physical Health & Home
- Financial Flow & Wealth
- Emotional Health & Happiness
- Creativity & Self-Expression

which I call the "Harmony Wheel," illustrating the realms of a woman's whole life. Think of this as a different way to constellate and design your life. Notice the circular shape. It mimics that of a compass, and it cultivates wholeness and interconnectedness just by its natural design — without you having to do anything to make that so.

Each of the realms holds a specific part of our lives. Just like a compass needs all eight directions to be whole and complete, so too do we need these parts to feel whole and complete. What follows are descriptions of each of the realms of a whole and harmonized life — some of which will sound familiar and others new. This is intentional. Take a read; consider each realm. Get curious about which are in harmony for you right now, and which are clearly out of whack or desiring more attention.

The Realms of a Whole and Harmonized Life

1. Sacred Work & Career: Your jobs, projects, businesses, missions, and roles and also your mentoring, caretaking, mothering, and parenting. Your career is the path you walk and take throughout your life. Your sacred work is what you are here to cause and create and what you choose to give your life force to. It's the purposes you serve through your gifts and presence.

2. Spiritual Practice & Connection: What you do in your daily life to create a consistent and felt relationship with the greater Universe and to sense your part within it.

3. Creativity & Self-Expression: The ways — tangible and intangible — you express yourself, without needing the outcome to be productive or profitable. Although you can receive financial flow from this, the deeper, more meaningful reward is your free and full expression, feeling your power to create, and the energy and connection you receive as a result.

4. Emotional Health & Happiness: Your sense of inner harmony, joy, and peace. Your inner foundation of self-love. Your balance, stability, and capacity to respond from a centered place on the inside.

5. Beloved Relationships: The intimate relationships in which you are seen, supported, and loved unconditionally. They can include life partners, soul friends and family, children, and furry four-leggeds. The only rule is that there is a mutual love and respect, which makes it safe to have them close to your heart.

6. Tribes, Friends & Colleagues: The individuals — relatives, friends, and colleagues — you feel connected to and the groups and communities you choose to be a part of. These support your various interests and the different expressions of *you*.

7. Physical Health & Home: The strength of your life force and the overall wellness of your body. This includes your physical body, which houses your spirit, and the dwellings you live in that need to be your sanctuary. This is what gives you the energy and resilience to "do" your life and be radiant within it.

8. Financial Flow & Wealth: The flow of money and resources that enable you to feel sustained on the material plane, receive what you need, and care for yourself and those you love. This also includes the financial reserves that support you to weather the ebbs and the unexpected, and embrace opportunities when they arise. This is living a lifestyle that is maintainable and sustainable.

Look back at the Harmony Wheel and you'll notice the following:

The bottom – Tribes, Friends & Colleagues; Physical Health & Home; and Financial Flow & Wealth – forms your foundation. When these realms are strong and in harmony, you feel supported and connected on the material plane. This gives you the confidence, courage, and space to soar and expand in what you give through your work, creativity, and self-expression. When these are weak or imbalanced, it's much harder to be open to new possibility, focus on your personal growth, do things that don't "make money," give generously, grow new ventures or existing businesses and organizations, or excel in your work and career.

The center – Emotional Health & Happiness and Beloved Relationships (your most intimate relationships) – forms your heart line. When strong and in harmony, these realms keep your heart open and your inner life stable. You feel deeply supported and connected because you are receiving love and acceptance — from others and yourself — and experiencing a sense of belonging. Rooted in the strength of your self-love and self-worth, this heart line keeps you steady and stable when other parts of your life get wobbly or intense. When these are imbalanced, *you* feel wobbly on the inside.

The top – Sacred Work & Career, Spiritual Practice & Connection, and Creativity & Self-Expression – forms your potential and actual expression, expansion, and elevation. These realms signify what you give, share, and express in the world, which can include your job and what you do for money but encompasses so much more than that. When these are strong and in harmony, you feel present in the world, on purpose, and in alignment. You see your job or business in an expansive way, where it is part of your life's work — a channel to express your full self; make an impact; and receive an exchange of energy in the form of money, support, connection, and recognition. You feel part of something bigger than you, fulfilled and connected at a soul level.

New words empower you to create new realities.

As you look at each of these realms, most of them likely seem familiar. And some, like "Sacred Work" or "Beloved Relationships," might sound odd at first. Good! One of the ways we change our reality is by changing the words we use, to elevate how we think. Language liberates us from constructs that limit us. You can't change your world if you don't change your language.

For example, in the realm of Sacred Work & Career, notice I did not name this your "Job" or just "Work." The word *sacred* means "devoted to." Your sacred work is what you are devoted and dedicated to causing, changing, creating, and influencing in this world.

The work we do in this world may manifest in part as a job, but that job doesn't define us. It's part of what supports and enables us to "do" our sacred work and have the impact and experience we desire. It is often a major source of our financial flow and reserves, helping create a stable physical foundation.

The original root of the word *career*, the Latin *cararia*, means "road." The modern definition of the verb *career* is "to run or move rapidly along; go at full speed." This explains a lot. Careers, as held in the overculture, pressure us to move along quickly, at full throttle — no wonder they create more stress than joy for many of us. We are under the gun to always *be* where we are not yet.

But at the root, your career is simply your chosen path to give your gifts, presence, and life force. Your career is the road to your learning, growing, and expressing your full, true self. And like on any path, you will encounter stops, starts, hills, turns, and straight flats.

How can this help you create a more harmonious reality in which you feel successful and sustained? Ask yourself this: "If I embraced my career as a winding road, an unfolding journey, or an unfurling spiral, and released the pressure to keep running rapidly along, what could shift?" or "If I embraced my work to include more than my job, and expanded it to include those I care for, mentor, and mother, what could shift?" Open up your awareness beyond what you've considered before.

In the realm of Beloved Relationships, these are the intimate, close relationships in which you are truly seen and supported, or have a deep, respectful, and healthy bond. This can include a life partner or your "romantic relationship." I ditched the word *romantic* a long time ago because it means "in an idealized state." Imagine how often that idealized state leads to disappointment. Plus, you need more than one person to receive unconditional love from and be in intimate connection with. Reframe *intimacy* as "into-me-see" — the people who see you and whom you let see all of you. Intimacy is not just physical, and it's not just about sex. True intimacy stems from your heart and soul first, and physical expressions of many kinds emerge.

Beloved means "greatly loved; dear to the heart." When I first was introduced to the word, honestly I couldn't say it without feeling weird. But that was the overculture talking. Now I love *beloved*. But if *beloved* doesn't resonate, try *soul* relationships — soul family, soul partner, soul sister — which can include children, pets, friends, and relatives. If *soul* doesn't work, try *intimate*.

The other essential part we must acknowledge and take a stand for as women is motherhood and parenting. You'll notice that neither is called out in its own spiral, which is intentional. For too long we as women have had to fit in and slot in the relationships with our children, our responsibilities as parents, and our desires as mothers. In the duality reality of work/life balance, these relationships, responsibilities, and desires just get lumped into life. But most parents would say parenting is *work*, because it is.

Ask any woman who mothers her own children or someone else's, or uses her mothering energy to mentor or guide others, what mothering means to her, and if she had the words, she'd tell you that it is deeply soul-nourishing work that allows her to express a primal part of herself. If you have chosen to be a parent, parenting is part of your sacred work. In fact, I would say it's one of the most important and challenging jobs you have. For nonparents and those who care for, raise, or have an influence on children, this is also part of your sacred work. Until we stop slotting parenting, caring for children, and guiding young adults in on the side, we will never get out of overwhelm and burnout. If we as women never speak up for mothering as essential to the health of our world, we'll never receive the space, support, and resources we need to do it. And those who mother, teach, and care for the world's children will never be valued, and financially compensated, for what they are worth. Choosing to embrace parenting, mothering, and caretaking as sacred and as work — first within our own lives, and then in how we design our systems — is, I believe, one of the most impactful acts this generation of women can take.

This elevated language and perspective can just be between you and me right now. Explore this new language as a way of elevating your reality. For example, consider how expanding your definition of your work, career, and creative expression, or your relationships, beloveds, and tribe, could release pressure and open up possibility and lead to more harmony. We'll dive deeper into each realm in our daring act of liberation, but first let's relieve you of some of the roles you've perhaps unknowingly embraced that will keep you from standing as the clear, centered conductor supported to cultivate harmony.

Embrace your role as the centered conductor of your life. Release the jobs of overwhelmed juggler, plate spinner, or multitasker.

Have you ever said or heard words like "I am juggling so much! I am stretched in a million directions! I am just trying to keep all the balls in the air!"? Every time I hear a woman talk about how she is "juggling" to keep all the parts of her life in order so nothing crashes or gets lost or interrupted, I want to embrace her and say: "No! Don't do it. You are not a circus act."

Take a look at the woman standing in the center of the Harmony Wheel, and you can see how you could easily fall under the illusion that you must try to juggle all the realms of your life like balls. Or run around trying to keep the parts all moving like a plate spinner. If you approach your life this way, expect to be full of anxiety and exhaustion: if you pause, slow down, or rest, all the plates and balls come crashing down! Imagine the amount of mental energy operating this way takes. You can't sustain this level of focus for days. Even the best jugglers have never been able to juggle more than eleven balls at once. And the person who holds that world record practiced for two years, and he could do it for only four hours.

If you make it your job to juggle or run around like mad so nothing crashes, you will never find respite or serenity. How could you? Constantly tracking the many moving parts, you've taken on the exhausting task of keeping it all going for everyone and everything. It's like living your life in a perpetual sprint from one thing to another. Not sustainable. And not necessary.

Here's the point where we press the LIBERATE button, and you make the choice to "be" in your life differently. Look again at the woman within the Harmony Wheel as yourself. Are you willing to relinquish the role of juggler, plate spinner, and multitasker? To release yourself from the responsibility of having to prevent everything from crashing by keeping it moving? Are you willing to experiment with embracing your role as the conductor who stands balanced in the center, focused on cultivating harmony. I mean, why wouldn't you, right?

As we've talked about, this is not about doing more; it's about doing things differently. You don't need to know the how, yet. Let's start with three self-sustainability principles below — read them, and then choose one to experiment with in your daily life by thinking, feeling, responding, making choices, and moving into action differently. Remember, the first step is just awareness — start to notice what you haven't seen.

Self-Sustainability Principles for Cultivating Harmony within a Whole Life

Be in connection with all the parts, but don't take responsibility for keeping it all going and moving.

Notice that each realm is symbolized by a spiral shape. This is because a spiral, by nature, creates its own momentum as it grows. As wise women, we structure the realms of our lives to thrive, without all the energy needing to come from us all the time. See the lines between you and each realm? These are meant to be energetic connections — not umbilical cords. A conductor doesn't sustain the tuba player with her oxygen and nutrients, but there is an energetic exchange and connection. The parts have their own energy and momentum. Notice where you have created codependent connections versus an interconnected dynamic.

Vary your focus; do not play everything at the same time.

You can't give the same amount of life force to eight things simultaneously. For one, you'll feel like an octopus in a medieval torture device (like when you multitask). Two, if you as a conductor directed all sections of your symphony to play at the same tempo and sound level at the same time, you would not create a harmony; you would create a harsh cacophony and chaos. Your role is to make choices about what to interact with when, at what pace, and for how long. Notice the difference when you act as a multitasking machine, trying to interact with many parts, versus a centered conductor, focused on one or two parts at a time, shifting her attention over time.

Cultivate the inner strength – emotionally, mentally, energetically, and physically – to stand at the center of your dynamic life, grounded and balanced, with all the parts moving around you in harmony.

If you stand in the middle, balanced within, in relationship with all parts but not *holding* all the parts, your feminine wisdom will sense when something is out of whack or needs attention. This empowers you to catch imbalances early on, making it much easier to bring things back into harmony. For example, think of a relationship or a project in which you had a sense that something was amiss, but you were either so focused in one realm or moving so fast that you missed the subtle signs. Rather than turning to it, you ignored it. Until eventually it got louder and louder so you had to deal with it, or like an unhappy tuba player, it threatened to quit on you. Notice and sense the disharmony before it becomes dis-ease in your body or emotions; drama in your relationships, finances, or home; or damage to your work, career, and self. This is where your power is. This is exactly where our first daring act of liberation will take us.

DARING ACT OF LIBERATION #1

Give Your Life a Harmony Adjustment

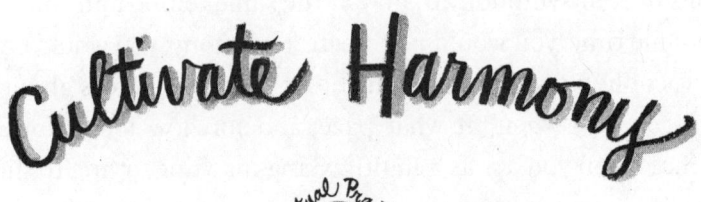

Cultivate Harmony

Self-empowerment and enlightenment are not about never experiencing symptoms of imbalance and disharmony but rather about becoming more aware and then consciously choosing to do things differently.

Wise women use the signs of imbalance to alert themselves to what needs attention in their lives so they can take empowered action to make shifts — before the imbalances progress to drama, disease, despair, distress, or destruction. This is what the Harmony Adjustment can do for you.

I take myself through this process once a year at the March equinox and whenever I sense the signs of imbalance in my life — crabbiness, frustration, sugar-intake increases, missing my daily walks, lashing out, my partner cuddling more with the dog than with me, working ten hours a day for too many days in a row, and feeling like everything is on me and up to me. I know my signs of disharmony well, and they will likely be the same for the rest of my life. Yours, too.

Your Mission

Reveal the current imbalances within your life so you become more enlightened and empowered to do things differently.

Embark on this daring act of liberation with the intention of cultivating more harmony within your whole life, now. If you take the steps I've outlined here, while I can't promise you nirvana, I can say that you will feel more empowered, instead of like you can't change your circumstances. You will be more enlightened as to what can transform and where to focus to create the greatest impact.

STEP 1: Assess the Current Harmony Level for Each Realm of Your Life

Referring back to the Cultivate Harmony glyph, tune in to each realm, one by one, and take a read to assess its current level of harmony, on a scale of 0 to 10.

- **10 – totally in harmony:** feels like a vibrant orchestra playing, or like this realm is good, solid, and well cared for
- **5 – needs attention:** feels like there's an imbalance, as if something is wrong or out of whack, is being ignored or avoided, or is calling for more attention
- **0 – totally in disharmony:** feels like the realm is draining life force

and resources, to the detriment of other realms, or like it's been so long since it received attention that it's gone dormant or disappeared

The best way to do the reading is to give your feminine wisdom the microphone. Slow down, take a breath, and tune in to that particular realm of your life (refer to the definitions on pages 50 and 51 if that helps) by asking: *What is the current level of harmony, on a scale of 0 to 10?*

- Sacred Work & Career
- Spiritual Practice & Connection
- Creativity & Self-Expression
- Emotional Health & Happiness
- Beloved Relationships
- Tribes, Friends & Colleagues
- Physical Health & Home
- Financial Flow & Wealth

Write your rating next to each of the spirals on the Harmony Wheel so you can see it; this is important. Don't skip this part. You can write the rating in the book, draw the wheel in your journal, or go to the www.OverwhelmedAndOverIt.com book readers' kit to get a full-size worksheet.

STEP 2: Acknowledge and Maintain the Harmony That Does Exist

Acknowledge the harmony currently present in your life. And acknowledge your part in cultivating this harmony. Challenge yourself to *feel* the strong foundation that already exists by answering the inquiries below. Feeling the harmony here now will give you the fuel and focus to turn your attention to what needs tending to and reharmonizing, and will keep the strong realms growing using the momentum you've already established.

1. *Where does harmony already exist in my life* [anything 7 or above]?
2. *What has contributed to cultivating the harmony?*
3. *What is needed to maintain this harmony for now?*

STEP 3: Be Honest about the Imbalances and Their Impact

One of our intuitive superpowers as women is to reveal the patterns and relationships between things. Remember, the realms of our lives are not separate; they are interconnected and interdependent. If you illuminate the pattern between the imbalanced realms, access to deeper wisdom arises. Circle the disharmonies, and then draw a line between them so they are all connected visually. Answer the inquiries below to reveal the wisdom.

1. *Where are the imbalances currently* (anything lower than a 6)?
2. *What is the impact of the imbalances on my life, now?* (Consider this physically, emotionally, financially, and relationally.)
3. *What is the relationship between the imbalances?* (Look for the bigger pattern.)

STEP 4: Choose to Cultivate Harmony by Making a Harmony Adjustment

Last, we need to get you tuned in to your fierce feminine heart. Remember that your heart is where your power lies. If you can feel the greater reason why making different choices going forward matters to you and get real about the cost if you don't adjust, you can move into empowered, supportive action, now. First, let your fierce feminine wisdom speak your truth; then let her illuminate some simple but significant adjustments you can make. Write out and/or speak these — don't just consider them mentally, or nothing will change. Look at your Harmony Wheel assessment and ask:

1. *What do I desire?* (You don't need to know how it could come to fruition; the first step is naming and claiming your desire.)
2. *What's the cost if I don't make an adjustment?* (Get honest about the consequences of keeping the status quo; your power is here.)
3. *What could become possible if I do make a shift?* (Allow yourself to step into the center of the Harmony Wheel and imagine what new reality is possible.)
4. *What small but significant adjustment* could *I make to restore or cultivate harmony?* (Choose the realm in which you feel empowered to make a shift and one action you can take in the next week.)
5. *What action* will *I take in this next week?* (Commit. Tell another person for accountability. Experiment! Remember that this is support for you, not another to-do.)

Embracing your power to cultivate harmony starts with one simple but significant adjustment you can make this week — don't ask for permission; give yourself permission, by the power within you. Taking simple yet mighty acts allows you to see and feel a shift in your reality; this gets the flow going and motivates you to keep doing things differently. Before you know it, momentum is creating more harmony within all the parts of your whole life.

I asked one of the women I've advised and mentored, Susan — Chief Technology Officer and mother of three — to share how she used the Harmony Adjustment as the starting point to create momentum for the bigger shifts her heart and soul were calling for. Once she became more self-aware, she didn't wait or put pressure on herself to hatch a big plan to "fix" things. We started with one simple action she could take — something she had the power to shift that gave her a feeling of what she desired immediately. Susan's story, in her own words, follows.

I Want to Be a Mom, but I Have to Make the Money

I felt something was seriously off-kilter in my marriage and family. I knew I was spending way too much time at work and way too little with my kids, not to mention the man I loved. While I had "made it" to the position and title of Chief Technology Officer, I still felt totally stressed about money. I was at a loss as to how to "fix" this. I was so overwhelmed already with the pressure of being the sole "breadwinner" in my family. I was running so fast, under pressure to perform in a reactive three-year-old tech company — where I was only one of two women on the executive leadership team. I was running on fumes as it was. I had nothing more to give, and what I was giving was not enough.

Honestly, I didn't want to just "fix" it. I'd been holding it all together for three years. And now, what had begun as intermittent imbalances were now full-on deep resentments swirling between my husband and me. My resentment of having to carry the burden of making all the money and his of feeling trapped at home. I wanted to liberate us out of our chaotic reality, where there was never enough time, space, or money. I needed something different — something that gave me perspective on *me*, and tools that had the power to change this dynamic.

When Christine first shared the Harmony Wheel with me, what emerged were three realms suffering from a significant lack of harmony: (1) Beloved Relationships (my partner and my children barely saw me); (2) Sacred Work & Career (I was giving seventy-five hours a week and about 175 percent of my life force to an industry that had 0 percent meaning to me); and (3) Financial Flow & Wealth (our previously two-income family was now down to one, and while money did flow in, a lot was flowing out).

As I drew lines between the disharmonies, I started to see a web of interconnection between them. And a very clear pattern of dissatisfaction, disconnection, and misplaced loyalty emerged. One that I had unconsciously created. I was pouring everything into my work — my loyalty, love, life force — when what I really yearned to be loyal to, love, and give my life force to was my family. I became aware that my overfocus on work was connected to my unsustainable financial foundation and the instability in my marriage. It was hard to admit, but truthfully it was easier to excel at work than it was to feel the feelings in my heart and get real with myself and my marriage.

Once I was able to get in touch with my heart — by letting myself feel the cost of the disharmony — I was able to admit to myself: "*Yes!* I have a great desire to make an impact in this world through my work, *and* I had children because I wanted to be a mother. I have a *deep* desire to mother." Just writing those words now gives me chills: "I have a *deep* desire to mother." It was so true, yet I was denying myself. I was mothering my team more than I was my kids, and myself. This struck a deep chord that woke me up, I think, because I allowed myself to *feel* my desire.

With self-awareness and systemic awareness, now I could do something about it! My first act of liberation? Change the way I started my mornings. I chose to connect with my three children and partner each morning instead of connecting to my email and work. This small shift created the momentum to making bigger shifts, which included eventually leaving the start-up and taking a role within a bigger organization, changing how we as a family spent holidays and vacations to create more connection, and creating space with my partner to connect and have meaningful conversations weekly versus numbing out to television at night. Cultivating harmony consciously so things don't become imbalanced again is a practice that's now part of the structure I've put in place. I still feel overwhelm and still have to watch my habit of overworking; the difference is, I don't wait until my life, health, and relationships get to a dramatic state before I respond. Cultivate harmony. It works.

PART TWO

Liberate Your Life Force

*Wise women choose to retain
and protect their life force,
as if it is the most essential resource
they possess.*

Chapter 3

RELEASE: **Drain Your Energy, Get Sick or Burn Out, Then Refill**

EMBRACE: **Cultivate and Retain Your Life Force, Daily**

Wise women have a relationship with their physical bodies; their energetic bodies; and the life force they consciously cultivate, retain, and spend wisely.

Your life force is your juice. Life force is the vital energy within you responsible for maintaining your life and your health. If you were a cell phone or an electric car, it would be your battery charge. If you were a fuel-based car, it would be your gas tank. Your life force plays a major role in how your physical body, mind, and emotional and energetic systems feel and operate. When your body has plenty of life force, you experience harmony and health. When your life force is weak, you *feel* weak physically and mentally. When your life force is low, you feel unstable emotionally and so are more likely to react from your emotional triggers or habitual imprints, rather than from your centered, clear core. If your life force wanes too far, you get sick.

You cannot see your life force with your eyes, but you can see its presence or lack thereof. When a person looks healthy, feels radiant, and seems vibrant, you may say, "Wow, that person is so full of energy." They have strong life force. Contrast that with a person who looks physically unwell, mentally fried, and emotionally drained. What you see are the effects of a deficient life force.

Life force is not a new concept. You can trace its origins back thousands of years in multiple parts of the world. The Sanskrit term *prana* — dating to as early as 1200 BCE — means the vital life force within. *Chi (qi)* has been a foundational part of traditional Chinese medicine for over three thousand years. If you visit Egypt, you will see depictions of life force etched in the glyphs of the ancient temples, some said to be built as far back as 2500 BCE.

Prana, *chi*, *vitality*, and *life force* are all synonyms. You can call this energy within you whatever you like; just call it something. I use *life force*. I see my life force as a *resource* I possess, and that therefore, as the conductor and designer of my life, I have a *choice* as to how I direct and spend it. But to direct and spend it wisely, you have to understand some things about how life force works, become aware of the ways in which you yourself are depleting your own energy and reserves, release the imprints not serving you, and embrace different choices in your day-to-day — ones that nourish and sustain you, instead of stress and drain you. This is the focus of this entire section. We'll start by illuminating some wisdom about life force, and about how you and I have been conditioned to operate that is *so* not working to our benefit.

Your life force powers up your physical body; moderates your mental bodies; charges and stabilizes your energetic bodies; and determines how clear, calm, and vital you feel.

Your life force has an impact on much more than your physical body. Most of the modalities for wellness that address the human as a whole system acknowledge and work with multiple bodies that make up your entire system. Yes, you have *multiple* bodies. When I first learned this in my yogic science studies, it kind of blew my mind. *I have multiple bodies, what?* Tomes of wisdom are written on this subject, and if you are unfamiliar, I encourage you to expand your understanding of your whole human system and how it works. In the book readers' kit, I created a list of some of my favorite books and resources for you. For now, just consider these three possibilities:

1. You are more than your physical body. You have a pranic body (a breath body), mental bodies (different facets of your mind), an emotional body (stemming from your heart and feelings), subtle bodies (the energy fields around your physical body), and energetic bodies (like your nervous system).

2. Your life force is something you need to cultivate, daily. Life force is something you have to choose to cultivate. Just like you plug in your cell phone or laptop to charge the battery, your batteries need recharging, daily. Sleep, healthy food, and staying hydrated, while essential, are not enough. There are specific methods, modalities, and practices for cultivating life force. There is so much to share. But let's start with waking you up to how you drain your life force because of your choices. Then we can put structures and practices in place that sustain your life force.

3. Your physical body is the last place dis-ease and the effects of overwhelm and burnout show up. By the time you feel exhausted or foggy or show other physical symptoms, you've already depleted yourself. The *disease* has rooted itself into your physical body or your mental mind, and it takes much longer to recover and return to a state of harmony. Consider the word *disease* — not just as physical symptom or a diagnosis but as a state of *un-ease* within you. *Dis-* means "apart." Disease is to be apart from ease, apart from harmony. When you are more aware of the dis-ease you experience mentally in the form of anxiety, worry, or negative self-talk, or experience energetically in your nervous system as frustration or feeling flooded, you become empowered to make changes sooner, before becoming completely depleted or physically sick.

Recall a time you hit your wall, got sick, or crumbled under the pressure. Weren't there signs that may have been subtle, but upon reflection, you can see how your whole system or parts of your system were overtaxed? We tend to associate burnout with our physical body or mental state because those are the areas we've been taught to focus on.

In my experience, there are at least eight kinds of burnout, only one of which is physical burnout. These other kinds of burnout often show up before the signs of exhaustion and disease appear in your body. When you can articulate what *kind* of burnout you are experiencing, versus just saying you are burned-out, exhausted, or overwhelmed, you are more empowered to see the root, and get what you need before you get sick. Read about the different kinds of burnout below, and consider which you may be experiencing now, noting that you have likely experienced many.

The 8 Kinds of Burnout

1. **Mental burnout:** *My mind cannot process any more; it's fried.*
2. **Emotional burnout:** *These heavy or anxious emotions are exhausting me.*
3. **Compassion burnout:** *I cannot hold any more loving space for anyone else; I'm tapped.*
4. **Relational burnout:** *I've been overgiving to others, my organization, or my community/family, and I am over it.*
5. **Survival burnout:** *I'm exhausted from trying to make ends meet and stay afloat.*
6. **Superwoman burnout:** *The weight of taking on so much is too much; I can't hold it all anymore.*
7. **Passion burnout:** *I love what I do, but I've given too much and pushed too hard.*
8. **Physical burnout:** *My body is revolting; I have depleted my life force.*

Know Yourself
What kinds of burnout are affecting me?

- Which types of burnout have I experienced in the past?
- Which am I experiencing now?
- What are the signs or symptoms that I am experiencing these kinds of burnout? (Be specific.)

These concepts may be new to you or familiar. In either case, what I just shared is pretty logical and rational, don't you think? Interesting, given this wisdom is often called *alternative* or not taken seriously by the mainstream systems, when in fact it's been around for a lot longer. What's even more interesting is how we've accepted ways of giving our life force to work and other people that are not rational, logical, or smart. For example, see if these next two pieces of wisdom resonate with you.

It is not normal or smart to drain yourself to the point you get sick. Or to get so overwhelmed that you wish you could get sick just so you could rest.

You already know this. It is common sense not to push yourself to your breaking point before you allow yourself to rest or drain your energy tank to zero before you refill. Just like a cell-phone battery or a gas tank takes more time to recharge or refill when at zero charge or on empty, if you drain yourself to exhaustion, it will cost you more time — and usually more money — to fill yourself back up.

Yet if you are like any of the rest of us overworked women, on more than one occasion you have drained your energy, gotten sick, and burned out, before you refilled. Maybe you even wished you could get sick just so you had an excuse to stop? It's okay; you can admit it. You wouldn't be the first woman who told me she was glad she got a cold or the flu so she could rest or who had to get sick before she let herself rest. We all know better. Yet we don't stop the cycle. Why?

Well, for starters, in the overculture we've assimilated into, it has become *acceptable* to work this way. We all know it's not healthy or smart to drain ourselves completely, but we complain and sympathize with each other over just how depleted we are. We go to work and push ourselves when we don't feel well, and we often have to send our kids to school or daycare when they don't feel well. Our systems are not designed for humans to rest and replenish, unless we get really sick and have no other choice.

Instead of calling out this cycle of depletion — individually and collectively — as a warning signal that we need to make a change, we take a pit stop, recharge just enough, and plow back in. Only to find ourselves in the same cycle all over again some months later. Take a look at the glyph below to see what the "deplete, get sick, burn out, repeat" cycle looks like.

Drain Life Force

GET SICK • BURN OUT • REFILL • REPEAT

Notice that the drain continues over time, depleting your life force until you get sick, but even then you don't stop to truly replenish; instead, the drain continues until you hit burnout. Eventually you begin the slow refill, but rather than stopping the cycle, you repeat it.

Why would you do this to yourself? I've witnessed this in so many women, and lived it myself, so don't feel bad if this sounds like you, too. And if you've already righted this disharmony, good for you. In any case, keep reading, because we are all susceptible to depleting our life force, especially in intense or chaotic times. Here's what I've come to believe. We keep burning ourselves out because either (1) we cannot see the cycle, or (2) we do not see how to change the cycle within the current reality of our lives or the systems we work within and interact with. Without another option, we suck it up and just accept the cycle of depleting ourselves and getting sick before we can rest and refill as "normal" when it's anything but.

Consider this: If you train your body to get sick or depleted before you recharge, that is what will become acceptable for it and you. If you train your body to monitor and maintain your life force, then you'll be more empowered to make choices that support you to refill and replenish before you crash into burnout. I asked my former assistant Sarah if I could share her experience of this with you, to help you reveal and shift your burnout and depletion cycles. Here's what she said.

> For years, I thought it was completely normal and acceptable to every December get sick with a cold, bronchitis, or a nasty flu. After a year of giving everything my all, I would crash hard, get sick for two weeks, and then pop up in the new year with just enough juice to do it all over again. I just accepted this as a normal winter reality. In fact, at some level, I think I expected it. Because I had so much going on and so many people and things to care for — five kids, my clients, three dogs, two goats, sisters, a partner, a business — I had conditioned my body to run on fumes because my life was designed that way. I didn't

know I had a different choice, or there was another way of working and taking care of my family. It wasn't until Christine suggested it was not normal to always get sick in December that I woke up to my unconscious burnout and depletion cycles. Self-awareness was the first step — I couldn't change what I couldn't see. Aware, I began to understand the power I actually possessed to maintain and cultivate my life force, even within a full life with many demands and people in it.

My invitation to you is similar to the one I made to Sarah. Start by becoming aware of your current burnout and depletion cycles, so you can release the insane ways of operating we've come to accept as normal. Then I will give you the wisdom and practices to embrace your power to no longer become emotionally or energetically drained, mentally fried, or physically sick before you rest or replenish.

Know Yourself
What is my current burnout and depletion cycle?

- *How often do I crash into burnout or get sick? Weekly, monthly, quarterly, yearly?*
- *What events in my life tend to end with a crash into depletion; getting sick; or feelings of despair, depression, or deep resentment?*
- *If I look upon burnout as a cycle I choose to accept versus just the way I have to live, what do I notice?*

When you embrace that how, when, and if you spend your life force is your choice to make, you become empowered to liberate yourself from the cycles of burnout and depletion.

It wasn't until the age of forty that I finally met a very wise man who in one word unlocked the code for me of *how* to stop the cycle of burnout and exhaustion I could not liberate myself from. I was three years into my journey as an entrepreneur, doing work I loved, feeling on purpose, and making a difference. But I was still working, creating, and giving until I dropped — which usually involved getting sick physically, feeling exhausted emotionally, or becoming so mentally fatigued that I just couldn't work. Only then would I give myself and my neglected workhorse of a body a break. I would have no choice but to refuel.

So I would, for a few days. And then, when I had filled my tanks enough — never full, just enough — I would charge back in, only to start the cycle all over again. I had cobbled together some self-care strategies that would keep me going like the Energizer Bunny for a while so I had the juice to meet a deadline, birth a project, or do what was needed to keep everything afloat. And like clockwork, every three to four months, I would end up depleted, exhausted, and tapped out. I was stuck in a burnout pattern and depletion cycle. I knew it wasn't working for me, but I couldn't stop it.

Then I met with Dr. Alex Feng, my acupuncturist. I had been seeing him for a year as part of my self-care strategy to "fill up" every three months. Apparently, this was long enough for him to get wise to my burnout cycle. I'll never forget the session that broke the cycle. This visit, instead of just sticking needles in me, giving me herbs, and saying, "Get some rest, and come back and see me in two weeks, Christine," Dr. Feng put his hands on my belly and spoke one word that changed my life forever: "*Retain.*"

He repeated it three times: "*Retain. Retain. Retain.*" And in that moment, I got it, the wisdom that would break my quarterly crash into burnout cycle, forever:

Retain, *don't drain, your life force.*

Have you ever had an epiphany? Where you hear or read something that pierces through you, and like a thousand-watt lightbulb was turned on by the Universe, you see what you were blind to before?

78   *Overwhelmed & Over It*

That's what this was like for me. It's called an *awakening*, when you become consciously aware of something that was always there but you could not see. If you embrace the wisdom and apply it to your life, you become empowered to do things differently and, as a result, elevate your reality.

I went home that day and wrote the word RETAIN in my journal in big bold letters. And then I said to myself, "*Retain*, don't drain, your life force, Christine!" Duh, why had I not considered that before? Such a better strategy, don't you think? To retain and maintain your life force, versus give it all away before you pay attention to your own physical, emotional, and mental needs?

Drain Life Force | Retain Life Force

GET SICK · BURN OUT · REFILL · REPEAT | RETAIN · REFILL · RETAIN · REFILL

Pause to take a look at the glyph above and consider which approach you want to take in your life — drain your life force until you get sick and burn out, or retain your life force, "refilling" as the intentional way you live and interact with your work, others, and the world. If you are up for liberating yourself from your burnout cycles, next I can show you how to make the move over to retaining your life force and creating a more sustainable reality in your life.

Self-Sustainability Principles for Retaining Your Life Force

What follows are six self-sustainability principles I believe are essential to embrace if you desire to stay centered and sustained in the now, have the energy needed to achieve and tend to what truly matters to you, and stay feeling vital along the way. Read and take in each one, and we'll end with a powerful stand for your personal sustainability.

Never serve from your reserves.

If I could etch this potent piece of wisdom into your brain so that big bells would go off as warning signals whenever you were about to make a choice that would tip you into depletion, I would. This is that critical for you to remember.

Your reserves are your deeper life-force tanks. If you deplete them, you get sick, and not just with a cold you can shake in a couple of days. Whacked-out thyroids, autoimmune disorders and hormonal imbalances, chronic fatigue, migraines, anxiety and pain, and much more and much worse can take root when we serve from our reserves. These deeper stores of life force are more challenging to refill and, in some cases, could take you months or years to replenish.

It's kind of like being a vehicle with multiple gas tanks. Once you empty one tank, you start pulling from your second. While it's good to know that the second tank is there, you should tap into your reserves only in emergencies or in unexpected situations that require additional stamina and resiliency. You want your reserve energy to be there when you need it. You don't want to make it *normal* to dip into your life-force reserves as the way you work and operate. You don't want to run on fumes. That's how you got here in the first place.

One way to visualize this is to see your body as a chalice. A chalice is a vessel often used to serve wine or water — water nourishes us and keeps us alive, and wine allows us to savor the sweetness and spirit of life. You may have heard the saying "Don't serve from an empty cup.

Only serve from the overflow." But have you ever tried to drink from a teacup sitting on a saucer? There's not enough fluid in that little teacup to get us through our morning routine, let alone a whole day! And we are supposed to serve from the overflow?

Take a look at the glyph of the chalice below. You want to serve from the top round part, which is more than enough to take care of what you have going on in your life daily. And if it's not, you'll know, because your cup will be dry at the end of each day, drained, and you'll be faced with a choice. *Do I refill in the evening? Or do I start my next day serving from the stem?*

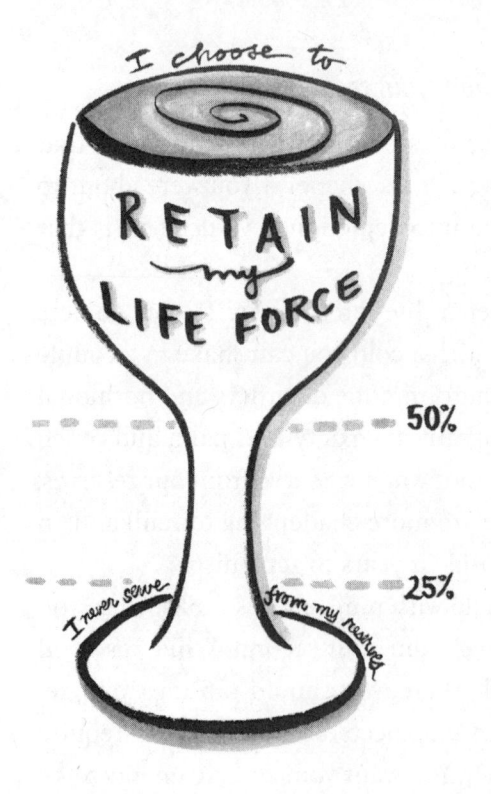

Think of the stem like your first reserve tank, which pulls from the energy stores needed to keep your whole system functioning properly. When you serve from here, you sacrifice the harmony of your system and steal from the life-force supply you need to be healthy.

Notice the stem isn't that big. It does not hold a lot of juice, so the life force here gets sucked up fast. And when it does, you drop into your second and last reserve tank, the bottom of the chalice, its base. Here you serve from your deepest reserves, which really should not be shared with anyone. This is where chronic disease, emotional distress, and mental overload set in. Most women are so resilient that they will operate from here for months or years out of sheer willpower, or survival instinct, until one day something fails within them. Then they must take a break, because they have reached their *breaking* point. But it didn't have to go down that way.

You *need* life force to survive. And to thrive. You have a choice. Keep waiting until the physical, emotional, mental, and energetic symptoms of dis-ease show up, or pay attention to your life force every day so you maintain your energy levels and don't dip into your reserves. Or if you dip into the reserves, instead of sucking your life force dry, make adjustments to how you live and give.

Monitor and check your life force, daily.
And you won't run out of fuel or cross the threshold into burnout.

Okay, now let's take all this wisdom and make it practical. I can't wait to share the harmonizing practice that has kept me out of the burnout cycle ever since I created it. I am going to teach you how to check your *life-force level* so you never dangerously deplete your reserves, because when you get close to serving from your reserves, your feminine wisdom will alert you. Stop everything else you are doing, and *do* this with me now, really.

How to Check and Retain Your Life-Force Level

1. Get connected to your body. Put your feet on the ground, one hand on your belly, one on your heart; close your eyes; and take a few deep breaths to tune in to your physical, energetic, and emotional bodies.

2. Take a reading of your current life force. Imagine your body like a chalice, and ask your inner wisdom *What is my life-force level?* on a scale from 100 to 0, with 100 being full, 50 being half-full, and 0 being empty. Keep breathing until you get a number. The first number is generally right, before your mind tries to make up something else. Stick with what comes to you first.

3. Receive what you need, adding more life force than you spend, so you stay sustained. Hands still on body, eyes closed, ask your inner wisdom a second question: *What do I need to receive today?* Whatever the answer, promise to give that to yourself by how you design your day, make choices during your day, and receive throughout the day. When you find yourself feeling overwhelmed, drained, or frustrated, you pause and give this to yourself. You check in with yourself as you complete your day to make sure you received what you needed.

The response is rarely *a seven-day trip to Tahiti*! Sometimes the responses are feeling words like *peace*, *love*, *harmony*, and *faith*. Other times they are specific actions, like *get hugs*, *drink lots of water*, and *take a walk*. The point is, if you don't know what you need to receive, you won't get it. And if you keep giving life force without receiving more, you will deplete yourself, leaving you feeling like all the nourishment, joy, and sweetness has dried up.

Your role is to make this your daily practice to ensure you keep your life force at a healthy level — which you do by always making sure you are receiving what you need and not serving from your reserves. Look back at the glyph on page 78, which illustrates the power you possess to retain and refill your life force. If you monitor your life force daily like this, when you get close to serving from your reserves or you find yourself in the depletion zones or you start feeling overwhelmed or drained, you adjust how you give. Take a look at the chart below to see what I mean.

If your life-force level is…	You are serving from…
Above 75	**A full chalice. You have plenty to give, even if you don't replenish deeply.** Maintain your life force and receive what you need so you stay nourished, resourced, and sustained. Even if you give a lot, it's unlikely you will serve from your reserves.

If your life-force level is...	You are serving from...
Between 50 and 75	**A chalice that has enough to give, for now. You need to receive and replenish today.** Make sure you refill, and receive what you need, or you risk waking up tomorrow having to serve from your reserves.
Between 25 and 49	**Your reserves, the stem. Alter how you give your life force today.** Shift how you work, how you interact with others, how much energy you put out — and make sure you receive what you need, and replenish, no matter what. Be aware of emotional drains. You must give, interact, and work differently until you have risen above half-full.
Below 25	**Your deepest life-force reserves. If you are not already feeling it, physical, mental, and emotional dis-ease is coming if you don't make a change.** Clear your schedule, create space to regenerate, replenish your reserves, get support, get emotionally balanced within, clear your mental and energetic fields of other people's energy, and make lifestyle changes. Your life depends on it.

Take a pause here with me. What is your current life-force level? Where does it fall on the chart? What does this tell you about how you can sustainably interact and work today? About what you need in order to replenish and retain your life force? When I do this with a group, over half usually report they are below a 50, and at least a handful below a 25. Which means over half of people are making themselves physically sick or mentally and emotionally exhausted because they are running on their reserve tanks.

The lowest I've been since taking daily readings is a 43. I got the reading on Wednesday, and by Friday, I cleared my schedule and spent the weekend doing what replenished me. When I awoke on Monday, while I was not a 75, I had risen above half-full. Sometimes life will not allow you to clear the space for the deeper replenishment you need, so what do you do?

When your life-force levels are low, work, respond, and give differently.

What do you do when you are at a 50 or a 33 or a 7? Call up your work or clients and tell them, "This lady whose book I am reading said I can't come in today because my life-force levels are too low, and I don't have energy to give"? (LOL.) Or tell those you care for, "Sorry, you must take care of yourself today; I have to fill up my life force!"? Of course not, although that does sound liberating, doesn't it? But it's not realistic for our dynamic lives in which we do have responsibilities and people who depend on us.

So here is what you do. You make conscious *choices* about how you give your life force. And you make sure you replenish your life force. You may have to show up at work or help your kids or travel, but the *how* changes. You choose to give, work, "effort," and interact differently. You give less, effort less, and work slower when your life-force levels are below a 50. You ask for more support. Clear space by releasing things that don't need to happen now, things that can wait and flow to another day. Say no to what subtracts from your life force. Seek out what adds to your life force.

When you make your daily choices in alignment with the life-force level you have each day, the Universe takes notice and small synchronicities happen. Meetings are canceled and create space. People show up offering to help. You see different solutions that don't require you to do all the heavy lifting. You retain your energy and give only in ways that are truly needed and valued. You start noticing how much energy you waste. It's really quite fantastic, but it can only happen if you first make the choice to give differently based on your life-force levels.

I also use the life-force check-in with my team as a way to keep all of us healthy. I refuse to run my organization in ways that burn us out or sacrifice our personal well-being. We do the life-force check-in at our weekly meetings and daily when we are running a weekend workshop or when we are in an intense time of outflow. Everyone has full permission to let the team know when their tank dips below a 50, so they don't serve from their reserves. It doesn't matter whether it's a personal or professional reason for the dip. We don't separate the human being from the person who shows up to work. We are whole beings with diverse lives doing our best to cultivate harmony at the core, and sometimes it all just gets too intense to handle. Instead of hiding our emotional or physical stress, putting on a strong facade, or pushing through, we alert the team with a text or email, or verbally: "Hey, everyone, I just wanted to let you know I am at a 45 today. So I need some support." Or "I need to go slow." Or "I need [fill in the blank]." Now we know this person requires support, so we can assess what the collective needs to operate, and we can pitch in based on our individual life-force levels.

Harmonizing Practice
Take a Morning Life-Force and Receiving Reading

Every morning before you start your workday, check in with your life force and inner wisdom with these two simple inquiries. Never start a day without them.

1. *What is my current life-force level?* (This informs how you give, work, relate, and create.)
2. *What do I need to receive today?* (Design your day to receive this, or when the swirl hits, give yourself this.)

> *Know your warning signals for overwhelm onslaught and burnout so you don't get blindsided.*

Your body and emotions will tell you when you are giving away life force you cannot afford to. Your job is to take notice of the warning signals and not ignore them, but make changes. This means you need to know how your individual human system works. What are the emotional, mental, energetic, and physical symptoms that, like flares, try to warn you that you are depleting your life force or serving from your reserves? Here are some common signals. Which show up for you?

Common Signs You Are Serving from Your Reserves
- You wake up feeling anxious each day.
- You wake up with a sore lower back or puffy eyes, really thirsty, or still tired.
- You go to sleep with a mind that won't stop.
- You walk around with stress balls in your shoulders or tension in your jaw.
- You emote frustration or lash out in ways that seem out of whack given the situation.
- You get short with others because your nervous system is fried.
- You cannot focus. You feel like you are reacting to the world around you.
- You feel a tingle in your throat, signaling you are starting to get sick.
- You crave sugar almost every day.
- You binge-watch TV two or three nights in a row.
- You are superwoman-sobbing but don't know why.
- You feel despair, defeated, or like you just can't do it anymore.
- You want to quit — your job, your family, your life.

Remember, awareness is everything when it comes to stopping the burnout and overwhelm cycles. So let's slow down here and get really specific by naming your particular emotional, physical, and mental signals that you are serving from your reserves. Answer the three "Know Yourself" inquiries below. Use the list above for inspiration, and also think back to times right before you got sick, burned out, or completely drained yourself. How has your body, heart, mind, and spirit been signaling you? In your wisdom journal write the warning signs you reveal. Start to notice them in your daily life as your feminine wisdom signaling you to make a shift and replenish, and realize you have a choice — *Do I choose to retain, or drain, my life force?*

Know Yourself
What are the warning signals that my life force is waning or draining?

- *How do I start feeling or reacting emotionally when I'm serving from my reserves?*
- *How do I start feeling physically?*
- *What do I notice about myself mentally?*

Practice retaining and cultivating your life force, every day.

There is so much I could say on this last self-sustainability principle. It is really like a big marquee flashing: "If you want to stay healthy and vibrant, you must practice both *retaining* your life force and *cultivating* your life force every day." Your life force is a *resource* that you are responsible for cultivating — you grow, generate, and receive it to make sure you stay strong and healthy. You don't need to be a life-force hoarder, but you do want to be a life-force *steward*. Just like the earth's resources do not have an endless supply, neither does your personal life force.

If we lived in a different time, you would have grown up learning how to keep your life force healthy and strong. Like Wonder Woman learned to condition her full superheroine self, you would have been trained, with practices to deal with the stressors that drain your life force, and taught how to generate life force, daily. So as an adult, you'd make choices to structure your daily life in ways that naturally cultivate and retain life force. You would not feel like it was another to-do to add to your list, or something that was optional. You would expect that the ways in which you worked and interacted with your responsibilities were designed to support your whole human system to thrive and stay healthy.

Learning about your life force and how to cultivate and retain it is a lifelong practice that in my experience many people either don't know or don't think about. You can practice yoga, meditate, and eat healthy but not be cultivating life force. My intention in this book is to create a stronger connection between you and your life force, make you conscious of the ways in which you yourself drain or retain it based on your choices, and give you simple practices as a foundation. If you want to go deeper, I've included ways for you to explore more at the end of the book. For now, you can start embracing your power to cultivate and maintain your life force by elevating your awareness of which habits, relationships, and ways of working and living are currently sustaining versus draining it. And then taking a stand for doing things differently.

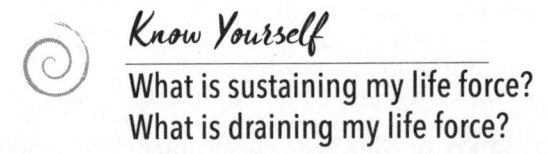

Know Yourself
What is sustaining my life force?
What is draining my life force?

Answer these questions now, and also take them into your daily life to start noticing what is draining your life force and what is replenishing it. Increase your awareness. Consider not just the physical and material but also the emotional, mental, and relational.

- What drains me and subtracts from my life force currently?
- What regenerates me and adds to my life force currently?

Take a stand to retain your life force, no matter what.

As you become more familiar with your burnout cycle and overwhelm onslaught warning signals, you will be more empowered to take action to stop draining your life force. But in my experience, awareness alone is not enough to get you to make the self-sustaining versus the self-sabotaging choice. Remember, your personal internal operating system is programmed with all kinds of burnout and self-sacrificing imprints, which make you believe you have no choice but to keep working, giving, and pushing and draining yourself.

Self-Sustainability Stands
for Retaining Your Life Force

In the moments when you feel the overwhelm approaching or your body signals that you are draining your life force to unhealthy levels, you need something strong enough to break the burnout imprint and neural pathways. I often use a harmonizing practice I call "Take a Stand for Your Sustainability." Taking a stand involves you speaking your choice for self-sustainability from that fierce feminine heart of yours. Like you were stepping back and drawing a line in the sand to proclaim: *I am OVERoperating in ways that don't sustain me. This is the new way I choose to operate.* This is you making an empowered choice to take the self-sustaining action. Taking a stand is both about telling yourself that things are shifting now and about intentionally putting out to the Universe that you choose to change the ways of working, interacting, and giving that are not working for you. The stand, your line in the sand, is the first step to freeing yourself. This doesn't mean things magically change overnight, but it does mark a pivot point, which opens the possibility and path to creating a new reality.

Here are a few common self-sustainability stands I have taken myself. Read these out loud and consider how your life would change if you lived by each stand.

1. I choose to retain, not drain, my life force.
2. I never serve from my reserves.
3. I regenerate and refuel before I crash.
4. I refuse to make myself sick in order to rest.
5. I refuse to get sick, burn out, or sacrifice myself for my work, my mission, or another person.
6. I promise to replenish my life force, daily.

These aren't just nice sayings or empty promises. You use these self-sustainability stands proactively as an intentional act to release the old way of operating that's not working for you. First you embrace them within yourself and proclaim them to the Universe, and then the external world responds. When you release something, you need to replace it with something more, or as, powerful. In this case a self-sustainability stand. You use these words in the moments you stand at a choice point — where you could take either the sustaining or the draining action. Like staking a claim to new territory by pounding a staff in the ground, you say these out loud to break the old cycle — habit, pattern, neural pathway, and imprint — so you can make a different, more sustaining choice.

Harmonizing Practice
Take a Stand for Your Sustainability

As we complete this program upgrade, choose one of the preceding self-sustainability stands that feels most potent for you now, or make up your own.

1. Write the self-sustainability stand where you can see it – your journal, a Post-it, a screensaver, a mirror, the outside of a candle.
2. When you're about to drain yourself, press the HARMONIZE button and restate your stand. Slow down, breathe, and say the stand out loud like a mantra, until you feel your power rise. Put your hand on your body – heart, belly, or solar plexus – for extra mojo. Then choose to retain, not drain, your life force.

Chapter 4

RELEASE: **Start the Day Harried and Hacked**

EMBRACE: **Start the Day Connected and Protected**

Wise women don't interact with the outside world without connecting with themselves first.

Your power to maintain and retain your life force starts with the choices you make within the first hour of every day. You know it's not good to reach for your phone first thing or plug into work or the world before you've even had a chance to wake up and get your bearings. You know rushing through your morning makes you more stressed. But you make these self-sabotaging choices anyway. Why?

My research over the years has revealed that most people just don't know the full *impact* of the choices they make in the first hour of their morning. We don't equate the overwhelm, anxiety, frustration, confusion, doubt, and stress we feel throughout the day with the choices we made with respect to how we woke up, who and what we interacted with, and what we put into our bodies.

But from the moment you register *It's time to wake up*, you've initiated a string of choices that either (1) give you the strength to meet and rise above the swirl and stay clear, confident, and calm within; or (2) program your internal operating system for a day of overwhelm. Because of *your* choices. Answer these few questions honestly.

In the first hour of your morning, have you *ever*:

- Checked your email or text messages before you brushed your teeth, peed, and looked at yourself in the mirror?
- Jumped out of bed without taking a few breaths to connect with your body?
- Hopped on social media or the internet, connecting to what's happening with others or in the world, before you've checked in with how you feel?
- Turned on the TV or radio, inviting the world's chatter into your personal space?

Don't feel bad if your answer is *yes* to any of the above. In fact, if it wasn't, I'd be skeptical. Every one of us, including me, has chosen to start our day in at least one of these self-sabotaging ways, on more than one occasion. Mostly because we just don't know how much the choices we make in the first hour of our day affect us. Or we fool ourselves by starting to doubt that our small choices have a significant impact on us, until we fall so far out of rhythm that we have to struggle to get back in alignment.

How you start your day is how you live your day.

Think of the first minutes and hour as the most important of your entire day. The choices you make with respect to how you relate to your body, others, and the outside world will tune your mind, body, emotions, and energetic systems to either harmony and clarity or chaos and clutter. What you as the conductor of your life attune to before you start your workday has a direct impact on how the parts play together.

Look at the glyphs on the next page. Which one reflects how you start your mornings most often? Which reflects how you would desire to start your mornings, if you felt like you had a choice?

Many people start their days as shown in the glyph on the left — harried and hacked. If you start your day with an alarm, short on

HARRIED & HACKED | **OR** | **CONNECTED & PROTECTED**

time, moving fast, flying out the door, or ingesting caffeine and sugar to get your body going, you've just programmed your internal operating system for a harried day. When you let in the outside world — people, news, work, media — before you've connected with yourself, you start your day hacked. You've opened the door wide for other people's emotions and energy to muck up your personal energy field. So now not only do you have your own anxiety, frustration, or stress to deal with, but your thoughts, physical life force, and emotions are being infiltrated and influenced by the swirl of others.

You can just look at the "Harried & Hacked" glyph and feel the *dissonance* versus the harmony you likely desire. *Dissonance* is such an appropriate word. It means "inharmonious or harsh sound," a "cacophony." When you are swirling in dissonance, you feel discord, divisiveness, strife, conflict, harshness, jangle, and incongruity. You and I both have had more days that felt like a frenetic cacophony, versus a harmonic symphony, than we would like.

My first *awareness* of how much impact my morning choices had on my entire day hit me like a two-by-four at the age of thirty-three. I had left the house harried and hacked to get to work, again. Running late, I flew out the door, fighting with my partner. In my rush, I forgot my tampons. Harried, I spotted the closest drugstore, parked, and returned to my car to find a big fat ticket for failing to see the NO PARKING sign. When I finally arrived at work, I was so swirled up inside that I turned a vice president's face red in a meeting. Starting my day this way cost me $100, a cleanup with my guy, and a talking-to by my boss, with an apology to Mr. VP. That day I promised *never* to leave my house or start my workday without connecting with myself. I've kept that promise ever since.

My dear soul sister Kristine Carlson, author of *Don't Sweat the Small Stuff for Women*, is the one who gave me the exact words: *How you start your day is how you live your day.* It really is feminine wisdom for all of us, a must if we want to stay above the swirl. I'm not perfect. I don't expect you'll be perfect, either. There are days, although very few, when I make the sabotaging choice to look at my phone before I tune in with myself. But when I do, I'm extremely aware of the impact. That's where we start with you, too.

You can't control the energy of other people or the state of the world, but you can control your personal energy field.

I have a question for you: "How would you prefer to start your days — harried and hacked or in harmony, connected, and protected?" I imagine "in harmony" gets your vote. Whenever I ask a group of people this question, all hands go up in favor of harmony. Of course, who wouldn't want to feel spacious versus stressed during their mornings? But when I look closely at their faces, I see the doubt; they don't believe it's actually possible. Do you?

Imagine having space to connect with yourself every morning and take care of what you need before engaging with work or taking care of others' needs. Most women, because of their current morning routine and life design — with all the things they need to do and places they need to be — just don't see how to create harmony instead of cacophony in their mornings. Or they approach making changes to their mornings like another to-do or thing to fix. So they give up, don't try, or try for a few days but then get swept back into the swirl. Defeated, resigned, and overresilient, they fall back into the sabotaging habits that drain their life force and lead to overwhelm.

I don't want you to suffer that fate. You are here with me now reading this book, which must mean you desire change, yes? Something different for yourself? So, here's what we are going to do. First, let's be real. You do not have the power to change how others show up, nor can you control the craziness happening on the world stage on any given day. There may be time constraints and responsibilities you have to deal with daily that you can't modify. But you do have the power of *choice* regarding how you set your personal energy field every day, even if you live with other people. And you have more control over the first hour of your morning than you realize.

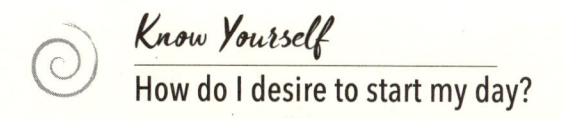

Know Yourself
How do I desire to start my day?

- What three words describe how my mornings currently feel?
- What three words describe how I would like my mornings to feel?

Our next step is to expand your wisdom about how your personal *energetic* system works and then illuminate the *impact* of your current choices about the first hour of your day. Then we can put in place a simple structure that empowers you to make changes in your morning flow so you can stay centered and clear within yourself regardless of what's happening around you. Let's get you connected.

Connecting with Your Magnetic Field

Here's a dose of potent yogic wisdom you may or may not know: just like the earth has a magnetic field that surrounds it, keeping our environment stable and protecting us from destructive forces, you have a magnetic field that surrounds and protects you. This energetic field keeps your inner climate stable and protects you from other people's "swirl," but only if it's strong.

Modern science teaches that the magnetic field of the earth protects the planet from space radiation. Without it, the solar winds — streams of electrically charged particles that flow from the sun — would strip away our atmosphere and oceans. It is Earth's magnetic field that helps make life on the planet possible.

Yogic science, sages, and healers have long taught that when your magnetic field is strong, it's like having a personal force field around you that shields you from taking on other people's "stuff." This includes people you live with, work with, stand in line next to, and interact with via the internet or media. Imagine your magnetic field like a golden bubble around you, like Glinda the Good Witch in *The Wizard of Oz* but without the superpower to levitate. Think of it like a force field that protects your life force and your personal energy. Check out the glyph below to see what I'm talking about.

My Magnetic Field

I choose to cultivate a strong & harmonious magnetic field

Your magnetic field supports your internal personal space — physical, mental, emotional, and psychic — to stay clear and stable so *you* can stay centered and focused. If your magnetic field is weak, you get overwhelmed and drained, because other people's energy and emotions — their drama, projections, fear, anxiety, frustration, and anger — seep into your personal space and swirl up inside you.

Have you ever felt someone walking up behind you before you could see or hear them? That's because they have entered your magnetic field and are now mingling with your personal energy field. You don't register their presence with one of your five senses — sight or hearing, for instance — but you sense them because your subtle body and their subtle body are now touching the same physical space.

Do you ever walk into a room and feel the energy? Or sometimes feel like you are a sponge taking on other people's feelings and "stuff"? Or have you suspected you are empathic? Many women are (it's one of our superpowers). And it's a function of your magnetic field, which tends to merge easily with the surrounding environments and people. Being able to "feel" other people's emotions or sense what's happening in a group is not a weakness; it's a powerful way to tap into your feminine wisdom. But without a strong magnetic field, it's too easy to get swirled up into the world's chaos or others' emotions and thoughts and lose yourself and your center.

Consider all of this in the context of your day, and all the people you interact with. How might the weakness or strength of your magnetic field be contributing to the drain, dissonance, and overwhelm you feel?

Wise women consciously cultivate a strong and harmonious magnetic field.

You want to be in relationship with your magnetic field, just like with your life force, every day. Just as you brush your teeth daily to keep your gums and teeth strong so you don't end up toothless, you must clean and strengthen your magnetic field daily. Then it can protect your personal atmosphere from absorbing people's stuff. Healthy self-care practices, exercise, and meditating, while all good, are not enough. You don't need to buy another exercise device you won't use, take a litany of supplements that break your bank, or start meditating two hours a day. There *are* actions to take, which I will share with you, but first, you need to get a sense that this magnetic field surrounding you is real. Take a minute with me now to connect with it (no one's watching, so just try it!).

1. Put your hands out to your sides, parallel to the ground.
2. Then move your hands *slowly* up above your head and then down toward the ground. That's your magnetic field above and below you and to your sides. If you move very slowly, and are open to *feeling* energy, you may feel your fingers tingle. That's your energy field! If you don't feel anything, that's okay; as with any relationship, it takes time. Just choosing to interact with this field to increase your awareness of it is a start.
3. Now do the same with your arms outstretched in front of you and then behind you. This is your energy field front to back.

When strong, your magnetic field naturally creates healthy boundaries so you can interact with others without taking on their emotions and problems or being negatively affected by them. This force field also does wonders for lessening some of the overload from technology that's overwhelming you. Your role is to become more aware of your magnetic field, start to notice the impact of technology and other people's energy on you, and make more conscious choices, starting with the choices of what you interact with and ingest in the first hour of your day.

Start your morning connected to yourself. Set and protect your magnetic field. And you'll stay centered and sustained.

I am going to be straight with you, wise woman to wise woman. The swirl out *there* isn't stopping. It's speeding up. If you have been waiting for the swirl around you to abate — in your work and relationships or the world at large — this is a wake-up call to stop waiting. If you've been turning a blind eye to how much the choices you make in the first hour of your morning are affecting your thinking and being and your feelings throughout the day, this is a reality check that until you change how you start your day, nothing can truly change.

If you start your morning connecting to email, social networks, news media, work, or people other than those you live with, you've just set yourself up for a day in which you will be like a windsock with no pole — *reacting* to the demands, desires, expectations, and energy of everything and everyone around you. Picking up all the anxiety, frustration, and emotional commotion out there. Next time you grab your phone before you brush your teeth, or you let the outside world in before you connect with yourself and set and protect your magnetic field, notice what happens to your thoughts, emotions, and inner sense of calm and centeredness. Here's a glyph to give you a picture.

Compare the two women. Yes, the one on the left looks like a set of disembodied heads. This is you when you forget or fail to connect with yourself and set your field — a harried and hacked woman, caught up in the reactive thoughts in her head, stirred up by chaotic emotions, ungrounded and uncentered because she's disconnected from her body. Notice the other woman on the right, who is standing centered while the swirl and chaos move around her — connected and protected, she's harmonized on the inside. This is you, having embraced your power to set your magnetic field as an act of sustainability, sanity, and straight-up wisdom before you interact with the outside world.

Look closely and you'll see that it's as if there is a vertical energetic pole that holds this harmonized woman centered within herself. She's connected at a physical level in her body and to the earth; to her heart, personal needs, and feelings; to her intuitive wisdom and clear intellect; and to the universal force above that has her back. Connected, she gains the inner power to stay aligned, centered, and upright, no matter what is swirling around her — and you can, too.

Notice the magnetic field around her: it's strong. She isn't isolating herself; she has created a field of protection — healthy boundaries — so she can be aware of what's happening in the world and consciously choose what is allowed into her personal field. She's not merging or overidentifying with other people's or the world's drama or emotions, or assimilating into the swirl; she's standing sovereign within herself. Rooted to the physical realm and connected to her elevated feminine wisdom, she's able to see what's really happening around her so she can respond discerningly and wisely, versus react impulsively.

When your magnetic field is strong, it does the work to keep out the swirl without you having to think about it. You feel overwhelmed and drained less. You feel clear and sustained more. You still come into contact with the chaos of the world and other people, but now their "stuff" doesn't infiltrate your personal field. Or if it does get through, you recognize it as an outside influence, because you are more aware, and there are practices I can teach you to reharmonize your field. You become insulated from the swirl, able to rise above it or stay still within it. You become empowered to respond from a place of personal integrity, courage, clarity, and compassion instead of reacting or taking it all on.

Now don't get overwhelmed thinking, *How am I ever going to do that?* This is not about more to-dos. You don't have to meditate for an hour; learn fifty yoga poses; or move into a house without pets, kids, or other adults. This is about doing what you are doing — like waking up, starting your day, and interacting with people and technology — differently, in ways that will actually make you feel better, happier, and calmer. This is about you embracing your power to set the rhythm and energy of your home and your body, mind, and emotions to harmony versus cacophony — even if the people around you or the systems you work in or interact with don't support you to make these changes. We start, as always, with self-awareness and small but mighty actions that lead to real self-empowering shifts in your daily life.

We'll bring this all together at the end of this section with a daring act of liberation, but for now, I invite you to embrace these three self-sustainability principles for how you start your mornings, every morning for the rest of your life: *Set. Connect. Protect.* Then I'll give you a few simple ways to make these practical and actionable now.

Self-Sustainability Principles for Starting Your Day, Every Day

SET your field for harmony by choosing what you interact with and ingest in the first hour of your day.

You set the *frequency* and *rhythm* of your personal field by your choice of what to let into your mental, energetic, emotional, and physical fields from the moment you wake up through the first hour of your day. Sounds, images, information, conversation, stimulation — all affect the frequency of your field. Do you want your morning to feel like a techno rave, a four-alarm fire, an enlivening festival, a peaceful garden, a vibe-setting yoga class, or...? Consciously choose the feeling and frequency you desire via the sounds and images you wake up to and the information you engage with and conversations you engage in.

CONNECT with yourself before connecting with the outside world.

Connect with yourself — body, mind, spirit, and heart (all four) — before you connect with the external world, which encompasses anyone who does not live with you. Remember this the next time you reach for your phone or computer and are tempted to let the outside into your field.

PROTECT your energetic and emotional fields so other people's stuff does not seep into your magnetic field.

Imagine walking out the door of your house stark naked and then getting on public transit. You would *never* sit on a city bus or train with nothing covering your body. You know to protect your physical body by wearing clothes. Your energetic and emotional bodies are the same. You may not be able to see these bodies with your eyes, but they are just as real, and they need to be zipped up so you are protected.

Remember this self-sustainability stand to support you to take the space you need each morning to set yourself up for a day in which you stay centered, clear, and calm:

I set. I connect. I protect.

That simple. That significant. Living this way is a practice. I'll share the "how" that is doable for any woman (I've tested it with myself and many others) in the daring act of liberation at the end of this section. For now, I just want you to start becoming more aware of what is happening in your first hour every morning and of some simple shifts you can make to set your field to harmony.

Embrace your power to set the rhythm and reality of the first hour of your morning, even if that means doing things differently or asking others to do things differently.

It can seem impossible to change how you start your mornings without having to rob your sleep or get up at four o'clock just to find some peace. Whether it's kids or animals climbing into bed, people in your house running around making noise like dissonant banjos, or the pressure of having to be someplace by a time way too early for any human being to start work, I want to say to you, "I get it; those pressures and people are real." And it's my job, also, to remind you that you are the leader of your life, the matriarch of your family and home, the arbiter of and advocate for your reality.

We cannot wait for an organizational policy to change or for our kids to go to college before we take back our power to set the rhythm of our mornings. We cannot expect the people around us to admit they are adding to our *dis*harmony. We teach people — whether those we work or live with — how to treat us.

So what's a wise woman to do? For starters, make the choice to set the tone in your home in the early-morning waking hours. Mornings are meant to have an easeful "up" cycle that gives you time to warm up — to rise so you can shine. If you don't give yourself space to warm up, like a car in the winter, your engine will clunk along in those first hours of your workday. If you start off hitting the ground running, you will pound the pavement all day, until you drop. If your house feels like a techno rave or chaotic circus, you will feel the *thump-thump* all day in your nervous system. But if you choose to embrace your power to set the field at home, while I can't promise you that you will forever live stress-free, I can assure you that you'll feel and be more empowered to handle the morning pressures and swirls and less likely to get caught up in them.

I have a library of practices and rituals for cultivating a harmonized field in your mornings, but here are four to get you started. Remember, it's all about doing things differently, not adding more to-dos. Choose to release the sabotaging choice and replace it with a supportive choice. The way we make lasting shifts is to consciously release one thing and then embrace a new action, ritual, or practice to put in its place.

Release	Embrace
Waking up to the havoc of a jarring alarm. This sets off your internal fight-or-flight system so now you live your day in an alarmed, reactive state.	**A harmonic start.** If you need a sound to wake up to, choose one that feels expansive and gentle, not jarring.
Media mornings. Allowing the news to invade your psyche in the first hour amplifies your feelings of fear, worry, uncertainty, and frustration.	**Wisdom mornings.** Consciously connect with sources of wisdom that give you a sense of calm, faith, possibility, and connection. Preferably printed, offline.
Connecting online. Email, texts, social media — in the first hour, just don't do it. As you reach for the device, see yourself like a Las Vegas slot-machine addict.	**Connecting to your body and Mama Earth.** Do things that cleanse your body (pee, brush your teeth, drink hot lemon water) and connect you to yourself or the earth (walk, yoga, stretch to music). Sit, look out the window, earth-gaze, sip tea, stand barefoot on real earth (grass, sand, rock, dirt). Breathe.
Accepting chaos caused by others. Stop being a windsock in your own home, allowing your kids, roommates, pets, or partner to get you swirled up. Stop allowing the pressure to get to work make you speed through your morning.	**Creating harmony in your space.** Play sound — music or mantra — as soon as you wake up; this will harmonize you and others. Make shared space technology-free. Empower others to take care of their basic needs. Create meaningful conversation and loving connection. Invite others, including teaching your kids.

During the process of writing this book, I have been so inspired by the stories that the women I mentor and teach have reported back to me about how they've used these simple but mighty shifts to affect not only their lives but the lives of those they love, influence, and lead. Rebecca, a single mother of a four-year-old boy, Joaquin, shared this story with me; it made me smile, so I thought I'd share it with you.

> Between kids and dogs in my bed and my own lack of focus, I was aware that my mornings were anything but harmonious. My first step to doing things differently was to get the dogs and my son into their own beds so I could wake up in my own energy field. Second, I knew I had to invite my son to be part of setting the harmony in our home each morning, because otherwise it wasn't going to happen. We now have a few rituals we do as part of our morning flow, but the one we love the most is to both ask ourselves, "What does my heart say today?" (a variation on "What do I need to receive today?" that works for a four-year-old, too). Then we share with each other. And when I forget, guess what? Like a true accountability partner, my son reminds me.
>
> I decided to start writing down the words Joaquin says, because they warm my heart, and sometimes, I'm like, *Yes, I need that wisdom, too!* Here are a few: "I am great and I am beautiful"; "I need to have a nice day and not be rude to my cousin"; "My heart needs love and fresh air."

Only four years of age, and such wise life-force-cultivating and self-aware words! Imagine that young boy growing up into a man who has been speaking to and from his heart for his whole life. All because of a simple — significant — choice to connect each morning. You have more power than you realize to cultivate harmony in your life and with those you love and lead. Let's start by becoming more aware of what is currently happening with your morning choices.

Know Yourself
Are my morning choices cultivating harmony or chaos?

- What am I interacting with or doing in my first waking hour that cultivates harmony?
- What am I interacting with or doing that creates chaos or dissonance within or around me?

Chapter 5

RELEASE: **Manage Stress**

EMBRACE: **Release Stress**

Wise women don't manage stress.
We release it, daily, in ways that support, not sabotage, us.

Living stress-free is as mythical a state as work/life balance. Trying to manage your stress keeps you stuck with something you don't even want. Instead of trying to become stress-free or manage stress, wise women cultivate the power within to meet stress, release it, and rise above it. We expect stress; we condition ourselves emotionally, physically, mentally, and spiritually to work with it. But we don't become tolerant of the toxic degrees of stress that have become normal and acceptable in our society today.

Stress can be your ally, or it can be the force that silently runs you into dis-ease, physical sickness, emotional instability, and mental overload. As in our previous program upgrade, there are things you may not know and choices you are making as to how you deal with stress that are adding to your overwhelm. Choices you can change with a dose of self-awareness, a combo of yogic and modern scientific wisdom, and a path for doing things differently with respect to how you "downshift" — wind down and complete — your day. Let's start with releasing the ways of dealing with stress that just don't work in these intense times we live in.

You have heard of "stress management"? Of course. This is how humans have been trying to deal with the increasing levels of stress since at least the early 1900s, when a Hungarian-born endocrinologist, Dr. Hans Selye, considered one of the fathers of stress research, borrowed the term *stress* from the field of physics. He observed that all his hospitalized patients, no matter what they were hospitalized for, suffered from what then didn't have a name but he coined "stress." In the world of physics, *stress* describes the force that produces strain on a physical body, like bending a piece of metal until it snaps because of the force, or stress, exerted on it. Pressure. Snap. Sound familiar?

I am grateful for the research people like Dr. Selye did to give us language to describe this root cause of much disease. I am grateful for all the people who have since dedicated their lives to developing strategies for stress management to get us this far. And yet now we need a different strategy. Managing our stress isn't working. And not only is it not working, but if you really think about it, it's ridiculous to try to *manage* stress.

Why would you try to manage something that you don't *want*?

Especially something that is impossible to "manage"?

Choosing the strategy of managing your stress to deal with the intensity of your life is like trying to manage a room full of two-year-olds. You can hold them at bay, keep them occupied, or keep them going for only so long without one or all melting down into a puddle or erupting into a tantrum. Managing the stress present in your life is the same. Just like you cannot keep a group of two-year-olds from melting down, trying to handle your stress and hold it all together will eventually lead to your meltdown. The stress you face in the world today from so many places is too much to "manage." The levels of stress we have come to accept as normal are way too much, even for strong women like us.

Too much stress for too long is not natural or sustainable, even for strong women.

We women have become so tolerant of the increasing thresholds of stress that we now think it's normal to operate under these intense stress loads — it's not! The overculture has brainwashed us to believe that being able to handle extreme levels of stress for prolonged periods of time is a sign of our strength versus a warning sign that something is out of alignment. We have a distorted understanding of what is healthy and stretches us in a supportive way and what is toxic, unsustainable, and frankly unacceptable. I mean, who taught you how to discern the difference for yourself? And even if you could, have you felt like you were at liberty to do things differently?

This is a big part of why I practice and teach yoga. By doing the yoga, you train your body, mind, and energetic systems to discern between *stress* that hurts you and *stretch* that holds you as you expand into your growth edge. The pressure you feel as you stretch yourself should feel like a good stretch, or a challenging exercise that lasts for a short burst of time. This is how the natural world works. If you've ever birthed a baby or midwifed anything into the world — a project, a mission, a piece of work, a company — or had to stretch to meet a goal, desire, or achievement, you know stress is part of the process. This kind of stress is healthy stress — it's called *eustress,* a term also coined by our friend Hans. Eustress creates positive pressure and supports you to move into action; birth new ideas, projects, and possibilities; and get what matters done.

It's the *buildup* of stress that creates overwhelm and, with time and repetition, leads to burnout and disease. It's the *acceptance* of the level of stress we deal with daily and carry within us that is not natural but in fact toxic. The posture we hold or activity we are engaged in should never cause prolonged physical pain or stretch us to the point where we feel like we are doing the splits over the Grand Canyon and at any moment are going to snap. Whether it's on the mat, a bicycle, or a run or in a relationship or work situation or project, this is when we enter the realm of toxic stress, which is called *distress*. And it's something each of us will experience in our lifetimes.

Wise women acknowledge when they are in distress.

Distress is the kind of stress that does, and will, make you sick — not just physically but also emotionally, mentally, and spiritually. While you will have times in your life when real distress hits — a death or illness of a loved one, unexpected disasters, or changes out of your control — distress should not be and cannot be how you live your everyday life.

It does not make you strong and smart to push yourself so hard or equate your inner strength with how much burden and responsibility you can carry. It makes you sick. It doesn't make you strong to think you should be able to handle it all on your own. That makes you an isolated she-woman who chooses to self-sacrifice versus a wise woman who asks for support when she's stretched too far.

Admitting you are in distress before you snap and get sick is wise. So much of the disease we are experiencing in our bodies is because we have come to accept distress as the normal operating mode. We keep pushing through, hoping we'll get to the place where things will change, but usually we hit our breaking point first. I imagine there are parts of your life that may be causing you distress. While many different kinds of stressors can lead to toxic distress, here are six common to women that I've found through my study of yogic and modern science but also my own personal experience and observation. Read each and then pause to reflect on which may be adding to your overwhelm.

6 Distress Creators: Which Are Overwhelming You?

1. CONTINUOUS STRESS – you have been operating at a high level of intensity or output or have been experiencing a highly stressful or toxic situation, for a prolonged period of time (anything more than a few weeks).

For example, you work long hours or multiple days in a row with no break. Or there is a constant source of stress in your life that never seems to shift, like debt that's always weighing on you or a sick child or person you are responsible for. Or you are in a toxic relationship, living situation, or job. There is no rest from the stress.

2. Repeated hits – you keep getting hit with a stressor, without time to recover. Your life feels like one of those blocks that football players run into and hit hard during practice. You keep getting hit, knocked down, or pushed around from events happening in your life — including stress in your relationships, work, health, money situation, and home — without enough space to recover. Just as you feel like things are stabilizing — *boom* — another hit.

3. Personal misalignment – your work, relationships, or life design is out of harmony with your heart and soul. You know you are not living in alignment with who you are and what you desire. Just like if your spine was out of whack, putting pressure on your nerves or joints, you're living out of alignment with your truth. This creates toxic emotional and spiritual stress, and eventually physical distress.

4. Survival stress – you don't have the resources financially or materially to take care of your basic needs. You are just barely scraping by. It's like living in a hole that you attempt to climb out of, but just as you are about to finally emerge, a big pile of "not enough" dirt comes down on you, and back into the hole you go. You keep trying to climb out of the hole but can't, which is exhausting and disheartening.

5. Superwoman stress – you feel like the weight of the world is on your shoulders, and it is. You are carrying a burden at work or in your relationships that is too much. You've taken too much on yourself for the organization, the team, your family, other people, or your community, and you are suffocating or about to buckle at the knees. You are attempting to be like Atlas, the Titan god condemned to hold up the world for all eternity, when in truth, you are just one mortal woman.

6. HOLDING / LACK OF RELEASE – **you experience a stressor, but instead of releasing it when the event is over, your mind and body hold tight and stay stuck in the distress.** For example, something happens that makes you feel unsafe, but instead of releasing it when the threat goes away, your mind and body continue to perceive the danger, even though the threat has passed. Or you hold on to a stressor — like a test or a conflict — and ruminate over it, making it repeat in your mind like a bad record, and maintain high levels of stress even after the event has passed.

Now slow down and take a pause. Identify one or two of the above distress creators that have been or are present for you and feel relevant to explore. First, admit to yourself that you have been experiencing distress in this way. Then use the inquiries below to go deeper and gain some more self-awareness.

Know Yourself
Which kinds of distress am I experiencing, currently or recently?

- *What has been the impact on me physically? Emotionally? Mentally? Spiritually? (Answer for all four realms.)*
- *What have I been telling myself I should be able to handle?*
- *What is the truth?*

The rest of this chapter is about choosing to practice *releasing stress* as a way you live, daily, and an invitation to take a stand that you are no longer willing to accept distress as normal. Until we take a stand as women to stop pretending we can handle these levels of stress, nothing will change. More will just keep getting added on. Until we snap. We've all snapped, but instead of taking a stand, we snap back. When you can't see another way, of course you feel like you have no choice but to pick yourself up and do the same again. But there is a different way, and you are in the right place to find it for yourself.

I can't promise you that you will wake up tomorrow stress-free or that the stressors in your life will go away, but I can offer you wisdom and practices that empower you to meet the stressors you face, discern between toxic stress and sustainable stretch, release the stress in healthy ways, and get the support you need. Start with this next self-sustainability principle. I invite you to embrace it as a way to think about, relate to, and deal with the stress you will inevitably face as part of daily life and the ups and downs of life.

Instead of managing stress, release it.

There is a name for the amount of stress you carry around — it's called your *allostatic load*. Allostatic load is the cumulative wear and tear on your body that results from stress, especially chronic stress. This isn't new to human life, although the term *allostatic load* just appeared in 1993 as a "thing" when coined by neuroendocrinologist Bruce McEwen and behavioral neuroscientist Eliot Stellar.

Yogic science has long known and taught that life on this planet is one full of stressors, and if you aren't releasing that stress, it's running and ruining you. I love when ancient wisdom and modern science collide — it gives us superpower to understand things at a deeper level, intuitively and intellectually. Take a look at the glyph on the top of the next page. You can keep trying to manage your stress, and you will look and feel like the woman on the left. Or you can embrace releasing stress as a proactive practice you consciously do, daily, like the woman on the right.

Just like you want to know how much life force you have to give in any day, you want to be aware of how much stress you are carrying around so you don't go into toxic levels of distress, where the recovery time and cost are much greater. Or if you are in distress, instead of acting like everything is normal and you should just be able to "handle and manage it all," you do things differently and get more support.

Manage Stress — *Release Stress*

The metaphor that really helped me embrace that I needed to be attuned to how much stress I was carrying, and that I had to make a conscious choice to release it daily as an essential practice, was this: Think of your mental, physical, emotional, and energetic bodies like a dump truck. You keep driving along all day, picking up energy, emotions, stress — yours and others' — like the garbage. If you don't empty the load, eventually the garbage starts falling out the sides, and the load becomes so heavy that the truck can barely move — or the person driving it can barely stand the stench. Your mind, emotions, and energy start to get stinky, clogged up, and foggy, and you get overwhelmed. If you empty the truck regularly — release stress daily — you can handle more coming in without feeling overloaded and overwhelmed. The key is to make sure *how* you are dumping that stress is actually releasing the stress for good, not just providing temporary relief.

Choose to release stress in supportive ways, or you'll default to sabotaging habits that give temporary relief but add to your allostatic load.

In our efforts to manage stress, we have all picked up unhealthy ways to deal with it that don't release it from our system but instead add to our allostatic load. These are the self-sabotaging habits we default to for managing stress but seldom speak of. You have them. I have them. Every woman I know has them, too. We reach for what we think will give us temporary relief from the stress of the day or the lull in our life force. We fall into habits that numb us or distract us from dealing with the deeper drivers under the dissonance and distress that we feel but don't have the emotional bandwidth or support to deal with.

I am inviting each of us to be real and stop pretending we don't all do things to manage our stress that are self-sabotaging. We need to stop beating ourselves up about them. Start embracing that we are human. Choose compassion for and curiosity about ourselves instead of self-criticism and judgment. Only then can we gain the power to do something differently.

I'll share my stress self-sabotagers with you, no shame here. In fact, one of the actions I've found most liberating and empowering is to become super self-aware and honest about how I react in sabotaging ways to deal with whatever challenge, stretch, or stress I am facing. I know my self-sabotaging habits. I treat them as warning signals that I am carrying too much stress, stretching myself too far, trying to move too fast, and not getting what I need to be sustained and feel supported. Then, aware and honest, I can be compassionate with myself, instead of adding more pressure from self-judgment or numbing out in avoidance or shame. It's hard to do things differently when someone — especially you yourself — is criticizing and judging you. Easier to make changes when you feel supported and empowered.

For me it's all about the sugar. When I feel the burden is too much or as if there is no space for me, like clockwork, at 4 PM I want a brownie. At 7 PM I want a glass of wine. At 8 PM I want another. It's the sweet treat I give to compensate myself, to deal with my underlying fears, and to downshift from the intensity of the day. But ultimately, while all this sugar feels good in the moment, and it helps me ramp either up or down, it depletes my life force and creates a habitual pattern that's hard to break. Using the sugar to cope, hovering just above the hole of distress. I'm not as sharp in the morning, and my body doesn't feel as strong and vital. And worse, I am avoiding looking at what is driving this unsustainable level of stress, which makes me less powerful and wise.

Over the years, I've trained myself to be really aware of the three to five self-sabotaging ways I "manage" stress versus consciously release it, and the emotional indicators that tell me so. When these habits show up for more than a few days or weeks, I push the HARMONIZE button, get curious, and start making different choices. I have found that it is the act of becoming aware that I'm stuck in a self-sabotaging cycle that empowers me first to *release* it and then *replace* it with a self-sustaining choice. In my case I've learned I need a different habit/action to take to replace the sugar, or the shift does not stick. I'll share more next about how to find what works for you as a self-sustaining replacer. But for now, let's get aware of how you may be releasing stress in ways that are draining your life force.

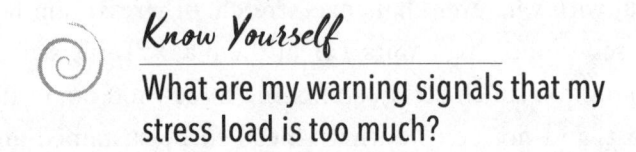

Know Yourself
What are my warning signals that my stress load is too much?

- *What do I physically reach for?*
- *How do I feel or react emotionally?*
- *What habits relating to how I work or interact with others are warning signals I am headed into distress?*
- *What habits for completing my day feel good in the moment but have a negative impact the next day or long-term?*

The Evening Downshift: Relax and Replenish

Last chapter we got wise to the fact that how we start our day affects us throughout it. The same is true on the opposite end. Consider this piece of wisdom: how you complete your day affects how you start your next day. Then ask yourself:

"Are the choices I am making to complete my day sabotaging me — draining my life force and adding to my stress load — or sustaining me?"

Unless you have already made a conscious effort to design how you do what I call "downshift your day," it's likely some of your choices, habits, and patterns are draining your life force, adding to your allostatic load, and giving you a false sense of stress release, which impairs your ability to get the rest you need. So you start the next day with less life force and emotional resilience than you require. And the cycle repeats.

Think about it this way: you know you should get the sleep you need to thrive; you want the sleep — you *know* this. But how aware are you of the link between the choices you make in the last hours of your day, getting the sleep you need, and the mental clarity, emotional stability, and physical vitality you start the next day with?

Wise women choose to downshift daily in ways that support them to release stress, replenish life force, reconnect with themselves, and rest.

Downshifting is the practice of proactively setting the flow of your evenings. It is the routine, rhythm, and choices you make with respect to how you wind down from work; take care of your body, family, and home; engage in evening activities; and complete your day. Downshifting, as the set of conscious choices, routines, and rituals that take you from the intensity of work; to the demands at home; to the needs of your own body, heart, mind, and spirit, is one of the most powerful practices you have available. But few of us were trained *how* to downshift in ways that set us up for what we really need to do as the sun goes down. What follows is some simple but significant wisdom about downshifting — some choices to embrace and some others to release. Take a read and consider what embracing your power to consciously create the rhythm and rituals for the end of your days could transform for you.

Self-Sustainability Stands
for Downshifting Your Day

Embrace These Self-Sustaining Choices as What You "Do" Every Evening

1. I slow down.
2. I release stress.
3. I replenish my life force.
4. I reconnect with myself.
5. I rest and regenerate.

Makes total sense, right? Five simple but mighty acts you are at complete choice about. Reread them. They sound good. Makes me take a deep exhale when I imagine this as what I *get* to do each evening. But how often do you actually "do" these? Don't feel bad or guilty. It's not like you had a "How to Downshift Your Day" class in school! Without the words to articulate the conscious practice of downshifting as the *wise* way to complete our day, we have all defaulted to habits, patterns, and choices that give us temporary relief or keep us running until our batteries die. Here are a few I've employed myself to manage stress and pressure.

Self-Sabotaging Choices for Completing Your Day

Release These as Self-Sabotaging Options for How You Downshift

- **The second shift:** You start a second day of work after you get home, or maybe you don't go home and keep working into the night hours.
- **The wine-down:** You use an external depressant to unwind and slow down after an intense day of work or taking care of others.
- **The numb-out:** You pour mindless TV, movies, or media into your mind prior to falling asleep, taking it into your dream time.
- **The crash-out:** You pass out on the couch or in your bed still in your day clothes, without cleansing body or mind.

Which of these have you tried? Or do you have other destructive downshifters we can add to the list? What are they? Be honest; it's just us women here (we all have these!).

Then press the HARMONIZE button, and get curious — what actions could you replace these with instead? Remember, you need something to take the place of a self-sabotaging pattern — something to fulfill the need not getting met that actually feels more nourishing, deeper down, because it's filling an emotional void and is something that interrupts the pattern. You need something that indicates you are *downshifting* now. Not upshifting or numbing.

I have lots of simple practices for downshifting — like replacing the crash-out with a ritual that includes putting on yummy PJs or a robe (I have a long black silk robe with gold threading that has become my transitional wardrobe shift to let my body, brain, and heart know: *Okay, time to slow down*). Or replacing the wine-down by embracing what I call "magical cocktail and connection hour," which is where my partner, Noah, and I sit watching the sunset, sipping bubbly water with lemon and lime wedges in a fancy glass, and share about our day — a transition ritual in which I receive sweetness and slowdown, sans the depressant.

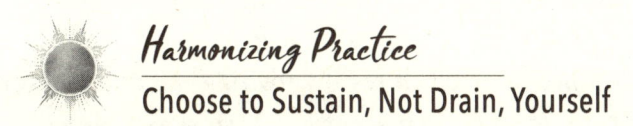

Harmonizing Practice
Choose to Sustain, Not Drain, Yourself

In the evening hours (after 7 PM), when you are about to make a choice you think may add to your allostatic load, slow down, breathe, and tune in by asking:

1. *Is this going to drain or sustain my life force?*
2. *What will replenish my life force?*

Then take the self-sustaining action.

Downshifting is a life-force saver! And a practice. Also, as an important side note, it's not that occasionally upshifting at night to get some things done, or choosing to enjoy some vino as you wind down, or even watching two episodes of your current favorite TV show is harmful. Doing these things consistently or in excess, whereby they become habitual coping mechanisms, is where the self-sabotage and negative impact happens. And it's pouring the stimulant, media, work, or outside world into your body, mind, or magnetic field the hour before bedtime that robs you of the rest and replenishment you need.

For more about downshifting, go to the book readers' kit to get a video and suggestions for self-sustainability replacements for downshifting your day. There's so much to share, and I don't want to overwhelm you. So just like last chapter, where we focused on the first hour of your morning, let's zoom in on the power of the last hour of each day. Read the words below and remember this wisdom every night as you make your choices about what you interact with and ingest in that last hour.

What you choose to put into your body, mind, and energy in the hour before you go to bed, goes to bed with you.

Yogic science teaches us that what you put into your body, mind, and heart in the hour before you fall asleep goes to bed with you. I can personally attest to this fact. If you fall asleep with a screen streaming, you've just robbed yourself of rest by inviting the outside world into your sleep time. If you watch a movie, TV show, or video that is emotionally disturbing or triggering, or full of drama and weirdness, all those people and their stuff climbs into bed with you and goes into your dream time. If you ingest sugar or eat late, now your body must spend its energy processing that versus releasing toxins from the day and replenishing your life force. If you are working, emailing, and interacting on technology, your mind is in an active state connecting with all the to-dos and could-dos. And you've just said okay to letting work and other people's demands invade your sleep time, and bedroom.

Just take that in. What you choose to ingest, connect with, and interact with in the last hour of your day is going to bed with you, remaining in your brain and body and energy field as you sleep. No one but you is the cause of that. You may have convinced yourself that your life must be this way, but we teach people what to expect from us and how to treat us. So if you email people at 10 PM, that is what they will expect.

What I have found to be true is that we need rituals, routines, and things to "do" that help us downshift, unwind, and release stress to sustain and support our physical, mental, emotional, energetic, and spiritual systems. Or else we will default to sabotaging choices that impair our ability to get good rest and rise and shine. Downshifting is the practice. You start it by becoming more aware of the choices you make in the last hour of your day. And when you choose to sabotage yourself versus support yourself, get curious and compassionate instead of critical. The inquiries below and the daring act of liberation we do next to complete this section will give you the path.

Know Yourself
How do I downshift in the last hour of my day?

- *What do I do to downshift that supports me to get good sleep and wake up fresh?*
- *How do I downshift in the evening in ways that sabotage me?*
- *Why do I downshift this way?*
- *What do I need that I am not getting?* (Really pause to tune in to the unmet need or desire underneath.)

DARING ACT OF LIBERATION #2

Bookend Your Days

Honor Your Rhythm

Rise & Shine — *Relax & Replenish*

Bookend Your Days

I don't prescribe a lot of "you must do this" kind of things, because in my experience every person and every body is different. But when it comes to having a *consistent, intentional* morning practice that connects you, protects you, and sets your personal energy field for the day, it's a must. I do not know how to keep you out of overwhelm, burnout, or self-sacrifice without one.

Yet, what I have noticed in my research is that few people have a *consistent* morning practice they do every day. I often start my professional workshops and personal retreats with the question "Who has a daily practice you do every morning, consistently?" In a professional setting, fewer than 5 percent raise their hands. Even in the retreats with people on a personal development path, fewer than 15 percent have a practice they do, every day. And few have a practice that connects them on the level of all realms — physical, mental, emotional, and spiritual — or that protects and sets their magnetic field. Virtually no one has a conscious flow to downshifting at the end of the day.

Wherever you are on the continuum of a consistent daily morning upshifting and evening downshifting practice, it's all good. We start where you are. If this is new to you, great! It was new to me at one time. Honestly, when I first committed to a daily morning practice, I would fall asleep, drooling on myself! But I stayed committed; that was the key. If you already have a consistent practice, this will deepen and strengthen it. We call it a *practice* because you never stop practicing or learning.

Rather than give you a litany of to-dos, I will teach you a "recipe" for creating a simple morning and evening flow, which you apply to the first and last hour of your day — the "Daily Bookend." The Daily Bookend empowers you to choose the rhythm and feel of your morning, no matter how much time you have or who you live with. It ensures you don't start your day open to being hacked or go through your day like an untethered windsock. You'll use the same recipe to downshift in the last hour of your day so you can receive the physical, emotional, energetic, spiritual, and mental replenishment you need.

Your Twofold Mission

1. **Create a flow for the first and last hour of your day, every day.** This supports you to stay centered, clear, and calm all day.
2. **Become aware of how your choices in the first and last hour of your day sustain or drain you.** This empowers you to make wiser choices that support your life force, and you, to thrive.

Take the following three steps to experiment with and elevate how you start and complete your days, embracing the Daily Bookend as a structure for how you "do" your daily life.

STEP 1: Become Aware of What's Draining and What's Sustaining You Because of How You Start Your Morning and Downshift Your Day

For one week, observe how you start your morning and end your day by becoming keenly aware of what you *ingest, interact with,* and *invite in* during the first and last hour. Notice what you put into your physical and energetic bodies and your mental and emotional fields. And notice the *impact*. Use the following inquiries to illuminate what's really happening; you'll be surprised. Write the inquiries in your journal and reflect on them each evening or morning or at the end of the week. Capture both weekdays and weekends to see what differs.

MORNING UPSHIFT: *What Am I Ingesting, Interacting with, and Inviting In during the First Hour of My Day?*

1. *What are the first things I "do" every morning?*
2. *What are the first things I "ingest" into my body and mind? The first information inputs I allow in?*
3. *Who are the first people I interact with?*
4. *What makes me feel harried or mucks up my energetic and emotional field?*
5. *What makes me feel connected or harmonized?*

EVENING DOWNSHIFT: *What Am I Doing and Consuming in the Last Hour of My Evening?*

1. *What do I "do" in the last hour before I go to sleep?*
2. *What do I regularly consume and ingest (food, information, media)?*
3. *Who and what do I interact with?*
4. *Which choices and routines drain me (and rob me of the rest I need)?*
5. *Which choices and routines sustain me (and support me to wake up regenerated and ready for my day)?*

Liberate Your Life Force 125

STEP 2: Experiment with Your "Daily Bookend" Practice and Create a Conscious Flow for the First and Last Hour of Your Day

You have to start and end every day anyway, so why not do so in ways that naturally cultivate harmony, self-sustainability, and vitality? Relax. I have no list of one hundred things you must do, or unrealistic expectations of you sitting on a cushion for an hour in silence meditating. After twenty years, not even I do that! Instead, I give you the superpower tool of the "Daily Bookend." As always, think of this not as more to do but as the choices, rituals, and actions that create a supportive flow for how you start and complete your day. Together, these create a pattern that harmonizes you to your natural rhythm and connects you to your needs and center.

As with any superpower, there are levels of depth and mastery. We start with the foundational recipe, the 4 Points of Connection. Take a look at the glyph below and read about each. I have included brief descriptions and a simple list of the kinds of practices that strengthen each one.

Vertical Line – Your Center Pole

1. **PHYSICAL CONNECTION – Connect to your physical body and the earth.** Rooted to both your physical body and the earth, you will feel more grounded. Like a tree with strong roots, you'll have the strength to stay stable within the swirl.

   Practices include yoga, tai chi, qigong, conscious breathing (pranayama), standing with bare feet on the earth (earthing), and walking/exercise with the intention of connecting to body (not ingesting outside chatter).

2. **DIVINE DOWNLINE CONNECTION – Invite your inner wisdom and the Universe in to support you.** Connected to the Universe, Spirit, God, Presence, or whatever you like to call this universal force, you will feel held, guided, safe, and protected. Plugged into what I like to call our "divine downline," you'll feel less alone and more connected to a greater web. And you'll be able to see from a more elevated and enlightened perspective above the swirl.

   Practices include guided or unguided meditation, intentional journaling, intuition-strengthening exercises, prayer, and wisdom readings.

Horizontal Line – Your Heart Line

3. **HEART CONNECTION – Receive love from yourself.** Connected to your heart, you'll be in tune with your own feelings and needs, so instead of responding to everyone else's, you'll make sure you tend to yours. In tune with yourself, you'll feel clearer, calmer, and more confident, naturally, and show up more compassionately with others and yourself.

   Practices include anything that strengthens your awareness and connection to yourself, such as taking a life-force and receiving reading, or that brings you joy or deepens your self-love.

4. **HEART CONNECTION – Receive love from others.** Connected to the feeling of receiving love and connection from another, you'll feel more seen and less isolated. This stabilizes your emotional field and makes you feel more courageous, confident, and calm. You can do this with the people or animals you live with, and if you don't live with anyone, any "love line" — a text, call, or hug, for instance, from a being whose energy makes you feel supported and seen — works. Even a smile from the barista or an act of kindness from another human can do wonders for your heart.

    Practices include hugs, cuddling, meaningful conversation, gratitude, and smiles.

Your action is to consciously connect each morning and evening to all four points. You don't have to do them all at once but can string them together to create a simple but mighty Daily Bookend practice that takes less than eleven minutes. Just remember to connect on all four points each morning before you interact with people you don't live with, including online. There is much more to teach about this. I made you a video in the book readers' kit that will lead you through more practices for protecting your magnetic field and connecting with all four points in a way that works for you.

STEP 3: Embrace Your Power to Set Yourself Up for Harmony

Wise women don't ask for permission; we take a stand for what we need and teach others what to expect and how to interact with us. The dynamics in your family or work may not be set up to support a Daily Bookend practice, yet. But remember, you can't receive what you need from others if you don't take a stand for it first. Which is why, in addition to embracing your bookend practice, using the 4 Points of Connection as a recipe and guide, I dare you to make one small but mighty change. Lock in this daring act of liberation by choosing one self-sabotaging habit and replacing it with a self-sustaining one, on both sides of your Daily Bookend practice. Then you can start resetting expectations.

Morning Upshift

1. *My current self-sabotaging habit is...*
2. *I choose to release the self-sabotaging habit of...*
3. *I choose to embrace the new self-sustaining choice to...*

Evening Downshift

1. *My current self-sabotaging habit is...*
2. *I choose to release the self-sabotaging habit of...*
3. *I choose to embrace the new self-sustaining choice to...*

The key to success is to choose a self-sustaining habit that *feels* supportive to you, not a stretch or a regimented rule that stresses you out or makes you feel like an ascetic monk who can have no fun. Choose what truly nourishes you. Choose what brings you joy. Choose what may require more discipline on your part but that results in you receiving the benefit of feeling more vibrant, connected, and aligned. Then go into your life, and as you observe yourself about to self-sabotage, make a different choice. Remember the four stages of personal transformation — *awareness, reflection, change in the moment,* and *integration* — and when you waver or falter, apply self-compassion instead of self-criticism to come back to the commitment you have to your sustainability, wellness, and true heart's desires for your life.

PART THREE

Liberate Your Heart

*Inside the heart of a woman
lie distorted cultural imprints and
unconscious impulses that cause her to
overgive and sacrifice herself —
including unseen and unspoken desires for
recognition, acceptance, love, and security;
and fears of missing out, not belonging,
and not being enough.*

*The question is,
"Do you know which are running you?"
(By the end of this section, you will.)*

Chapter 6

RELEASE: It's Better to Give *Than* Receive

EMBRACE: It's Better to Give *And* Receive

When women give and receive in harmony,
the whole world thrives.

"It's better to give than receive" — six seemingly innocent words you have likely heard but don't give a second thought. Seems like good counsel for being a good human, right? But look more closely. Instead of seeing just another nice saying, use your wise-woman eyes to see another unconscious program running your thoughts and actions.

If it's better to give *than* receive, how might that affect your choices for how you show up in your relationships? At work? For yourself? If it is better to give *than* receive, wouldn't it follow that you should give as much as you can, even if you don't have it to give? If it is better to give *than* receive, what might be the impact on your capacity to ask for or receive support from others?

Is the lightbulb turning on yet? If it is better to give *than* receive, no wonder why when someone tries to give you support — a compliment, help, money, kindness — you experience a knee-jerk response to give back. We women cannot just receive. We feel we must give, too.

If we don't return the giving, we feel guilty or selfish, and proceed to sacrifice ourselves in some other way to make up for it.

Give *or* receive. It's another duality reality! Here the internal tug-of-war makes us believe we must choose between giving (to others, our work, and the world) and receiving (for ourselves) what we need.

But why should you have to choose receiving *or* giving? Why can't you have both? It makes no sense to have to choose between supporting others and receiving the support and resources you need. If this is an abundant Universe, as the ancient sages teach, with infinite possibility, as the scientists say, shouldn't there be enough for everyone to *both* give to others *and* receive for themselves?

Don't let the simplicity of what I am sharing fool you. The "it's better to give than receive" program seems harmless, but within our hearts it's wreaking havoc. I see it like an insidious parasite that's wormed its way into our internal operating systems, making it crazy challenging to stop sacrificing ourselves for the good of others, and we can't see why. Did you know that parasites can make the animals that host them act unnaturally, in ways unhealthy to the host but beneficial to the parasite? This particular self-sacrificing parasite compels you to work and relate in unnatural and unhealthy ways, including giving too much and draining your reserves even though you know better. The result? You bankrupt yourself.

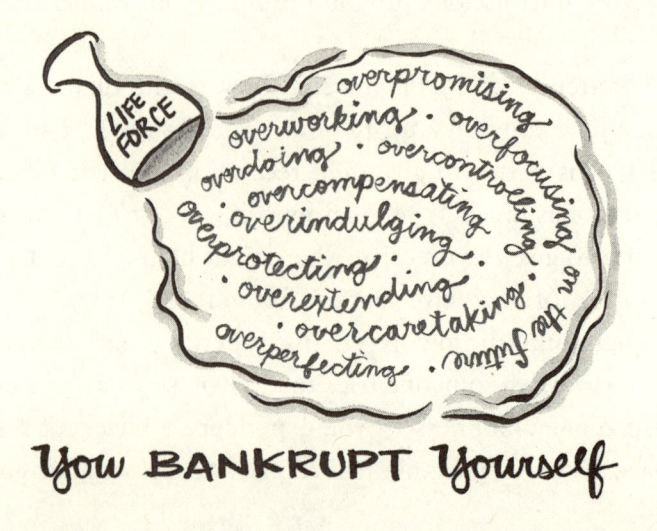

You BANKRUPT Yourself

Women operate like banks that give more withdrawals than receive deposits, blindly bankrupting ourselves.

We work and run our lives like banks with significantly more withdrawals than deposits. At times, we even refuse deposits altogether. You don't have to be a business whiz to know that if a bank gives out more money than it takes in, the bank goes belly-up! This is exactly what's happening to us. More often than not, we are teetering on the edge of bankruptcy — emotionally, mentally, physically, spiritually, even financially — because we keep giving more than we receive and can afford to give. We just don't see it, so we can't stop it. We don't see that we are doing this to ourselves, so we don't know we have a different choice.

If you can't see how you are *over*giving and *under*receiving, you can't help but drive yourself into a deficit. Women have been overgiving and underreceiving within their lives, families, and organizations for so long that today we just accept this as a totally normal way to operate, work, and be in relationships. See if any of these bankrupting scenarios sound familiar to you:

1. You give more than is needed. You give 110 percent to a project when 80 percent would have been enough. You give hours of time and mental space to a person or project, but upon reflection, it wasn't worth it. That extra percentage of your life force, money, mind space, and time is wasted, unnecessarily. If you had retained it, you would not have depleted yourself.

2. You give more than is in harmony. The exchange of energy, time, and money — between you and another person, between you and the organization you work for or with, or even between you and your mission or family — is imbalanced and not in your favor. Eventually you get resentful. You don't have what you need because you gave too much for what you received in exchange.

3. You give more than you can afford. You want to be generous, to "help" or pitch in, but in truth you just don't have the time, money, or energy to give. Rather than be honest or give what you can afford, you overgive of the resources and life force you truthfully need to retain for yourself. You've managed not to disappoint someone else, but what about you? You betray yourself for the sake of helping another.

Women tend to show up this way in our relationships and in our work not because we are sadists who want to create suffering for ourselves. Without language to see and articulate *how* we are overgiving, our reality feels like one big overwhelming swirl. We have no idea where to start altering the exchange of input and output. Which is why we begin by beaming self-awareness into what's going on within our hearts, driving us to bankrupt ourselves.

If you can reveal the specific ways you overgive, you become empowered to shift the imbalance.

I am going to break down for you the most common ways women overgive of their life force (that is, energy, love, and attention) and their resources (including time, money, and support) and as a result deplete themselves. I call these the *OVERgiving Imprints*, or the "OVERs." This will give you language to illuminate the deeper emotional imprints that, like a parasite, drive you to keep sacrificing yourself. One thing to note before we dive in. This will require self-honesty. Because the ways in which you overgive in many cases are how you have come to value and define who you are. How's that for deep?

The 13 OVERgiving Imprints

Read through each of these OVERgiving Imprints with the intention of revealing which might be running in your internal operating system. Pause after each to consider if it rings true for you, by asking, *Have I been or am I...?*

1. **OVERcaretaking:** You overempathize with and caretake others.
   You feel, take on, and carry other people's stuff — worries,

concerns, needs, and life or work challenges. You take over-responsibility for people, projects, organizations, issues, or the world.

2. **OVERcompensating:** You feel the gaps or the needs with a project, organization, or family member and then fill them in or fulfill them with your life force, money, or time. You make up for what other people can't, don't, or won't show up for.

3. **OVERconnecting:** You spend a lot of your energy and time connecting with others — at home, at work, online, at networking events, and more — but leave little space for connection with yourself. You spend too much energy and time "out," not enough "in."

4. **OVERcontrolling:** You plan, strategize, and organize, leaving nothing to chance. You allow no space for others to step in or lead. You overcontrol how things work and flow.

5. **OVERdoing:** You rarely stop moving. Resting makes you anxious. You are perpetually busy. You find it hard to do things that are not productive, just for pleasure. You go to sleep and wake up with your to-do list.

6. **OVERefforting:** You work harder and longer than is needed, giving 110 percent when 80 percent would do. You believe hard work is what makes you successful or valuable, so you work harder than others, giving everything your all.

7. **OVERextending:** You give, spend, or invest more money, time, and energy than you have. You stretch yourself to the point of stressing and depleting yourself. You don't have the resources and time *you* need, because you've given them to others or spent beyond your capacity.

8. **OVERfocusing on the future:** You obsessively think about what could or will happen. You get so focused on the goal, outcome, or plan that you pressure yourself to keep moving until you "get there." You waste your life force on all the anxiety or frustration you feel about the future. You don't receive or savor the joy of the present in the process.

9. **OVERindulging:** You eat, drink, spend, or binge-watch TV more

than is healthy, to compensate for the lack of nourishment, support, love, and care you receive. In the moment, your indulgence feels good or numbs you, but you end up with a physical, emotional, or financial hangover.

10. **OVERperfecting:** You put too much time, energy, and effort into make something an A+ when a B would do, stressing yourself and others out. You pay attention to details no one else sees, wasting life force for little return. Or you procrastinate about completing things, trying to perfect what no one else cares about.
11. **OVERpromising:** You say or impulsively blurt out "Yes, I can!" when you know you can't or before you've even paused to consider whether you can do what's being asked. You take on more than is possible to do in the time or with the resources you have available, and then you have to deliver.
12. **OVERprotecting:** You've learned to protect yourself so much that you can't receive the love, attention, and care you need. You block physical affection, support, and intimate connection, or you waste energy chasing relationships that are not fulfilling or supportive.
13. **OVERworking:** You give so much to your work that your relationships, health, and happiness suffer. You tell yourself that one day you'll have time for fun, love, and pleasure, which never happens, because there's always more work.

Chances are, you relate to more than a few of these imprints; most women do. But usually one, two, or three are most present and pervasive now. Circle up to three that resonate in your current personal and professional situations and relationships. At the end of this section, you'll choose one OVERgiving Imprint to transform, in your everyday life, to make a significant impact. First, more self-awareness. Answer the inquiries below, and for extra support in identifying your OVERs, you can take the online "OVERgiving Assessment" in the book readers' kit or at www.AmIOvergiving.com.

Know Yourself
Which OVERgiving Imprints are running me, and what is the impact?

- Which three OVERs most resonate for me currently?
- How is my overgiving currently showing up? In my work? In my relationships?
- How is overgiving in these ways affecting me?

What we are revealing here together is much deeper than a few mental beliefs you can positively think or "affirmation" yourself out of. Self-sacrifice and taking it all on have been imprinted onto the psyches, cells, and hearts of women at deep generational and cultural levels. These ways of doing, being, working, mothering, taking care of others, and valuing our worth have been passed down from generation to generation for centuries. Now it's up to *our* generation of women to break the cycles of self-sacrifice for ourselves, each other, and the girls and women to come.

If you look at your family lineage, you will likely see a long line of women who have also been afflicted with these OVERgiving Imprints. Perhaps they sacrificed themselves for the good of the family, a partner, the community or a cause, or maybe even you. Or the opposite, they had a hard time giving, which left you feeling like you didn't receive what you needed. Maybe the women you watched as role models growing up seemed like they were able to do it all. This is just what our mothers, grandmothers, guardians, aunts, and sisters "did," because in many cases they had to. And in the situations where they could have done it differently, they didn't have the support, guidance, or strength to know how.

And as if our family systems didn't imprint us enough, advertising and media continue to condition and domesticate us into unsustainable — and unconscious — expectations we keep striving to live into. There are so many to choose from. Like the campaign to sell perfume in the 1970s and '80s that suggested a woman should be able to bring home the bacon and fry it up in pan and still never let her spouse forget he was a man. Chew on that. We make the money *and* make sure everyone is fed. That may have been before your time, but it still lingers in our collective female psyche. Even the resurgence and focus on an archetype like Wonder Woman can have a negative impact if we overidentify with her as the image of what a strong woman should be able to be and achieve. You and I are not superheroines whose job is to stop bullets and save the world, although I know many a woman who has approached her career, relationships, and life this way. While you and I do have superpowers, we are also human women with fears and needs. This doesn't make us weak. Our spectrum of emotion is what makes us strong.

We are holding ourselves to unattainable, unsustainable images of what a good, strong woman looks like, and teaching our girls to do the same.

When I became conscious of the impact of these cultural imprints, first I got sad and then I got mad. Sad that for generations, women have been unknowingly passing down to their daughters these "invincible superwoman" and "self-sacrificing martyr woman" imprints. Of course, not on purpose. It's all unconscious. That's what makes these imprints so damaging and dangerous. The stuff you can see is easier to shift, to stand up for and say, *No! That won't work for me or my family*. The unseen stuff is what wreaks the most havoc. Oblivious, we just keep working and operating unnaturally and unhealthily by some standard we never consciously agreed to:

"To be a *good* woman — mother, wife, daughter,
sister, friend, team player, leader —
you must sacrifice what you need for the good of others."

"To be seen as a *strong* woman, you must be able to do it all, keep it all together, and suck up any feelings or needs you have."

Were the women you witnessed growing up self-sacrificers? Invincible superwomen? Or were they not able to show up and support you the way you needed? Perhaps a mix of all three? How about the women you modeled your aspirations, career, and life design after? Reach back. What do you notice?

When I reach back, I have a visceral remembrance of a back-to-school shopping trip, preparing for seventh grade, where my mother and I had been rambling through a mall for hours. My hands were full of bags; hers held one very small bag, which contained a pair of sensible underwear. With all the culturally untainted consciousness of an eleven-year-old, I directly asked my mother, "Why aren't you buying anything for yourself?"

She instantly replied to me, compulsively reacting from the self-sacrificing imprint she'd inherited: "Everything I do is for you girls. I don't need anything for myself." Whoa! Though my grade-school vocabulary didn't contain the word *self-sacrifice* at the time, my consciousness did. I could feel the energy from which she was speaking. It felt wrong and heavy, and I wanted no part of it. I rejected embracing this self-sacrificing imprint and said, "I don't need you to give me *everything*. There's enough for both of us." I would have gladly had less so she, too, could have left the mall that day with things that made her feel beautiful — so both daughter and mother could give and receive.

My mother, like many, was a blend of both self-sacrificing good girl and invincible superwoman. She never sat down or rested. The OVERdoing imprint ran constantly within her, which I inherited. I never saw her rest or sit without "doing" something. I am not sure if she ever considered she had another choice. You've likely inherited some OVERgiving Imprints, as well, from the women you grew up watching. For most of us, there were also ways that our mothers, like any human mother, didn't and couldn't give us what we needed to receive. Not because they didn't love us or want better for us, but because of their unconscious imprints. This also programmed us to overgive in the ways we've started to explore. We don't need to lament about these for the next ten years of our lives to liberate ourselves — and future generations — from these imprints; we just need to reveal them, articulate them, and invoke compassion for ourselves and the women who came before us.

Know Yourself
What overgiving and underreceiving imprints did I inherit or take on?

Reflect on the women you grew up around in your family or community. Recall the women in your educational and work environments who influenced your imprints of what a good, strong woman looks like.

- *How have I witnessed the women in my life overgiving and underreceiving?*
- *Looking back, what was the impact on these women?*
- *What OVERgiving Imprints or habits have I inherited or modeled after them?*
- *What OVERgiving Imprints or habits might I have taken on due to a lack of receiving what I needed?*

You have the power to rewrite the code and birth new realities.

Calling this code forth isn't about blaming the people who raised us or influenced us. They were doing the best they could with the consciousness they were living in. What matters now is that you and I embrace our power to be system and cycle breakers within our own families, communities, and work systems. We do have the superpower to stop these toxic imprints of self-sacrifice and the superwoman facade, for ourselves and the generations growing up and to come.

You don't have to play by the rules or norms — the codes — set by the overculture. You can choose to redefine what a strong, successful woman or girl looks like, which cannot just resemble an invincible superwoman or self-sacrificing martyr. Our images for strength and self-empowerment must include our ability to both achieve *and* receive. I invite you to rewrite the code for how you give and receive in your work, organization, community, team, family, and whole life from one that is bankrupting you to one that sustains and supports you. The time of you working and giving to your detriment and not receiving what you need can be *over*. We start with one simple yet significant act of rewriting the code by changing just one word that doesn't take anything away from others:

> *It's better to give* ~~than~~ *receive.*
> *It's better to give* and *receive.*

Rewrite the code in your handwriting as an intentional act to break the cycle and choose a new way. Really do it. First, write the outdated program on a piece of paper. Then cross out *than* and plug in the elevated imprint with the word *and*. Every time I rewrite this code, crossing out the *than* to make it *and*, I exhale. With that small act, the potential for a different reality opens, which creates more possibility for everyone. Our hearts feel at ease when we embrace that we do not have to choose between giving to others and receiving what we need. We can have both.

You are more compassionate, courageous, and confident when you give *and* receive in harmony in your relationships, your work, and the world.

If it is to better to give *and* receive, then it would logically follow that the more you receive, the more you can give, and that simply cannot be selfish. Don't you show up as a better human — mother, sister, leader, friend, partner — when you have more than enough money, time, energy, love, and resources for yourself?

Aren't you more able to show up as the compassionate, courageous, and confident woman you are when you feel supported, sustained, and cared for? Have you ever noticed that when you are not receiving what you need, it's hard to be there for others or show up as your best self?

GIVE & RECEIVE create HARMONY

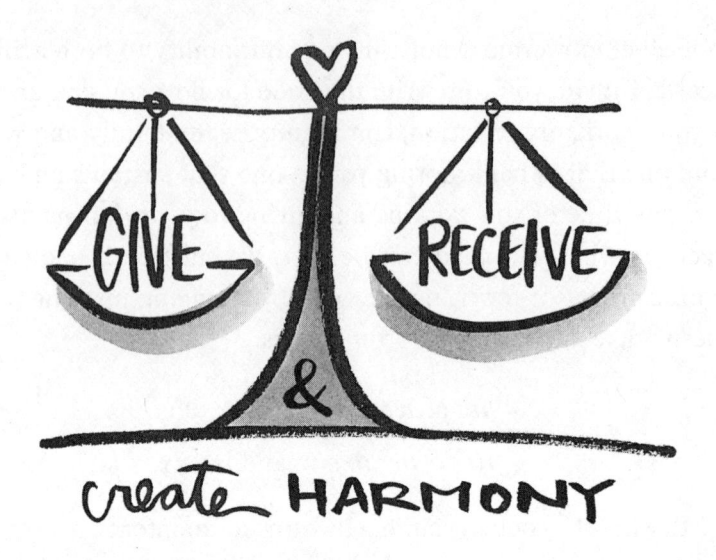

Recall a recent time when you did not show up in a way that made you feel good and proud of yourself. Maybe you snapped? Had what I call a "Superwoman Banshee Blowout," where you reacted in frustration because the pressure was too much? Or you passive-aggressively took a jab at someone and did a "Cut-and-Run"? Or you blamed and criticized versus sought understanding? Or overindulged? You were likely not at your best because you were depleted, were stretched too thin, or weren't feeling sustained or supported.

Don't beat yourself up about it. Do wake up and make the connection between how when you overgive and underreceive, you don't have the strong, stable foundation you need to stand on. So it's much harder to be the woman you desire to be. Which is why you and I, and all women, must take a stand together to stop bankrupting ourselves by overgiving. And then find new ways of working and supporting others that support and sustain us, too.

Self-Sustainability Stands
for Giving and Receiving in Harmony

Consider embracing the self-sustainability stands on the next page for how you give to your work and others.

1. I stay conscious of how much I give to work and relationships.
2. I refuse to give or work from self-sacrifice.
3. I stop equating my strength with my ability to do it all.
4. I stop equating my self-worth with how much I give.
5. I am at my best when I am receiving what I need.
6. I make choices that create harmony between what I give and receive.
7. I am honest about what resources – time, money, energy – I can give.
8. I give myself permission to give less if I start to feel depleted.
9. I model giving and receiving in harmony for those I love and lead.

Now let's make this practical with a small but mighty act: *choose one self-sustainability stand to work with and bring into your daily life.* Choose one that would support you to bring your giving and receiving more into harmony now, to reverse the flow of some of that overgiving. Write down the self-sustainability stand where you can see it daily, or in your journal. When you feel yourself about to overgive, take a stand by saying these words out loud, until you feel empowered to make the harmonious choice. This is how you begin to break the neural pathways in you and the energetic agreements between you and others, and even between you and the organizations you work with or founded. This change happens over time, remember. These OVERgiving Imprints run deep. But it's all good; you and I will spend the rest of the book giving you what you need in order to be aware and empowered to do things differently.

The next step is to go into your daily life and become more aware of both the *physical* and *emotional* signs that you are overgiving and underreceiving. Your body and your heart will signal when you are about to make a choice that sacrifices too much or stretches you too far. We all have different signs, ways our feminine wisdom speaks to us through physical sensations and emotional reactions. I included a list of some common signals in the book readers' kit. Your mission is to reveal how *your feminine wisdom* signals you, which will empower you to start making different decisions. Pay attention.

Know Yourself
What are the physical and emotional signs that indicate I am overgiving and underreceiving?

- *What do I feel in my body when I overgive?*
- *How do I react emotionally when I overgive?*

Harmonizing Practice
Receive Before You Overgive

Notice when you are overgiving, and before you react, get harmonized. Slow down. Breathe. Tune in and ask: *What do I need to receive?* Do your best to open to receive by giving this to yourself, advocating for yourself, and being aware of when other people and the Universe show up to give this to you.

Chapter 7

RELEASE: **Work Hard to Succeed**

EMBRACE: **Work Wise to Thrive**

*We often give more than is needed or valued
and then waste our life force and resources in ways
that could have been directed to what nourished
and sustained us and made a greater impact.*

"You have to work hard to get ahead."
"If you work hard, you will be successful."
"If you just work harder, you will have everything you need."
The overculture loves to dangle these work-hard ethoses for success over us like carrots, promising us if we just work harder, we will get ahead and have what we need. What I want to know is, work hard to get ahead of what? What I want to scream is, *Who is this working-hard motto really working* for? Who is reaping the benefits of all this hard work? Because when I listen to the stories of overwhelmed and tired women, we sure don't feel like the return we've received is worth the price we have paid.

All this hard work has had an impact on our hearts, physically as well as emotionally. One in three women are dying of heart disease — and not because we are eating too many french fries. The pressure and burden *emotionally* and *energetically* are too much. It's coming from all directions — from the external pressures, for sure, but also from the way we think and feel about ourselves, and the way we take on and process the struggle of the world and the people around us.

I imagine you, like many women, have worked your ass off, and damn if it hasn't felt like hard work. Most of us could even make a case that some of our success has come because we chose to work so hard. But this does not mean this is the only way to achieve success. It's just that working hard has been so ingrained into our psyches as *the* path to success, we never consider there could be a different one. But I believe there is.

I'm not about to lay down some platitude about doing less and simplifying your life. If it were only so simple to "do less" and "be simple"! No fairy godmother is coming by to free you from the systems and people that will keep taking everything you give. You cannot twitch your nose and instantly release the demands that form the current constellation of your work, life, and relationships. This "work hard" programming is so deeply equated with our sense of survival, belonging, and self-worth that doing it differently takes time, commitment, and frankly, courage.

For more than a decade, I've been committed to freeing myself from the toil and grind, from pushing hard and striving, and from the perpetual feelings of "not enough" the "work hard" program generates. I would be a liar if I told you I am completely free of it. But what I can honestly say is that I am completely *aware* of it. Aware of how I have accepted working hard as what I must do. Aware of the feelings and fears within my heart that make me believe I have no other choice but to give everything and everyone my all if I want to achieve my goals. Aware that I am no longer willing to sacrifice my heart's health physically, emotionally, and energetically just to appear successful, strong, or smart or reach some made-up marker of success or security. Aware that I actually need to feel joy, savor the moments and milestones, and have space to breathe and connect in meaningful ways as how I live, every day. I know there is a different way, and it starts with us rejecting the overculture's prescription that working hard is the only path to success.

Working hard as the path to success has taken us as far as it can.

If we looked back through time, we would see countries, infrastructure, organizations, and systems built off the backs of many people who had worked *really* hard. Working hard has been the path to making a better life for a long time for most people. Perhaps that is how it had to be. But to grow, a person or a culture has to let go of how they as an individual or a collective did things before. Traditional leadership theory teaches that the skills and strategies that got you to this point cannot take you to the next. To elevate into new levels of possibility where burnout and overwhelm are not the norm, we need a new equation for how we work.

Here is where we invoke our power to write new codes. You know the old program: "work *hard*." You've likely tried the current upgrade: "work *smart*." But that is not quite the key to liberation and sustainability, either. There is another option: "work *wise*." Look at the glyph below, then read for yourself what each really means and decide which option you want to employ.

The definitions below may be different from the way you've thought about working hard or working smart, but since our words form our reality, I thought you might want to be aware of what you're signing up for.

WORK HARD　　**WORK SMART**　　**WORK *wise***

Option #1: Work hard ➡ To do with great exertion; strenuously; or in such a manner as to be difficult to bear or endure, to be marked by resentment, or to inflict physical discomfort or pain.

>Root: Greek *keskeon*, to tow.
>Synonyms of *hard*: toilsome, burdensome, exhausting, severe, grinding, cruel, unfeeling.

Option #2: Work smart ➡ To be quick or prompt in action. To feel, cause, or be a source of a sharp, stinging physical pain or keen mental distress.

>Root: Latin *mordēre*, to bite; Greek *smerdnos*, terrible.
>Synonyms of *smart*: agile, brainy, brilliant, apt, clever, quick, shrewd.

Option #3: Work wise ➡ To discern and judge properly as to what is true or right. To possess discernment or discretion. To be prudent, sensible.

>Root: Old English *wīsian*, to see or know; to show the way, guide, direct; *wīse*, form, shape; melody, ballad.
>Synonyms of *wise*: sage, sensible, intelligent.

As you look at these three options for how to work, which has been your approach? Perhaps a combination? Which way are you working now? And most importantly, which way would you like to work? I have a suggestion.

Choose to work wise, and be smart.

Can we agree that working hard is a raw deal, a recipe for suffering? Working smart is certainly better, but I've advised and mentored many brilliant women who are so quick to think and act that they create realities — as well as organizational and business structures, projects, goals, and agreements — that trap them and strap them down versus support them to succeed *and* be sustained. I am a big *Yes!* to being decisive and having the agility to move swiftly. But I am a big *No!* to continuing to make choices too quickly because the systems we work in or create ourselves pressure us to make a snap decision and move fast into action. Then we are the ones left holding all the work that has to be done. Consider this feminine wisdom instead. I encourage you to read it a few times to really let it register.

To work wise is to seek the way or path
to creating the form or shape that creates harmony.

When you work wise, you are focused and intentional in how you work, discerning in how you direct your life force and resources. You marry the power of your intuition and intellect to work together to access your internal wisdom to know what is in right timing, in harmony, and real, versus reacting to external or internal impulses. You can sense when to move swiftly, and when to slow down. You consciously create constellations (shapes and forms) for your life, family, projects, and organizations and choose paths (timelines, milestones, and goals) that create personal and collective sustainability, true success. Imagine how much happier and healthier your heart would be working this way, in a manner that actually gives you the possibility to create a reality in which you, the planet, and the people you love and influence can thrive.

This sounds totally rational and smart, don't you think? So why the heck are we not working this way already? Well, one big reason is because working wise requires the courageous choice to take a step back and question what is *really needed* in any situation, before taking action. Which means you, and everyone else, have to slow down to consider what shape, form, and impact moving into action will cause. You need space for the path to emerge that will actually lead to harmony — short- and long-term. And in our current overculture, which values faster as better and is fueled by the fear of scarcity and competition, slowing down is seen as a waste of time, when in fact it's the path to saving time, money, resources, our sanity, and our planet. So even if you are wise enough to know to slow down, most of the current systems are rigged to keep everything and everyone speeding up.

Working Wise, a Path for Sustainable Creation

So much of our overwhelm comes from having to constantly react to mentally generated ideas and emotionally driven impulses — created by ourselves or others. There's no space to consider what's needed, necessary, healthy, and in harmony for the whole. All these ideas and impulses create more work, more projects, more tasks that put more pressure on you emotionally and energetically because you feel like you have to make it happen or put it all into action immediately. There is another way. Take a look at the glyph below, which shows the path for unsustainable creation — reflecting how the majority of the world operates and what has led to our unsustainable reality — and a root reason why you stay stuck in overwhelm and scarcity.

Unsustainable Creation

IMPULSE (Idea!) → *speed up* → **INTUITION** (feel, sense) → **INTELLECT** (Thought...) → **UNNECESSARY ACTION** (Form, Form, Form, Form, Form)

All creation starts in the first phase on the left — you or someone has an impulse. Like fire, this creates the spark of an idea. In a culture that values the intellect, logic, and fast action over feelings and slowing down, there is a tendency for people, teams, and organizations to skip the second phase, intuitive thinking, feeling, and sensing, which is the most powerful — it's where the wisdom lives.

Instead of slowing down to consider what is needed and in harmony, people have been trained to speed up — move fast, jump to the intellect, and make up thoughts that may seem correct, even smart, to the mental mind (as opposed to the higher mind). But in reality, what the impulsive mind often creates is void of the human heart. It lacks the deeper wisdom and a felt compassion, it misses the unseen and undiscovered possibilities, and it's blind to the long-term interconnection with the whole. The result? We go from impulse to thought, right into form or action, usually creating too much, too fast, leaving us and others with too many things to take care of and do (notice all the arrows and forms in the last step). And in some cases, we collectively create things that do more harm than good for people and the planet.

Now look at the glyph for sustainable creation, which illuminates how to work in a way that leads to actions and forms that create sustainability and harmony.

Sustainable Creation

IDEA! → slow down to feel sense, receive the wisdom → THOUGHT... → FORM

IMPULSE — INTUITION — INTELLECT — ALIGNED ACTION

Notice that the second step is to slow down to receive the wisdom — to tap into our human feelings and senses, our intuitive guidance, and a higher intelligence beyond the mental realm, which gives us access to deeper wisdom, imagination, and insight. Our thoughts — informed by possibility, clarity, and compassion — can then lead us to create aligned action and form, based on what is truly needed and in harmony.

Making the shift to bringing wisdom into our choices is essential to the sustainability of people and the planet. Think about it. If more wise choices were made in business, health care, government, education, and the organizations where we work, we'd all be wasting less life force and fewer resources and achieving more of what matters. We would be doing less, with greater impact. We wouldn't be reacting to the "go, go, produce, produce, grow, grow" overculture giant that keeps us all busy, doing too much too fast, working much harder than necessary. And perhaps humanity would also stop creating things that harm people and the planet, even if they seem like a good idea or the only way at the time.

Now slow down and take a breath. Don't get overwhelmed; as with all our shifts, you don't need to make big sweeping changes or take on the gigantic distorted systems. Your part is to stop reacting to the impulses of the system or your own impulses as you consider the projects, tasks, responsibilities, and actions you say yes to. Instead, choose to slow down — internally — to tune in to your feminine wisdom before responding. If you do, insight will emerge. You will see and learn things you can't when you work in quick reactive mode. The length of the slowdown will vary based on what's needed. For situations that require a quick response, like in an emergency, the pause may be just a minute to breathe, center, and tune in. Most situations, however, are not emergencies; we just make them so because we are so trained to react quickly or just push through.

Working wise and following the path to sustainable success, in which you and what matters to you can thrive, is a practice, one that supports and sustains your heart. So many people tell me that they want to experience more joy and meaning, to feel the freedom to authentically express themselves, to do work in which they feel they are making a difference — this is part of how you create that kind of reality. Remember, to find the harmonious path, shape, and form, you must slow down and tune in to your heart wisdom, which comes through your embodied feelings and senses. Your mental mind will want to react. But wisdom requires space to emerge.

This simple glyph for sustainable creation represents a big shift in consciousness. I don't want you to swallow this all in one bite. When one of my early teachers, Pamela Eakins, PhD, taught me this timeless wisdom, first I translated it into the practical application I just shared with you, and then I began experimenting with it for my business, projects, and goals. I started using it with my teams and the choices I could control. Then I started using it with the individuals and organizations I advise to support them to create sustainable success.

For you, let's start with increasing your self-awareness and systemic awareness by making this wisdom personal and practical with respect to the ways you have the power to do things differently. We'll look at a piece of fierce feminine wisdom — one I think all women need to know to have any chance of thriving within the current systems in order to then create new ones — and three self-sustainability principles. Remember, you don't have to *do* anything right now. Just wake up your awareness. Take a deep inhale and exhale. Let's dive in.

Self-Sustainability Principles for Working Wise

Systems love women who work hard. The harder you work, the more the system receives. Organizations are like insatiable Pac-Men that will munch up your life force until you are empty. Think about it. Is there ever an end to all the things that "need taking care of" at work? With your family? The world? Is there ever really enough of everything — time, resources, people? No. No matter how much you pour in, the system will take everything you have, if you'll give it. And yet there never seems to be enough.

Programmed to work *hard* and *fast*, we can't stop ourselves from filling the need. Whether it's an underresourced or understaffed project, organization, or team, or it's real people who need the services and support we supply. Our hearts and our heads react to the need without considering the consequences or questioning what is possible given the resources available. Instead of *wisely* stepping back to assess the situation to discern what is *actually* needed and possible, and then taking a stand for what is in harmony to give — which our feminine wisdom is screaming for us to do — we pour our life force in, and in the end, more is still needed. If the fierce feminine heart had the microphone, this is the wisdom she would have shared long ago:

*The systems will take everything you will give,
and there will always be more to give.*

Where does that leave you? The system gets what it needs, for the moment, but your life is rarely better for all you've given. Usually, you are left mentally fried and physically plumper, and your relationships have suffered. And you've just set up the expectation that this exchange is okay with you. You tell yourself this was a onetime thing, but you and I both know that the responsibilities, "fires," deadlines, and demands just keep coming, asking for more. So here's how we support you to start doing things differently. Three self-sustainability principles you can put into practice in your life without getting permission from anyone else.

Stop filling all the holes and gaps.

This is self-sustainability principle number one for working wise. If you keep plugging the holes and overcompensating for the lack of staff, resources, time, and so forth by working harder and more, the systems you work and live in, and the people around you, will have no incentive to change. Why would they? You are always there to pick up the slack; take on the burden; bridge the gap; and be the loyal worker, leader, daughter, or friend. That's a lot of weight on your precious and powerful heart.

Whether it's to the organizational systems we work within or to the familial or community systems we live within, until you and I stop overgiving, they will never reorganize themselves into a "shape" that creates a harmonious exchange instead of self-sacrificing bankruptcy. Chew on this piece of feminine wisdom:

Even if you love what you do; cherish your family; or feel deeply dedicated to your team, community, or mission, it is not healthy to give everything you have to any system, organization, or person just to make whoever or whatever it is function and stay afloat. Even if it feels like you have no other choice. Even if that means it flails, falters, or fails.

You have to stop plugging all the leaks like the Dutch boy who tries to save the village from flooding because the dike is failing structurally. More leaks keep springing up because the structure, agreements, and expectations must change. Have you considered that the dike might need to come down in order for change to happen? But until he and you stop plugging and patching all the holes, you will both stay stuck in the same reality.

Know Yourself
What leaks am I plugging that are creating distress for me?

- *What holes and gaps am I filling in my work – for the organization, team, or project – that are taxing my wellness or draining my life force?*
- *What holes and gaps am I filling in my personal relationships – within my family, with friends, or within my community systems – that are overstretching me?*
- *What is the impact on me physically? Emotionally? Mentally?*

Now I get that there are holes you cannot take your fingers out of, yet. But I've got a message for you, from the fierce feminine heart that's speaking to all women. Slow down, read these words, and take this in:

Just because you can, doesn't mean you should.

Just because it needs fixing does not mean you are the one to do it.

Just because the organization or others won't or can't provide the resources necessary to meet the goals they've set, or the needs of those you support, does not mean you take on five people's jobs and drain your life force to make up the difference.

Working this way will make you sick, and the ROI — return on investment — is not worth it.

Your role is to discern what holes really need plugging or what gaps need to be bridged because they truly are mission- or life-critical. See which needs or shortfalls can be left to leak or in some cases completely break apart, because the structure and agreements need to change. And get clear about how much you are giving and why, and what is actually in alignment.

Stop giving 110 percent when 80 percent would be enough, or you will never have enough for yourself or what truly matters.

This is self-sustainability principle two. There are two things I know for sure about us strong, dedicated women. One, we will consistently give 110 percent to everything we do, even when 80 percent would be enough. Two, our 80 percent is like most people's 110 percent. You go for the A when the B would do. You put that extra 30 percent — your life force, hours of time, worry, or concentration — into a project. Yet, the extra effort is rarely worth the time or your energy.

Think of a project that you poured 110 percent or more into, personally or professionally, because you were convinced it was the only way or the "right" thing to do. But in hindsight, you see all that energy and time poured in did not result in a return commensurate with the value you put in. If you were working wise, you would have given 100 percent commitment and 80 percent effort, and it would have been enough.

You would have had that extra 30 percent of life force, time, and resources to give to something that did matter, like your own wellness, a relationship, or a project that had greater impact. Something that would have felt meaningful, worthwhile, and appreciated — all of which is like superfood for your heart. One of the reasons we feel so burned-out, frustrated, and depressed is because our current way of working and living starves us of the appreciation, meaning, joy, and connection our feminine hearts crave and thrive on. Consider what would shift for you if you embraced these three perspectives for working wise to thrive:

1. Giving 80 percent effort and 100 percent commitment is a choice to support your long-term sustainability and now-term happiness and health.
2. If something requires 110 percent just to maintain it, something is out of harmony.
3. There's a difference between effort and commitment. You can give 100 percent *commitment* — be dedicated and engaged — and at times wisely choose to give 80 percent *effort*, because it's enough and in harmony given all that's happening.

Working or giving this way doesn't mean you don't care. It does not make you a slacker or lazy. It makes you wise. And you don't have to feel guilty or ask permission when you choose to pull back and give less effort, energy, or time. You are not trying to cheat anyone. Working wise is about giving effort and energy in a way that actually creates value and makes a difference, versus reacting to the impulses of people and systems tied to an insatiable overculture that always wants more — and rarely creates space to savor the effort given. And when there's no space for savoring the process, path, and people, our hearts feel starved, uninspired, and eventually resentful and burned-out.

Plus, it's so much more human to operate this way. If organizations want healthy people who are committed to long-term thriving and prospering versus just the short-term burnout and bailout, we must embrace that women lead *whole* lives. At times parts other than our jobs will require more energy. And that's okay. In fact, we have to not just be okay with this; we must design how we work to support it.

When I started graduate school, I made a conscious choice to embrace being a B student, giving 80 percent effort and 100 percent commitment. I didn't announce this; I internally made a choice for what was aligned with me. The reality was that I was working full-time during the day, going to school full-time at night, ending a fifteen-year relationship, and having a personal awakening that required deep healing work. My feminine wisdom, which was just a whisper at the time, pointed out that I had already been accepted into a top business school, and no one was going to ask me my GPA. I was there to learn. So yes, I would show up, be committed, engaged. But instead of killing myself to get the A, I would embrace that my energy was also needed in other places. I needed that extra 30 percent to focus on myself, my healing, and personal growth.

Know Yourself
Where am I giving 110 percent when 80 percent would be good enough?

- *In what parts of my life or what projects or relationships am I currently giving more than is needed, valued, or in harmony?*
- *When I consider pulling back to give less effort, time, and energy, what thoughts, fears, or feelings does that bring up for me?*
- *If I pulled back how much I was giving, what could I do with the extra life force and resources?*

How does the thought of giving 80 percent effort and 100 percent commitment sit with you? It can feel almost criminal to pull back, go for the B, stop filling gaps, and choose not to compensate for the shortcomings. Since grade school we've been imprinted with this "work hard and fast" program for how to survive and succeed. But the truth is, if you and I don't stop overgiving, nothing can change. And we all know things need to change.

To break free, you'll need two things. First, the clarity to discern between what really requires your all and when 80 percent would do. And second, in situations that beg for your hole plugging and overgiving, the courage to take wise action based on what your feminine wisdom is showing you, even if that means disappointing another or doing things differently, in ways that feel uncomfortable — often *really* uncomfortable.

To access the power to make wiser choices, you have to go deeper into your heart. Lurking in there are some significant subconscious fears that must be illuminated if you are going to have the inner clarity and courage to make different, wiser choices for sustainability and harmony. If you are willing to go deeper into your heart, I know the way. I've gone there myself many times — and still do — and have taken many women through. We'll just start by giving words to the fear that is unseen but has been driving you. Ready? Okay, here's the portal in:

> *You can't stop working so hard or giving so much,*
> *because you fear everything will fall apart if you do.*

Underneath every self-sabotaging OVERgiving Imprint is a deeper fear you may have no clue is there. You may not want to feel or deal with it. But as wise woman Melissa Etheridge says in her song "Heart of a Woman," "Our power ends precisely where our fear begins." So I say, let's dive into your heart, illuminate the fear, face it, embrace it, and unleash your power to do things differently. I asked a few women from my community if I could share their root fears and corresponding choices to help make this practical for you:

- **Stacey, overpromising coach and mother:** "Driven by a root fear of disappointing another, I would consistently take on more than I could do by saying yes to all the people I supported when they made a request. You'd find me consistently working until midnight to get it all done. I kept choosing to be loyal to another instead of myself."

- **Mary, overworking government employee:** "Driven by my unconscious root fear of losing love, I made excelling in my work my everything. I longed for deep connection, so I made the people at work my family. I longed for my parents' love, so I strove to be the person they wanted me to be. But my work was making me sick. It was not my true path. I knew I needed to leave. Because I had attached my source of receiving love to my career and work life, I chose to overstay."

- **Kim, overcaretaking leader within a nonprofit:** "Driven by a root fear of others not having what they need, I deeply wanted all the girls my organization served to be cared for. Truthfully, they needed support desperately. But the need was much more than I or the organization could meet. I chose to continually put my physical needs on hold, I gained fifty pounds, and I was on the way to body breakdown before I slowed down and made a shift."

Know Yourself
What root fears drive me to overgive and work too hard?

Let's take a look into what root fear may be lurking under your overgiving habits. Read each of the root fears below and put a check mark next to those that might be running under the surface.

Fear	Imprint	√
1. *It will all fall apart.*	"If I don't hold 'it' all together, everything will fall apart."	

Fear	Imprint	√
2. *I won't be needed.*	"If I say no, people will stop needing me, and if I'm not needed, I am not valuable."	
3. *I won't have what I need.*	"If I stop working so hard, I won't have what I need to survive."	
4. *Others won't have what they need.*	"If I don't show up and keep giving, another person [or other people] will not have what they need to survive."	
5. *I'll be seen as a fraud.*	"If I don't work hard, they'll see that I don't know what I'm really doing or that I'm not really smart enough."	
6. *I'll miss out* (fear of missing out — FOMO).	"If I don't do X or go to X, then I won't belong, be included, reach my goals."	
7. *I'll disappoint others* (fear of disappointing others — FODO).	"If I say no, I will be letting this other person [or these people or this organization] down. I have to be loyal."	
8. *I'll stop being loved.*	"If I stop giving so much to my family [or team, clients, friends], I will lose their love or be all alone."	
9. *I won't fulfill my purpose or reach my goal.*	"If I stop doing and giving so much, I won't reach my full potential or achieve my goals."	

Many of us choose to toil, push, and give everything our all because we do not want to feel these deeper fears. As warped as it sounds, we feel more in control when we focus on all that needs doing "out there" versus "being" with how unsafe, unseen, uncertain, and unsupported we feel *inside*. It's true. Underneath all the overgiving and burnout, we are trying to control the outcome, the process, and other people. All so we or others don't get hurt, so we have enough of what we need to survive, or so we finally meet whatever standard or goal we believe is what success looks like.

Avoiding these fears and the deeper feelings underneath will keep you locked into making choices that burn you out; fill you with anxiety and frustration; and drive you to struggle, grind, and strive. The other option is to get intimate with your heart — remember "into-me-see"? Don't just check the boxes on these fears — that keeps this mental. Dare to feel what is in there, inside that power center of yours. Your feelings are the key to liberation.

Know Yourself
What am I afraid would happen if I stopped working so hard or giving so much?

Be honest with yourself by finishing these heart starters:

- *If I stopped working so hard or giving so much, then…*
- *There is no way I can stop working or giving so much because…*
- *If I pulled back on how much I am giving and doing, people would think…*
- *If I was honest with myself, the truth is…*

Remember how we've been talking about how the first step in transformation is self- and systemic awareness? Well, self-honesty is part of self-awareness, and without it, lasting change just doesn't happen. So do yourself the great service of taking a moment and being honest about the deeper drivers within you that have made it near impossible to do things differently. What I, as a woman who has looked and continues to look deeply within my own heart for the path to making the changes I seek, can share with you is that once you get honest about *what is*, you release a whole lot of self-judgment. And then you become empowered to make your choices differently. As you choose differently, the system and the people will begin to respond differently.

I have one more self-sustainability principle for you to put into action to release working hard to succeed, so you can embrace working wise and actually have the potential to thrive. It's a permission slip, really, that will support you to take a step toward hitting the RESET button on the current expectations that are not working for you. This is where we start shaking loose the status quo to make the space for a new way.

Reset the expectations of the people around you, by choosing to do what is true and aligned for you.

This is the third self-sustainability principle of working wise to thrive. People will expect what you teach them to expect from you, so reset the expectations to support you. If you are always working late and over weekends and taking more on, that is how people and the system will interact with you. If you check email early in the morning and late into the evenings, they will come to expect that as normal. If you are the one in your family who takes care of all the gatherings, keeps everyone connected, or is always there to deal with a drama, the family system will constellate around this and keep taking this from you, until you stop giving it.

If you get what matters done and create healthy boundaries, people around you will change how they interact with you, eventually. Or you will find different people to work with. Or people will find others to soothe their drama or take care of their needs. This is a big shift that ultimately will benefit both you and the system and the people within it. But at first, people and the system will resist, especially if they are benefiting from your overgiving. Expect it. Just don't *react* to it. *Respond* to it.

As you pull back your energy from overgiving, note that at first there is an adjustment period. Be ready for it. Know that you will feel uncomfortable, and that the fear in your heart will get triggered. Observe it, versus try to fix it or stuff it down. Sometimes people will surprise you. Sometimes they will disappoint you. But you will learn a lot about your relationships to individuals, to family systems, and to the organizational and community systems you live in.

Know Yourself
What imprints, agreements, and expectations for how I work and give are no longer working for me?

- *What imprints about working hard have I received from the culture? My family? My work experience?*
- *What are the expectations and agreements I have set for how I work and how much I give that no longer work for me?*
- *What are the expectations and agreements I have set for what I give and do within my relationships — family, friends, and community — that no longer work for me?*

Harmonizing Practice
What Would "Enough" Look Like?

When you sense you may be pouring in 110 percent when 80 percent would do, or running one of your OVERgiving Imprints, hit the HARMONIZE button. Slow down. Breathe. Tune in and ask, *What would "enough" look like?* Just do that. Give enough, no more. Then spend the surplus on something that nourishes you.

Chapter 8

RELEASE: **Do It on My Own**

EMBRACE: **Receive Support and Sisterhood**

We have become so self-sufficient as women that we often don't consider the support we need, and even when it does show up, we struggle to fully receive it.

Asking for support does not make you weak; it makes you wise. Cultivating sisterhood isn't a nice-to-have; it's a necessity. When a woman feels supported, she thrives. When she feels connected and held in sisterhood, she exhales. When she tries to do it on her own, she flounders, drowns, and depletes herself. So why can it be so hard to ask for support? Why do we lack the deeper sisterhood and connection we crave, and just make do without it? Why is it that even when support shows up — whether it's a simple act, like a man offering to take your suitcase down from the overhead bin on an airplane, or someone making a bigger offer to help you with a project or personal situation that involves the giving of time, money, or effort — you refuse or repel the support rather than receive it with grace?

We have become so self-sufficient as self-empowered women that we have become overly self-reliant.

We've become so used to doing whatever needs doing that we don't pause to consider that we may need help to do it. We don't consider that if we don't have the resources we need, maybe we shouldn't take it on. We've grown so accustomed to having to fight for what we need or just barely scrape by that we've gotten used to making do and doing more ourselves.

We seem to be stuck in a vicious cycle in which the responsibility to do it all on our own, without sufficient support, is our reality. Like Olympic weight lifters, we've hoisted the burdens on our shoulders, and held them there. But truthfully, too many women are buckling at the knees, and our girls are feeling the pressure much too young. I've witnessed women break bones, get sick, lose breasts, because only then, when their physical bodies broke down or got slowed down, were they forced to *receive* support. And even still, they resisted *receiving*. Needing others made them feel uncomfortable and vulnerable. Not being able to take care of themselves made them feel weak, lazy. This was not their fault, nor is it your fault if you've experienced a major health or life crisis that required you to receive help. I am being blunt and real with my language because my fierce feminine heart is saying, *No more*, for any and all of us. This deep imprinting against receiving support has made it almost impossible for us to receive what we need — so much unnecessary guilt, shame, judgment, and overgiving — and it's costing us in significant, life-altering ways.

Our inability to receive as women has an impact on our physical, emotional, and mental health and quality of life, as well as our intimate relationships, families, desires, and work, in big ways. And in small ways with respect to how we block support — whether it's a compliment or an offer to take care of something for us. I see it every time I hold a retreat and women arrive to check in and are greeted by my partner, Noah, who offers to take their bags. Noah stands over six feet tall, is 250 pounds, and like a gentle giant can carry three times what we could without breaking a sweat. You would think most women would gladly hand over their heavy bags. After all, they are on a retreat. But oh no! Over half react from some deeply embedded protective response: "No, I've got it!" In other words, "Back off, Mr. Man. I'm a self-empowered woman who does not need a man's help."

The other half pause for a moment to take in what has just occurred. I watch their eyes and can see their internal operating systems shifting, hearts and heads upgrading. These wise women, instead of contracting or asserting their she-woman strength, open their hearts. They *receive* Noah's offer of support. As each one hands Noah her bags, I witness her exhale. Imprint breaker. Consciousness elevator. The bags, a metaphor for all the responsibility she carries in her life, have just been given to someone else to take away. The women realize they need to set down the burden of their lives. They received the unexpected support, and now they are free! The other half struggle and sweat their way to their rooms, once again choosing to carry the burden versus receive support.

This inability to receive support without guilt or apology has got to stop, now. Our lives, our missions, and the lives of our children depend on it. Keep reading for a different way.

Wise women choose to be strong achievers, generous caregivers, *and* gracious and unapologetic receivers.

If you logically look at this equation — be a strong achiever, plus a generous caregiver, plus a gracious and unapologetic receiver — of course you would choose all three; why not? The challenge is, most of us never received training on how to receive! And our overculture has made us believe that receiving is passive, weak, and selfish. Which is just not true. Receiving is a feminine superpower, and basic logical math. The more support you receive, the more you can give to others and what matters to you, without depleting yourself.

Look at the two glyphs on the next page. Which reflects how you would rather approach meeting the desires and demands of your life? I say we hit the REJECT button for the glyph on the left. We cannot keep attempting to be invincible superwomen holding up the world, strong because we can shoulder the weight on our own. Notice the invincible superwoman isn't standing next to her partner or being held by a community or sisterhood. She's solo. You could keep doing your life that way, refusing support. But why would you want to?

You have another choice — receive support. Take a look at the glyph on the right for a different way to operate. You don't have to hold the burden of it all to prove your strength or commitment. You can choose to stand tall, connected vertically to the Universe and the earth, like we practice in our daily morning flow. You can choose to be supported on both sides by the people, organizations, and communities around you — including sisterhood. Notice how the heart of the woman on the right is so much more open to give and receive. You don't need to go it alone. We need for you to both feel and be supported, because when you are, you have so much more access to your power center, and you become much more empowered to retain your life force versus give it all away. Next is the awareness and practical wisdom for how you expand your capacity and superpower to receive.

To thrive, you *need* support in four realms – emotional, mental, spiritual, and physical.

Look closely at the "Receive Support" glyph. Notice the woman has wings. I call these your "Wings of Support." When support is present in all four of these realms, just like a bird's wings support it to soar, you too gain the support you *need* to thrive.

You *need* support. Say that out loud to yourself, "I *need* support." In fact, actually write "I need support" in your wisdom journal, underlining the word *need*. Rewrite the code, even if writing the word *need* makes you feel uneasy, which it does for many women. Which is exactly why I am asking you to say and write the words *I need support*.

Admitting you need support doesn't make you weak or inferior, incapable, or lazy — although you likely have imprints that cause you to feel so. Needing support is not the same as being needy. Embracing that you need support to do your work, reach your goals, take care of yourself and your family, and meet all the diverse demands of your life is what a wise, empowered woman does.

If you think about your life right now, both your desires and daily demands, and I were to ask you "What support do you need?" what would you say? Many women stutter at first; they can't respond. Most of us have been so out of touch with what our true needs are for so long that we don't know what we need. But if you don't know what you need, you cannot ask for it, or recognize and receive the support when it shows up. As wonderful as support sounds, the sheer thought of all we need can even overwhelm us. We don't know where to begin. Which is why I've broken support down — so you can assess, articulate, and receive what you need.

The 4 Realms of Support

1. **PHYSICAL & MATERIAL – support that takes care of your basic human needs.** This includes all needs on the physical plane: your home, food, clothing, work space, transportation, financial flow and reserves, physical body and health, technology, and so on.
2. **SPIRITUAL – support from the Universe, or whatever you call the force that guides and holds you through your life.** Whether this is a practice, a teacher, a community, or a path of study, this provides you with faith and clarity to make choices that keep you true to your path. This support helps you stay stable when life circumstances and challenges stretch you.
3. **MENTAL & INTELLECTUAL – Support that teaches or instills the knowledge you need to do your job, meet your goals, and be successful at new endeavors.** This also includes what you need to keep your mind sharp and clear.
4. **EMOTIONAL & RELATIONAL – support that helps you stay centered through the ups and downs of life.** This includes supportive relationships, in which you feel safe, seen, and held. This strengthens your courage and confidence. Community, sisterhood, beloved relationships, healthy friendships, soul family, coaches, therapists, healers, mentors, and teachers are all part of this support. This also includes self-love, which is a deeply embodied practice — not a meme or affirmation — and is much more than self-esteem.

Know Yourself
How am I supported already?
Where do I need more support?

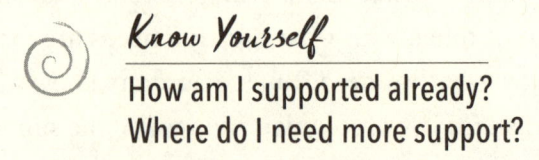

Take a moment and consider the responsibilities and to-dos in your life right now, professionally and personally.

- *In which realms do I have the support I need?*
- *In which realms do I need more support?*

Receiving is your superpower. Receiving support is nonnegotiable. Receiving is a practice and a choice to open your heart when support, love, care, attention, and resources come your way. Are you willing to open up to receive more support? If the answer is yes, the next question is "How are you blocking support?" Let's dive in and see!

In the past you may not have received the support you needed; that's real. And you have the power to feel and be supported now.

Before we can elevate to higher levels of awareness and operating, we always pause to acknowledge what has been. You cannot spiritually bypass, logically think, or self-help yourself out of the realities in which you are *so* not getting the support you need. In order for change to happen, two things must occur: (1) *you* acknowledge and feel the impact that all this pressure and responsibility has had or is having on you, and (2) *your experience* is acknowledged by another woman, a sister who has also carried too much. Then you can finally set the burden down, be free of what has been, and step into new possibility.

I would love to do this for you now.
Slow it down. Breathe.
Read these words. Receive them. Let them get through to your heart:

Wherever this finds you, dear one, I first want to acknowledge…
It has all been on you.
A lot.
Too often.
And it's too much.
Even for a strong woman like you.

For every moment you found yourself alone, with no one but you to do what needed doing, I witness how frustrated, mad, sad, exhausted, and isolated you must have felt.

*I witness how unfair it has been, for all the ways in which you had to shoulder the responsibility.
I witness that in the moments when shit needed to get done and you looked around, you were the only one standing.
There was no support to call on. No one but you could do the job.
No one but you could do what needed to be done.*

*Second, I acknowledge that at the time,
you didn't have another choice you could see.
You did not have the support structures in place you needed.
You did not have what you needed to change the reality you were in.
You were taught how to survive in an overculture that never had your best interest at heart.*

*Third, I acknowledge that in this moment,
you are standing at a different choice point.
It's time now to ignite the fierce feminine wisdom
within you and be truly empowered.*

Now here's where you pick up the thread of liberation, by being real with yourself, from an empowered and compassionate place. While it is true that in the past you did not have another choice, you did have a hand in setting up your reality. Just as there are ways in which you overgive because of your deeper fears, so too are there ways you repel or refuse support, take it all on, or make choices in your relationships and work that create the unsupportive realities you face.

What's important now is to not hold on to the past choices or place blame for the current consequences you may be feeling and dealing with. What is essential is that we move you into a place of self-empowerment, where you can make a choice to get the support you need, period. To do that, first we need to go a level deeper, to get to the heart of what makes receiving support challenging for you. Then we can move to the next stage, of opening up to receive the support you need. Sound good?

Here's what we do next. First, I'll share with you some root reasons why women push away, rather than open to receive, the support they need. It's all about the heart, of course. Then I'll share wisdom for doing it differently by the choices you make.

The Support Sabotagers:
Which Keep You from Receiving the Support You Need?

What follows are ten root reasons, compiled from years of observation, that illuminate why you may be preventing yourself from getting the support you truly need, and deserve. Read each, pausing in between. Circle the ones that resonate.

1. **You have equated not needing support with strength and needing support with weakness.** It feels weak, vulnerable, or disempowering to accept support. You judge that you should be able to do it on your own.
2. **You believe that if you receive support, you are taking away from others or putting a burden on them.** You don't want to weigh others down with your struggle. You tell yourself that others need the support more than you. You'll be fine.
3. **You do not know how to ask for what you need in a direct and healthy way.** You were not taught to be empowered to ask for what you need. So you wait until you are in dire circumstances. Or you ask in distorted or disempowered ways.
4. **You don't even really know what you need.** You are moving so fast, doing so much, or focusing so intently on what's going on at work, in the world, or with other people that you have not asked yourself what you need in a long time, if ever.
5. **You have stopped asking for what you need because in the past when you asked, you didn't get it.** You've experienced being met with something other than kindness, generosity, and empathy when you asked for support. It became safer and smarter not to ask.

6. **You have been fending for yourself for so long that you don't trust that you can or will be supported.** You've had to take care of yourself and others so completely that you don't believe it can be any different.
7. **You are seen as so capable and strong that others don't know you need help.** The image you present is so self-sufficient, strong, or stable that people think you've got it all together or have everything handled. So it doesn't occur to them to ask if you need support.
8. **You are afraid you will be disappointed or that others won't do what they say they will.** You have been let down by others in the past, so you would rather just do it all yourself. You'll end up having to do it anyway, so why bother getting others involved?
9. **Your standards of excellence are so high that other people cannot meet your expectations or do what needs to be done as well as you can.** You are smart and dedicated, and you expect others to be just as smart and dedicated. Either you don't trust that people can take care of things as well as you, or others feel they cannot do them as well as you. So they don't. Or you step in and take over.
10. **You are overprotecting your heart, so when people reach out, you contract instead of opening to receive.** It's like there is an energetic block where you cannot accept the support when it comes. You *want* to open up to receive it, but something inside you shuts it down.

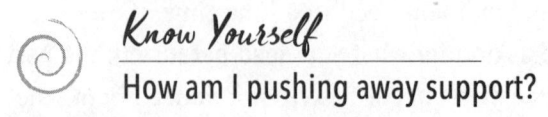

Know Yourself
How am I pushing away support?

Choose up to three support sabotagers that ring true for you. Write them out in first-person, "I am…" sentences. Then ask yourself these questions.

- *In what situations or relationships am I currently pushing away support or shouldering the burden?*
- *How could I be contributing to not receiving the support and sisterhood I need?*
- *How might my past experiences be affecting my inability to receive support or sisterhood today?*
- *What imprints about needing support, being supported, being self-sufficient, or having sisterhood did I take on — from the overculture, my family, or my education?*
- *What supportive reality would I love to create instead? Professionally? Personally?*

What could be possible if you embraced receiving support and sisterhood as being as essential as paying taxes, not optional? Except this will feel good — LOL! Are you willing to experiment with making receiving support a conscious part of your choices at work, in your relationships, in everything? I can't promise that you will wake up tomorrow and have all the support you need if you say yes. But I can promise if you take a stand for yourself now, affirm you deserve to be supported, and choose to open to receive more support, over time the Universe and people around you will begin to respond differently. What follows are three practical applications, self-sustainability principles, for putting this wisdom into action in your life right now.

Self-Sustainability Principles for Receiving Support

In times of stretch and stress, or when you are doing something new, ask for and receive more support, not less.

Here's practical application number one. In times of stress or stretch, you ask for and receive *more* support, even if it's challenging to do so, which in my experience it often is. When Noah, my partner in life, love, and business, had a stroke at the age of forty-two, I had no choice but to step in and take care of our business, make sure we had enough money, and help him get the care he needed. I also had to take charge of making choices about where we would live. We were six months into our nomadic dream to live and work around the world. Noah's stroke had not been part of the plan. I didn't have any choice but to take charge; however, I was at choice as to whether I took on the full burden of the business, our physical safety and security, and Noah's well-being. I could have very easily hoisted all the responsibility and pressure on myself.

Instead, I made a very conscious choice to release the first two support sabotagers: (#1) the need to appear strong, and (#2) the fear of being a burden on others. Then, I chose to get clear on what my part to do was in our business and in Noah's recovery, just focus on that, and receive support for the rest. I chose to acknowledge that I needed support, and I opened up to receive it. This did not mean our experience was easy or that I emerged unscathed. In the three years Noah took to fully recover, my body was negatively affected by the distress and the pressure of being the sole money generator. There were days my knees did buckle. Physical symptoms of distress showed up, almost to the point of chronic disease rooting into my body. I made it through this seriously stressful threshold only because I had my Wings of Support in all four realms to lift me up and guide me through — which included sisterhood.

This was a big, extremely challenging lesson for me in receiving support and surrendering control that broke open my heart and expanded my capacity to receive in countless ways. The whole deep heart story will have to be saved for another time, but the wisdom I gained and can share is as follows:

1. **In times of distress or significant stress, know this: it is okay to demand from the Universe the support you need.** But don't wait to create a relationship with the Universe — or a thriving sisterhood — until the two-by-four hits you. It is also more than okay — it is the humankind way — to receive support

from others without feeling like you have to give back. Allow people to support you. And receive it.

2. **In times when you feel yourself taking on the burden and overgiving, do this: pause, release the impulse to take it all on, and invite in and receive support.** Recall the two glyphs from page 168. Instead of hoisting the burden on your shoulders, open up your heart to receiving support. Get clear about what you need. Ask the Universe and the people around you for support. Be aware that you are in training, not for weight lifting but for strengthening your feminine superpower of receiving, so you can open your heart to receive support with grace.

3. **In times when you find yourself doing something you have never done before or have little experience in, be proactive: create a web of support and receive more support!** Do not attempt to figure it out on your own. Whether it's a new job or responsibility, being a first-time parent, or starting a business, before you jump in or consider putting your nose to the grindstone, remember: *I need more support!* Use the four realms of support to get clear on what you need, and work with the Universe and the people around you to create your web of support — make and write out a proactive plan for receiving the support and sisterhood you need.

Know Yourself
How could I release some pressure by receiving more support?

- *In what realms of my life am I feeling too much pressure or responsibility on me?*
- *What kind of support would help me release some of the pressure and burden?*
- *What belief or fear within me would stop me from receiving the support?*

*Invest in the support you need. You are worth it.
And you'll do more for others because of it.*

Practical application number two is this: remember that receiving is an act of self-love and love for others, so invest in support and feel good instead of guilty about it. One of the self-sabotaging choices we make as women that keep us from receiving support is not spending the money and time on ourselves or on things that create more space for us. We'll spend resources on our kids, family trips, relatives, home remodeling, work clothes, and dinners out. We'll invest in more degrees or certifications. But unless our company or insurance pays for it or we are in distress because of some major life crisis, we often won't invest in the emotional, mental, physical, or spiritual support we need to be the leaders, mothers, partners, and strong and fulfilled women we desire to be.

Where you put your money and time tells the Universe what you value. When you keep putting your real needs, not your pampering desires, on hold until there is enough money or time, they will never come off the back burner, unless there is a crisis. Don't wait for the crisis to come.

And also don't put yourself into tons of debt. Sometimes the money isn't there for what we want or even think we need, because we actually don't need it in the form we think. Often, when I've invested in myself or spent money on the support I've needed and desired, it's felt like a stretch, but it shouldn't feel like a *stress* that requires you to eat ramen noodles for dinner every night or puts you into levels of debt that create distress.

Sometimes there is another way for you to receive what you need. Be clear about what you need, articulate it, and stay open to how it comes.

Remember that conversation with Gloria Steinem I told you about in chapter 1? What I didn't tell you was that it took place after an intimate fundraising lunch for about forty women, for which the tickets were $2,500 each. I didn't have $2,500 in my budget or bank account. But I knew I needed to meet Gloria. So I reached out to the woman hosting the event, shared my story and need to talk with Gloria, and asked her if there was some way I could support the event in exchange for my attendance. And then I received a holy receiving lesson. This woman, whom I had just met a night earlier and who had significantly more financial resources than I, said to me, "I will pay for your ticket. Just come." *Gulp. Deep breath. Receive.* I said yes.

Most of us have one area among the four realms we have no problem investing in. Another we continually underfund, especially when money feels tight. For me, when money feels like it's ebbing, my tendency is to pull back on spending on the support I need for my body. But I don't stop working less. I don't stop giving to others. I just stop receiving what I need in order to support my bodily system to operate at the level of intensity I am working at. A few years ago, as I became self-aware of this pattern, I took a stand. I told the Universe, myself, and the organizations I had created, "No more!" Remember, taking the stand internally is often the catalyst that finally gets us committed to doing things differently. Then the outside reality starts to shift, sometimes quickly, sometimes slowly.

In this case, I took two steps to put my support structure into place, on the physical realm and the relational realm. One, I scheduled an acupuncture appointment at the new moon and full moon, for three months at a time. That way the space could be saved for me to sustain my life force. I told the Universe this matters to me. Two, I set up a Health Savings Account and put in money every month so I could fund my acupuncture without it feeling like a financial drain.

Know Yourself
Which realms of support do I underinvest in?

Look back at the four realms of support and name which ones you find it challenging to invest your time and money in. Then answer these inquiries:

- How is underinvesting in this area affecting me?
- What do I tell myself about why I do not have the money or time to spend for this kind of support?
- What is the truth about the support I need in this realm right now?
- What is the consequence of not giving myself what I need?
- What one action can I take to receive more support in this untended realm?

Proactively and actively cultivate support and sisterhood as a practice so it's there when you need it.

Lastly, here's practical application number three for receiving support and sisterhood: Do not wait until crisis hits before you decide to cultivate the Wings of Support you need. Don't wait for the need to emerge. Proactively assess the support you would love now, and just like you put money away in savings, put time, energy, and money into cultivating the support you desire as a *practice* for how you live. This includes sisterhood.

Sisterhood is not something that just happens; it's something you choose to seek out and cultivate. Sisterhood isn't just about the length of time you've known someone; it's about being in connection with others who see you, who have a similar level of consciousness and passion, who are also growing, and with whom you can grow together. Gathering conscious women in sisterhood, with intention, is a substantial part of my personal path and the work I do in my Feminine Wisdom Way school and my feminine leadership communities. Consider yourself invited. At the end of the book, I share ways to connect.

Self-Sustainability Stands for Strengthening Your Capacity to Receive

Next are some self-sustainability stands that can help you cultivate support and sisterhood now.

1. **I receive, versus refuse, support.** Whether it's a simple compliment or an offer of money, time, or effort, instead of contracting or blocking the support, open up to *receive* the support.
2. **I receive support without feeling guilty or like I have to give in return.** Embrace what is being offered as a gift, without feeling like you have to give in return or like you are a burden.
3. **I know what I need, and I name it, without apology.** Be direct and clear about what you need, instead of feeling like you have to prove or justify your needs. Then be open to how the support comes, as it often shows up in ways different than you think.
4. **I make choices based on the resources actually available.** In the running of your life, family, organization, team, and projects, operate based on the support you actually have, not the resources you wish you had or were promised.
5. **I cultivate a strong web of support and sisterhood so the support is there when I need it.** Create this support web for yourself as if your life depends on it, because it does. Don't rely on just one person or one community. Cultivate multiple *meaningful* connections with individuals and communities — it's about quality, not quantity — in which you connect in person and online; both are needed. This web will be what holds you when the challenges, doubt, and swirl stir you up.
6. **When I set goals for what I desire to achieve, I also name the support I need to receive.** When you set your intentions and plans for your business, organization, wealth, health, relationships, self-expression, and so on, use the four Wings of Support to identify the support you need. This way, giving and receiving will both be woven into how you work, create, relate, and operate.

You now know that in order to reach your goals, meet the demands of your life, and stay sustained, receiving support and sisterhood is a nonnegotiable. Your role is to get clear on what you need, ask for it, and open up to receive it, however it comes. This is a practice for how you design your life and meet both the expected and unexpected challenges and opportunities that come your way.

To strengthen your receiving muscle, a few small but mighty acts: One, choose one of the six self-sustainability stands for strengthening your capacity to receive (on the previous page) to experiment with proactively. Write it in your wisdom journal or somewhere you can see it. Just being more aware of it will start to create nourishing changes. Two, try the following harmonizing practice in your life in the moments when you feel unsupported or like the world is on your shoulders. Remember, it's not about doing more; this is about doing what you already do, differently. Three, let's complete this section with a daring act of liberation to get your giving and receiving into harmony.

Harmonizing Practice
What Support Do You Need?

When you feel yourself about to step into the *I have to do it all myself* reality and hoist the world on your shoulders, or when you feel unsupported or like you don't have what you need, press the HARMONIZE button. Slow down. Breathe. Tune in and ask: *If I am going to do this, what is the support I need?*

DARING ACT OF LIBERATION #3

Get Your Giving and Receiving into Harmony: Transform One OVERgiving Imprint

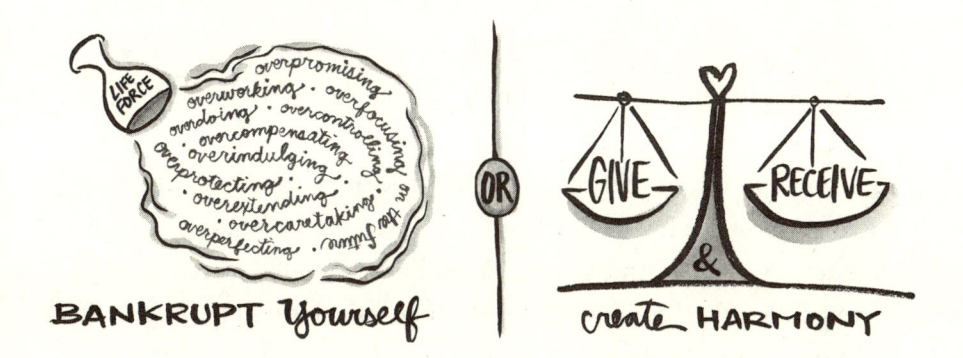

BANKRUPT Yourself (LIFE FORCE: overpromising, overworking, overfocusing, overdoing, overcontrolling, overcompensating, overindulging, overprotecting, overextending, overcaretaking, overperfecting...)

OR

create HARMONY (GIVE & RECEIVE)

The internal experience you desire to feel comes before the external reality you've been trying to achieve. If you want to feel supported, you must first choose to stop overgiving and start receiving what you need.

Feeling unsupported and not receiving the support you need is a self-fulfilling prophecy. Whether you are currently lacking the support at work or home to deal with the big stuff or the mundane details, the only way to change that reality is to take a stand to feel supported within yourself first. This is just how the Universe works.

This universal wisdom applies to everything. Freedom, money, love, and in this case, support. If you feel unsupported, you will stay unsupported. If you want to be supported, you first have to choose to feel supported inside, and open to receive the support when it comes. This is not self-help mumbo jumbo. I am not suggesting if you just whip up some affirmations, your life will change. That is much too simplistic.

You have to show up in your life and make choices that support you. When evidence of how unsupported you are appears, or when you feel like everything is on you and you have no choice but to sacrifice yourself, you have to take a stand and say *No more!* and find a different way. Which isn't easy. In fact, it can be damn challenging, because it pushes against all the deeply ingrained and distorted patterns, fears, relationship agreements, and imprints you've been operating within for years. But it is possible to change your reality and relationships so that how you give and receive comes into, and stays in, harmony. And as a result, instead of sacrificing yourself, you sustain yourself. I know, because I myself have done exactly what I share with you now — it's not a theoretical exercise I whipped up; it's a practice I've transformed through and taken many others through. If you follow it step-by-step, you'll come out with some potent insight into yourself. (To support you, I made a meditation in the book readers' kit that will help you tune in to your heart and drew out an example of one of my real OVERgiving transformations.)

Your Mission

Reveal the root fears and feelings underneath why you overgive to your work and relationships and underreceive what you need. Then start making wiser choices that lead to harmonious exchanges, in which you receive what you need in order to be supported and sustained.

STEP 1: Choose One OVERgiving Imprint to Transform

Choose one of the OVERs that seems like it may be at the root of the burnout, overwhelm, or self-sacrificing reality you can find yourself in. Refer back to the descriptions on pages 134–36. Identify which feels most ripe and ready for transformation:

OVERcaretaking • OVERcompensating • OVERconnecting • OVERcontrolling • OVERdoing • OVERefforting • OVERextending • OVERfocusing on the future • OVERindulging • OVERperfecting • OVERpromising • OVERprotecting • OVERworking

STEP 2: Feel and Reveal the Root of Your Overgiving

How does this OVERgiving Imprint show up currently, or how has it in the past? Really let yourself see the reality you're experiencing because of overgiving in this way. Close your eyes, take a few breaths, and imagine yourself in the situations where the overgiving is present, as an observer. Then use the inquiries below to *feel* the impact. Write out the inquiry; then tune in to your heart rather than answer from your head. To do so, close your eyes, put your hand on your heart (this works even if it feels weird), take a few breaths, and ask yourself the question. Write out the answer using the sentence starters under each inquiry.

1. What does the overgiving *feel* like physically and emotionally?
    When I am over_____, my body feels...
    When I am over_____, my heart feels...
2. What are you *sacrificing* by running this OVER program?
    When I over_____, I sacrifice...
3. What are the *underlying fears* or feelings driving you to overgive?
    If I stop over_____, I am afraid that...
    If I stop over_____, then I will...
    If I stop over_____, then others may...

Next, we create a blueprint of what this looks like within you. Don't skip this part. When you see the OVERgiving Imprint, the reality sinks in.

Overgiving Imprint

First, draw the glyph — a circle with an upside-down triangle in it — on a piece of paper or in your wisdom journal as you see it but *without* the words. Or you can just write it here in the book. Write your OVERgiving Imprint at the top of the triangle: "OVER_____." Then use the inquiries you just answered to complete your overgiving glyph. (Note: I correlated the question numbers below with the questions you answered above to make it easy for you.)

1. **Feelings:** Write three of your physical sensations or emotional feelings in the inner circle outside the triangle.
2. **Sacrificing:** Write what you are sacrificing in the center triangle.
3. **Fears:** Write your underlying fears, one at each triangle point.

STEP 3: Liberate Yourself by Naming the Loving Truth

Answer these questions honestly, using the sentence starters. Write the truths under the overgiving glyph.

1. How are you benefiting from this OVERgiving Imprint?
    Even though I know over_____ is not working for me, if I was being honest, I'm doing it because...
2. What are the cost and consequence to you if you don't stop overgiving? (Be specific.)
    If I don't stop over_____, I will...
3. What do you need to release in order to stop over_____? (Write one to three things.)
    I need to release...

As you dig in, you may find that other OVERgiving Imprints even more deeply rooted emerge. For example, one woman I worked through this process with started with overcontrolling. People told her she was a control freak. She agreed. She was always taking care of everything, not leaving space for others. As we dug deeper, we found that at the core she was overprotecting, first herself and then everyone she cared for — parents, daughter, partner, and team. This drove her to take overresponsibility for the safety and health of her family and the people who reported to her at work. That was a big burden to carry! We decided to focus on overcaretaking, because the distorted pressure of the responsibility was making it impossible for her to make choices that were about *her* needs and desires. Having raised a daughter, held the role of main financial provider for two decades, survived cancer, and supported her parents, she first needed to set down the weight of overcaretaking for everyone else if she was going to design the next phase of her life from an empowered place. Only then could she get to the heart of what she truly desired.

STEP 4: Embrace What You Need to Feel Supported

Now that you can see the imprint you don't want, let's elevate your internal operating system by embracing a new imprint that will support you to give and receive in harmony. What follows are a series of Receiving Mantras in the form of "I AM" statements. After many years of experimenting with what "receiving" actually is, and what's needed to release the fear and coping strategies that cause us to push or give away what we need, I learned that receiving is something you must *feel*, in your core.

I refined the core feelings into the Receiving Mantras you see below. They are written as "I AM" statements intentionally. Working with the "I AM" is a choice to embrace this feeling, to cultivate it within. As you do, you start to create a reality externally that reflects the inner reality. The "I AM" is the heart-powered imprint that replaces the fear-based imprint, supporting you to make choices in your work and relationships that lead to harmonious exchange. Read through the list and choose one or two that reflect how you desire to feel, or make up your own. Don't think too hard; go with what resonates in your body. If you need support sensing into these, try the meditation in the book readers' kit.

Receiving Mantras

"I am valued."

"I am whole and healed."

"I am met."

"I am supported."

"I am safe."

"I am sustained."

"I am nourished."

"I am seen."

"I am held."

"I am protected."

"I am connected."

"I am enough."

"I am worthy."

"I am nurtured."

"I am surrounded by love."

"I am just doing my part."

"I am divinely guided."

STEP 5: Create a New Harmonizing Imprint That Empowers You to Make Self-Supportive, Sustaining Choices

Now we make this practical and superpowered. Remember, we are revealing deeply ingrained imprints and fears that have driven how you relate to the world, work, and other people for many years. So expect resistance from yourself and others as you take a stand to get your overgiving into harmony. This next step will give you the awareness and practice to meet the fear when it arises and make a different choice. Wise women don't avoid fear or pretend we don't have it; we look fear straight in the eye, embrace our humanness, and step forward with fierce compassion for ourselves and others.

We start with harmonizing the three *fear* imprints you identified, the ones you wrote in your overgiving glyph. Go through this harmonizing process by writing out the three inquiries for each fear (there's an example below):

1. *If I stop over_____, then _____* [insert fear from the OVER glyph].
2. *If* [insert the "I AM" Receiving Mantra you chose], *I could embrace that _____.* (This transforms the fear into faith.)
3. *If I embraced this, I would I feel _____ on the inside.* (This transforms the fear-generating feelings into harmonizing feelings.)

Example from Stacey, mother of two, who did this after separating from her husband:

1. If I stop *over*compensating for my husband's lack of presence, then my boys will suffer.
2. If I am just doing my part, I could embrace that my boys will learn independence.
3. If I embraced this, I would feel calm and trusting on the inside.

Now make your new Harmonizing Imprint that reflects what both giving and receiving feel like for you (see glyph on next page). Draw the same shape as before but this time with the triangle pointing upward. This is a symbol for elevation through fierce compassion. Draw it on a separate piece of paper or on the other side of the page with the first glyph. Or write it in the book.

Harmonizing Imprint

1. In the center of the triangle, write your "I AM" Receiving Mantra.
2. At the three triangle points, write what you said you could embrace from sentence 2, replacing each of the former fear imprints with faith imprints. This is what you say to yourself when you are in danger of overgiving: *I can trust that…*
3. Inside the circle but outside the triangle, write the feeling words you would experience if you embraced the faith imprint from question three. These are your "harmonizing feelings," what you feel when you give and receive in harmony.

Remember, your internal feeling creates your external reality. The "I AM," the faith imprints, and the feeling words hold the essence of what you desire to cultivate within so your outside reality can harmonize to reflect this.

STEP 6: Work This into Your Daily Life and Choices

Put both imprints where you can see them daily so you can work this upgrade into your reality. I put mine where I do my daily morning practice. Every year, as part of my yearly visioning and goal setting, I choose one "OVER" to transform, and work with it for the entire year to strengthen my capacity to receive. I invite you to work with this overgiving pattern during the year by noticing how and when the OVER shows up, and then choose to see and do things differently. This will take some courage and practice. In the moments you sense you are overgiving, or are about to, pause, breathe, and tune in by running yourself through this harmonizing practice (which will require you to slow down but will save you lots of life force and time on the other side!):

- **_Feel_ the fear and your feelings instead of stuffing them down.** Get curious, tune in to your heart, and literally ask, "What am I feeling? What is the fear?"
- **_Feel_ the fierce compassion and faith by repeating your "I AM" Receiving Mantra to shift from fear to love.** This is most effective when done with eyes closed and your hand on your heart — that's where the feelings and fears are. Keep saying the mantra out loud or to yourself, with the intention of calming your heart so you can find clarity.
- **_Find_ the wise harmonious path. Reveal the wise choice to give and receive in harmony using these four inquiries.** Write these out yourself, or ask someone to run you through them:

  1. *What would* enough *look like to give?*
  2. *What would* too much *look like to give?*
  3. *What is* in harmony *to give?*
  4. *What do I* need *to receive?*

- **_Feel_ the liberation and freedom when you make a choice for harmonious exchange.** Feel it so it gets into your cells that you can trust this way of being. Even if others respond poorly, don't take on their stuff. When you can't make the self-supportive choice, reach out and ask for support before you overgive and sabotage yourself.

Remember, elevation happens over time. You will go through the four stages of personal transformation, starting with awareness of when you overgive. Notice what happens when you make the harmonious choice and when you make the choice to overgive — and see and feel the impact. Reflect on what you could have done differently. Your emotional feelings and physical sensations will alert you when you are in the OVER zone. Little by little, you will stop wasting your valuable life force and resources on what does not create a harmonious exchange. Remember, living this way is a practice, and we do it every day through the choices we make.

As we pass this midpoint of our journey together, I wanted to pause and share a story with you. One whose place I knew needed to be at the center of this book — at our deepest point. My intention in sharing this is that it will open and touch something in you that gives your fierce feminine heart permission to make your self-sustainability nonnegotiable from this day forward. And that inspires you to listen to and trust your deeper inner knowing, no matter what.

My Heart Could Not Take on the Burden, Again

I'd like you to meet a woman who cannot write her story but whose story needs to be told, so I'm writing it for her. Her name is Accalia. She was a force of nature, the heart of her home and family and the communities and organizations she served and worked within. I met her just one year before she beat breast cancer, for the second time. A chronic overcaretaking, overresponsible, overworking woman, she embraced cancer as a wake-up call to do things differently.

Mother of two, major "breadwinner" in her marriage, sales leader for Big Pharma companies, youth mentor, and board member for her spiritual community, Accalia overgave to every part of her life. Because she was so darn strong and capable, she was able to operate this way for a good forty-five years before her body shut down the first time. For the seven years I worked with her, Accalia knew two things: One, she didn't like the way people were treated in the business world;

she wanted to change this. Two, if she didn't get off the road, she was going to die.

"If I don't get off the road, I am going to die." Many times she voiced this to me. And when she did, I didn't brush it off; I slowed her down and said, "Pay attention — that is your feminine wisdom speaking." So our work began. She was financially shouldering her kids' college and a mortgage, so she couldn't just quit her job. So we worked first on getting her connected to her life force, teaching her how to stay grounded and keep her magnetic field clear. Then we started the deeper heart work, to reveal the roots of why she could so easily and generously give to others but could not receive for herself.

I wish I could give you a fairy-tale ending, but it's not that simple. On the upbeat, Accalia did get off the road, for a few years. She took a contract job mentoring salespeople. She did deep healing work and reset her sense of self-worth. She saw her children graduate college. She opened to receive the support of sisterhood. She faced her fears of not having enough. I smile as I write this, because I can feel the presence of Accalia having an impact on every person she touched — so full of joy, passion, laughter, and compassion. She could light up an entire room and did, often.

But here is where the story takes a turn to the darker reality we as women need to be talking much more openly about. Accalia's contract ended. She was the primary moneymaker. What she really wanted to do was write and speak about compassionate leadership, but she didn't have the runway to create that reality while faced with the financial needs present in her life. So she started interviewing for jobs doing what she had done before, managing large teams and traveling around the country. In early December, Accalia texted me that she was interviewing for a big job that would require her to have seventeen direct-report employees and go back on the road. She wrote, "I am already feeling the frenzy. I am doing my best to keep my head above the swirl." She had not even accepted the job yet and was already feeling the pull of the swirl. I am not sure why I didn't text her back with the message her feminine wisdom had so clearly stated: "If you don't get off the road, you will die." But I wish I had.

Three days after the text, Accalia took the job. Ten days later she was admitted to the hospital. Four days after Christmas, she died. Not of cancer, although that had compromised and weakened her body. She died because her heart failed.

Accalia was my first student to die. As I type this, tears flow down my face, because the absence of this bright light and force of feminine wisdom is a loss. She was about to go back to doing what she had done, but her body and spirit could no longer handle it, so her body said "enough." I imagine she felt like she didn't have another choice.

I share this story with you because I believe by speaking to us Accalia is doing her sacred work — encouraging us to listen to our hearts and bodies and find a different way. If at fifty-four, with a passionate fire in her heart to make a difference, *she* died, so could any one of us. We should not feel like our only option is to sell our souls and compromise our needs in order to have the material support we need — because this choice can have life-altering, even life-ending, costs.

I imagine if Accalia could speak to us now, she'd say something like this: "Sister, if you hear yourself saying things like 'I just cannot do this anymore' or 'Working and living this way is making me sick,' stop and pay attention. Do not just take a weekend off, refuel, and push back in. This is your feminine wisdom jumping up and down, saying, '*Wake up*, woman! This is real.' My heart could not take on the burden, again. We have to change things, now. And you don't have to do it alone. But you must go straight into your heart and stand up for what you need, without apology. Know you are not alone in this; we stand together, in sisterhood."

PART FOUR

Liberate Your Time

Change your relationship to time, and you'll not only be more productive; you'll become empowered to create the space you need and crave.

Chapter 9

RELEASE: **Make and Find More Time**

EMBRACE: **Create and Claim Space**

*Wise women know the truth about time
and the secrets of creating space,
and they choose to work with both.*

Just like work/life balance is a faulty equation for organizing your life, making and finding *more time* is not the answer to getting all that needs doing done. More time cannot be a solution for the lack of spaciousness you feel or the pressures you face, no matter how many time-management systems or strategies you try. Yet how often do you speak or think words like the following?

"I just need to *make* more time."
"If I could only *find* more time."
"I just don't *have* the time."

We are so used to relating to time from a deficit that we say things like this a lot but don't even realize what we are saying. We keep asking for more time, affirming our lack of it, yet nothing changes. If you think about this logically, why is pretty straightforward:

You cannot make more time.
There is no time kitchen.

You cannot find more time.
Time is not lost.

You cannot make more hours, find additional minutes, or squeeze in an extra day. According to the mainstream calendar system, there are only 24 hours in a day, 7 days in a week, 12 months or 365 days in a year. Time is finite. At some level you know this. Yet, if I were to stop by your house tomorrow and gift you with one thousand hours of time, would you take it? Of course! We've all wished for *more* time.

If you go deeper, however, what you are really seeking is not time; it's what you *think* time can *give* you, the freedom and feeling of *space*. Space to breathe; space to create; space to achieve your dreams and goals; space to enjoy the people you love, your home, and all the things you work for but rarely have the space to *savor*. This is good news! You don't need to find or make more time, which is impossible. What you need, my sister wise woman, is *space*, which is within your power to control.

This section we are about to dive into is perhaps the most challenging, because it requires you to open your consciousness to receive some secrets about time and space that your mind may struggle to embrace. Which is okay, because remember that in order to change your reality, you have to shift your consciousness, which includes changing how you think. We have become so run by — even enslaved by — the overculture's time structures and imprinting that it can be hard to see a different way. And even when we do see, it can feel awkward or uncomfortable. We have to unlearn so we can remember — which is why you are here. Breathe. Remember, I won't ask you to do more; I will show you how to access, experiment with, and trust a different way. And I promise it will be both enlightening and empowering, and even fun.

Let's press the ELEVATE button and go to where the wise sages and reality-altering thinkers like Einstein operated from — people who dared to stretch beyond the mental mind into a higher consciousness. From this expanded possibility, I can show you how to awaken a superpower that not only enables you to get more of what matters done — but, when applied practically to how you make your choices and design your reality, creates the spaciousness you crave, even within an intense, full life.

Wise women wield their superpower to "create space" instead of trying to manage and make time.

Have you ever had the experience where you start your week or day, and it's already jam-packed? Meeting after meeting, or to-do after to-do? And you are unsure how you are going to get it all done? You start to stress, feeling the pressure within you build. Your calendar and life feel like a puzzle with more pieces than fit. Your mind goes back and forth trying to move things around to squeeze them into too small a space, and eventually you sink into resignation. Your schedule is like a puzzle with no solution. You're going to have to push through, with no space for *you*, again.

But then something magnificent happens. A meeting gets canceled. A deadline shifts. A responsibility falls off your plate. You exhale. You feel expansion versus contraction. Your day opens up. The meetings and to-dos flow into another day that in the end is a much more effective way to work and operate. Miraculously, you have the space to do what's really needed, that day. *Ahhh!* This is you experiencing the superpower of "Creating Space."

The Feminine Superpower of Creating Space Is...

Your power to operate outside the limits of linear, fixed time by tapping into a field of infinite possibility and expanded space where more "time" seems to exist.

When you apply this superpower, you have enough "time" for everything that really matters, in right timing. Things happen, grow, and come together in ways that defy linear time and put everything into a harmonic flow.

I can personally attest to the fact that the superpower to create space is very real. I have it, you have it, all women have it. At first, the notion that you can "create space" can feel foreign or even irrelevant. We've been so trained to excel in a cerebral, consumption-driven world built to keep women operating like productivity machines and self-sacrificing martyrs that we doubt anything our rational brains haven't heard of or a scientific study hasn't validated. In many ways, we've become servants to time, blindly marching like ticktock robots to a manufactured rhythm we never considered could be different.

Before I knew about this superpower of Creating Space, I too believed if I could just manage my time better and make more time, I would be more productive and efficient, and everything would be better. I had to *wake up and see* things differently before I could embody the wisdom and power to *do* things differently. Which is where we go next for you.

Change your relationship to time, and you'll not only be more productive; you'll become empowered to create the space you need and crave.

Einstein taught that time is an illusion and, in general, the only value of time is so everything doesn't happen at once. Imagine trying to schedule meetings or set school schedules without time. There'd be chaos. Time gives us a common structure and set agreement. This is supportive. But the way time is used to structure your life, setting projections for how fast you are expected to get things done, and bartered in exchange for receiving money is more often a source of stress than support. Think about it. The time we start work and school; the length of a work/school day/week; the length of maternity leaves, lunch breaks, vacations — do the current time structures support how you work best as a human being and what your needs are as a woman?

Liberate Your Time   201

Yogic wisdom teaches: "When you are subject to time and space, you are just insane. You can never be happy because the pressure of time and space shall not let you be happy. You have to pull your head above time and space." Wise women understand the value and purpose of both time and space, and consciously work with both. We don't let time run us. We embrace our power to create space to structure our lives, work, and responsibilities and set expectations to create a sustainable flow to our days, weeks, months, and years. Take a look at the glyph below to get a better sense of how time and space function.

On the left, you see what time "looks" like. Notice the boxes, the straight arrow, the twelve ticktocks. The qualities of time are fixed, finite, linear, and limited. Time is contained in boxes, lanes, and lines with hard stops and starts. This is why we use language like "time *frame*," "time*line*," "*window* of time," "*track* of time." Because time is finite, it cannot be expanded, which is why it tends to create feelings of contraction and scarcity. You have to fit your project, life, relationships, and needs into the time frame/line/window/track available.

Have you ever considered that time is not a natural reality but a man-made system? You trust time and allow your life to be run by it because you have been trained to see it — in calendars and clocks. But you were not born with a watch embedded in your wrist. And humans have been monkeying around with time structures for thousands of years. Julius Caesar changed the start of the year from the vernal equinox, in March, to January 1 (so in the northern hemisphere we start our year in the dead of winter versus the emergence of spring). The calendar was also "de-lunarized" by chunking the year into twelve months versus the natural flow of the thirteen moon cycles (interesting that the moon, which is connected to feminine energy, was omitted). People in the 1900s decided a workweek should be forty hours and five days (which did shift horrific work conditions, but is this what's needed today?). There's a lot more, but I think you get the point.

Consider what this might mean for you personally. For starters, perhaps one reason you can't seem to get into a sustainable flow or find space for everything is because you've had to alter your natural internal rhythm to fit into a limited, fixed, fabricated system. A system dictating things like the hours you work and when you wake up, eat, exercise, and get the kids to school that is not attuned to how you — or the planet — naturally flow.

Now go back and look at the glyph on the right, and you will see what space "looks" like. Notice the spiral and how it expands on itself, creating and growing by its own momentum. The nature of space is flexible, infinite, cyclical, and expansive. Space can morph to meet the need, which is why when you work with space, meetings and to-dos often flow into their right timing. Space is what allows for unanticipated opportunities to arise.

You can't see space, but that doesn't mean it's not real. Remember the example where meetings move and you exhale? You don't see the space with your eyes; you *feel* the space within your body and magnetic field, which is evident in the release you experience. Your superpower to create space is a lot like the power of electricity before it was deemed "real." People wrote about experiencing the properties of electricity as early as 600 BCE, but humans had no word for it until 1640 CE (over two thousand years later). Only when electrical energy became harnessed in ways people could see it (like in 1882 when Edison brought lightbulbs to Manhattan) would they believe electricity was even real and useful to their daily lives.

Embracing your feminine wisdom and power requires you to go beyond what you can explain logically or see with your eyes and trust what you can feel and sense. And then apply the wisdom to your daily life. Are you willing to experiment with time and space with me, and go beyond what your mind knows? Let's start with one aspect of each — the linear nature of time and the cyclical nature of space — so you can experiment practically in your daily life.

Time is linear; it creates routine.
Space is spiral and cyclical; it creates rhythm.

Look back at the arrow on the time glyph. There is a start and an end, one straight line. Look at the structure of the week within a calendar: one straight line starting on Sunday that pushes you straight through. As you brace yourself for the intensity ahead, you think thoughts like *I just need to get through this week.* But then the following week, it all starts over again.

Have you ever experienced the Sunday-night or Monday-morning dreads when you feel the pressure of the workweek ahead seeping into your spaciousness and serenity? Or noticed on Wednesday people walking around saying, "Thank god it is almost Friday"? Or using phrases like "hump day," affirming that the week is like climbing an arduous hill? This is pressure-inducing "time talk" that keeps you stuck on the linear *track* of time. Pushing to get through. Pining for the future versus savoring the now. This is no way to live.

Creating Rhythm vs. Routine

Time, by its linear nature, creates routine. Space, by its spiraling, cyclical nature, creates rhythm. When we are stressed-out and our lives feel like chaos, routine can sound like a saving grace. But take a look at what focusing on a routine will create versus what focusing on rhythm can do for you.

Option #1: Focus on Creating Routine

ROUTINE: an unvarying, habitual, unimaginative, or rote procedure.

When you design your life to fit into a routine, you become like a ticktock robot focused on repeating the same fixed pattern over and over again.

Option #2: Focus on Creating Rhythm

RHYTHM: a flow or beat; movement or variation characterized by the regular recurrence or alternation of different quantities or conditions, as in the heartbeat.

When you focus on cultivating a rhythm to your life, you create a flexible flow that supports you and your dynamic, diverse, whole life.

Your choice. Routine or rhythm? I vote for rhythm; for one thing it's just more natural. Rhythm creates a consistency like a routine, but instead of having to adhere to a prescribed schedule made up by our minds, rhythm creates a *pattern* that by nature allows for flexibility — creating a reality that feels fluid and spacious, in harmony. Just as your heart beats to a natural rhythm that keeps you healthy and full of life force, how you operate, create, and regenerate best follows a natural rhythm. Your role is to find it.

What I've noticed in myself and with the women I work with is that most of us have no idea just how far away we've moved from our natural rhythm. We've been adhering to externally driven routines and schedules for so many years — from the day we started school and each day ever since — that we never consider how forcing ourselves to fit into these schedules has been and is negatively affecting our emotional, mental, and physical health. It's not usually until we have a health scare or get fed up and quit our jobs that we start to see the time constraints and constructs we've been blindly trapped in.

Let's not wait for that to happen to you. Or if it is happening, let's make a shift. Now that you have some context and wisdom about time and space, let's make your superpower of Creating Space practical with regard to what you can "do" differently within your daily life.

Elevate your "time talk" and you'll stop feeling so behind or like you never have enough time.

Practical step number one is to wake up to your "time talk" — how you talk about time. When you are unaware of your language about time, your words can keep you in debt to time, feeling busy and behind. Your language reflects your relationship to time, how you give your power away to a system that isn't the only "reality."

Often as we start to become aware and hear our time talk, we are initially shocked at how our own words are creating pressure, exhaustion, and overwhelm. We never considered our *relationship* to time. But when you embrace the practice of elevating your time talk, you start to see some of what the reality-altering sages and scientists know. The words you choose create the reality you live.

Next is a list of disempowering, pressure-inducing time talk that can cause you to give your power away, followed by some feminine wisdom to elevate your relationship with time. Read each and put a check mark next to the time talk you use sometimes or often.

√	Disempowering, Pressure-Inducing Time Talk	Feminine Wisdom about Time
	I need to find more time...	You can't find time; time is not lost.
	I need to make time for...	You cannot make time. There is no time kitchen.
	I don't have the time for...	You don't have to be a slave or victim to your schedule. Time is a resource you choose how you spend.
	I am running behind...I am running late...	You can't run behind time; time is not like a car you chase. You cannot "run" late. Saying so stresses you out and speeds time up. You may show up later than planned, but that may be just the right flow.
	I am taking time off...	What exactly are you taking time off *of*? You are not a prisoner released for good behavior or servant released from work duty. If you are no longer working in a work/life duality, and are creating a whole life, you don't take time off your life. You just focus in different realms as part of a healthy rhythm.
	I am waiting for when there is time...	Time does not have a waiting room like a dentist's office. If you wait for when there is time, you will be old, sick, or dead before enough time emerges.

√	Disempowering, Pressure-Inducing Time Talk	Feminine Wisdom about Time
	Let me find a [time slot, time frame, window of time]...	Slots, windows, and frames are limited space; if you try to squeeze into them, you will feel squeezed and other people will feel squeezed in.
	Let me find a few extra minutes or an extra hour...	You cannot find extra minutes or hours; there is only 24-7. Working this way is like trying to balance an overdrawn bank account. You will feel like you never have enough.
	I will try to carve out time...	You can't cut up time like a piece of meat or a pumpkin. Plus this sounds painful!
	I am going to block off the time...	When you block time, you block yourself into squares and boxes and set up a reality in which you have to stand outside that box and protect it from invaders. Exhausting!

Know Yourself

How is my time talk creating a reality of scarcity, disempowerment, and pressure?

- Which one to three examples of pressure-inducing time talk do I use?
- If I really look at the language, what reality could I be creating for myself?
- How could working with time in this way be adding to my overwhelm and feelings of not having enough time?

Take a moment to write one to three of the disempowering, pressure-inducing time talk phrases you tend to use, in your wisdom journal. Then, take this simple but mighty act of liberation: elevate your time talk. Become much more aware of your language around time (step one of transformation: awareness). Then, when you hear yourself using limiting time talk, and you feel the contraction and pressure it creates, pause, notice how you feel, call on your superpower of Creating Space, and choose your words and actions differently (step three of transformation: change in the moment).

Claim and create the space you need, or no one will give it to you.

As you awaken to your limiting time talk, you will need new language to replace it, of which I have some to share.

Self-Sustainability Stands
for Creating Space

Instead of time talk rooted in lack, fear, resignation, and helplessness, what if you spoke a self-sustainability code like this into reality?

1. I need more space.
2. I choose to create the space I need.
3. I choose to create space for what matters to me.
4. I choose to take the space I need, without guilt or apology.
5. If the system or people won't give me the space I need, I reset expectations.
6. When I claim the space I need, the Universe supports me to create harmony.

Pause and read these words out loud. Consider what would be possible if you truly lived by these words. Read them so they really sink in; *feel* them. These are self-sustainability stands that can empower you to liberate yourself out of time-created overwhelm. I encourage you to use these to take a fierce stand for yourself in the moments you feel the pressure created by time starting to push you to make a self-sacrificing choice that stretches you to the point you get sick or miss out on what really matters to you. I offer these words to give you an alternative, so you can receive what you need to do the job, achieve the goals, and meet the diverse demands and desires of your life and relationships in a way that supports and sustains you.

Taking a fierce stand for yourself is one of the simplest and mightiest tools you have; don't miss it. Just like with naming and claiming the support you need, if you don't name and claim the space and time you need, no one will give it to you. I have witnessed too many women feel pressured to make choices that did not have their best interests at heart because of the time constraints and expectations put on them by others, organizations, societal norms, even themselves. You've likely seen and experienced this, too.

We see it in the big life choices women feel disempowered to do differently. Executives and entrepreneurs having a baby and going back to work three weeks later because they felt they had to be there, or the company couldn't run without them. New mothers feeling pressured to return to work too soon because they had to make money or faced losing their jobs. There was no space to do the one job only she, the mother, could do — bond with the new soul who needed to feel safe and loved so it could grow up feeling rooted and secure. Many a woman, parent or not, has often deeply desired to stop working so hard or so many hours but, because of financial responsibilities and burdens, can't see any path out. So she sucks it up, until her body revolts.

We witness it in the socially imposed time constructs that drive women to treat their bodies like workhorses or machines that should be able to keep going no matter what. Women having major surgery and going back to work a week later. No space to heal. Women starting a new job immediately after finishing their previous all-consuming job, with only two weeks in between. No space to reset or regenerate, so they start at a life-force deficit. These are big life choices that have a big impact that should not just be "how it is."

We witness other women — and ourselves — suffering because of the time constraints in the day-to-day that seem small but that build up to create dis-ease, resentment, and burnout, unnecessarily. I asked a few of the women in my community if I could share how this has shown up for them; here's what they said:

- **Kristin, a doctor:** "I have to be at work for rounds at 7 AM every day, which means leaving my house by 6 AM. I know I need to connect to myself every morning, but I am not a morning person and can't get up any earlier. I feel like there is no time for me. I'm mad about it. My body is feeling it. *I need* space in the mornings and evenings for me to breathe and be a human woman, not just a doctoring machine."
- **Gretchen, a working mother:** "I was part of a sisterhood of women who meets virtually twice a month on Friday mornings. Even though I would 'block the time' on my calendar, people would continually schedule meetings at work over this. I had to quit this supportive group that had been a lifeline for me emotionally, mentally, and spiritually. *I need* a supportive sisterhood I can connect with consistently, and *I need* for people to respect my space and time."
- **Jan, a corporate employee:** "I was trapped in the 'back-to-back meeting' racetrack every day where I was lucky if I could pee more than once or get outside the building to breathe fresh air. There was no time to actually get work done because I was in meetings all day. Nine to five? Ha. Arriving early and leaving late was not an *exception*; it was the *expectation*. *I needed* space to get my work done during the workday, before 5 PM!"
- **Karen, a former teacher:** "I was in class all day, then told I must take on extra before- and after-school assignments, and then I still had papers to grade and lessons to create. I got twenty minutes for lunch if I was lucky. I loved the kids. I hated the nonhuman working conditions of what I was expected to do. Summers 'off' should not mean being an indentured servant

during the school year. *I needed* to stay focused on my job as teacher in the classroom, and other activities needed to be staffed in other ways."

I share all of this not to make any of us feel bad; you and any of the women this made you think of have been doing the best we could in the systems that exist. It is clear we are not getting the space we need to support us to be healthy, whole women, leaders, and humans. We have all acquiesced to the time demands and constraints of a job or organization and our family because we didn't feel we had another choice. And unless we wanted to risk losing our jobs or putting ourselves in financial peril, we may not have. We did the best we could with the consciousness, support, and tools we had at the time. But if we don't take a fierce stand now to claim and create space, without apology — for ourselves and those we lead and love — nothing will ever change.

I am not suggesting we take the systems head-on. What I *am* suggesting is that you have the power to take a stand; draw a line in the sand; and say *no more* to accepting time constraints, constructs, and expectations that do not provide the space and time needed. While the systems might not have had to change during the last rise of women's liberation because not enough of us were in positions of influence to change the systems, today, together, we are.

The question to ask yourself is, *What is not making a shift costing me?* And the question I then ask you is, "Are you willing to draw the line, and say *no more*?" You don't need to broadcast this to everyone around you. Or make some broad-sweeping impulsive change. Or even see how making a change is possible. Your power starts from the conviction, courage, and clarity you find first within yourself. Only when you become more conscious and rooted within, and stand committed to your needs and desires, does the outside reality shift around you. Take a breath. Sometimes the fierce feminine gets fiery, and then we slow it down to find the wise path forward.

Here's how we make this actionable — from the inside out. First, you honestly speak what is not working within the time constraints and constructs you find yourself in. And then you fiercely name and claim what you need. Remember, you don't need to know the how; the path will unfold once you get clear within yourself. As with the women who shared their stories and stands, the first step is giving voice to what's not working for you and what you need. Feminine wisdom teaches: "All creation is present within the vibration of the spoken sound. Once it is heard, everything changes." Once you've given it voice, then you, I, and the Universe can begin working together to liberate you and then others into a more sustainable, supportive reality. Which will take "time."

Know Yourself
What space do I need?

Imagine you and I are sitting together, fully committed to you receiving the time and space you need. I'm going to ask you four questions, and then you use the sentence starters to give voice to your truth and needs. To voice these, you have to speak or write them. So slow down and do this with me:

- Where are you feeling like you don't have the space and time you need?
    I don't have the time I need to…
    I don't have the space I need to…
- What is not working for you?
    What is not working for me is…
- What are you sick and tired of?
    I am sick and tired of…
- What do you need?
    I need…

If you have spoken out what you need, I witness your fierce stand for yourself. If you skipped the writing and speaking, go back and speak up for yourself. Then we and the Universe can work together to start creating space. You need to feel the power within yourself — embodied, through your words of truth and the feelings and conviction in your heart — to spark the fire of liberation. Remember that true empowerment comes from giving yourself what you need first, staying committed to those needs while being flexible and fluid as to what the form looks like. Results don't appear overnight, but there is a path, and you and I are on it. Let's take the next step.

Wake up to the time constraints and constructs running you. Get conscious of what's real, what's man-made, and what's made up in your head.

As empowering as it would feel, you cannot just go into work tomorrow, or wherever you are feeling sick and tired of the current situation, and demand they set you free from the time constraints that are not working for you. Even if you yourself created them. Although the image of you doing so makes my inner wise woman smile! The truth is, there are real "time constraints" you have to work within — these are the time-based agreements you are expected to adhere to, and at some level have agreed to. They can feel constrictive and unchangeable, like shackles. What time you have to be at work, what time you can leave, when your kids need to be picked up, and more. Most are either:

1. **Nonnegotiables that cannot or will not change no matter what.** If you want to operate within this system, these are the rules. Like the days you need to be at work, in person.
2. **Socially acceptable norms that are malleable.** Everyone else does it this way, but that doesn't mean you have to. Like staying at work until 6 or 7 PM, or working weekends and nights to get more done, because there's no space during the day.
3. **Guidelines that are flexible.** You've never considered whether you could do it differently, but if you did, you could create a different reality.

Here's where your superpower of Creating Space comes in. If you start looking around, through your wise woman eyes, at the time constraints put out by the systems you interact within, you will start to see which time constraints you can influence and shift. Name, claim, and take a stand to shift these. Also, be real about and name the time constraints you cannot influence or change. Instead of wasting your life force battling or complaining, or acquiescing to these, wisely seek to find ways to work around the time constraints Be stealth about it — don't ask for permission or give voice publicly; just do things differently, and know this may also lead you to make bigger changes.

In addition, become more aware of the "time constructs" running you — these are your mental beliefs about time that make it über-challenging for you to take the space you crave and need, even when the space appears. These constructs are not reality, although they feel as if they are. Created in your mind, often because of the time constraints culturally ingrained into your body and psyche for so long, they cause you to react against what you need. For example, when I left the structure of a job working as an employee to work for myself, I felt guilty, lazy, or unproductive if I wasn't working by 9 AM or if I did anything other than work till 5 PM Monday through Friday. I could not go grocery shopping or to a yoga class on a Tuesday afternoon because it was a "workday" during "work time." Even though I was my own boss, I was still shackled to a Monday-to-Friday, nine-to-five work schedule versus creating the space for the workflow that supported me best.

Know Yourself
What time constraints and constructs are stressing me? What is real? What is made up?

Again imagine that you and I are sitting together, with me asking the following questions and you answering using the sentence starters. Say your answers out loud or write them out.

- What time constraints are you currently under that are nonnegotiable?
    I have to...
    I can't...
- What time constraints are really social or culture norms?
    Everyone seems to...
    It's expected that...
- What time constructs have you created within yourself that make it challenging to take the space you need?
    I have to...
    I can't...

Stay committed to finding the supportive, sustainable, spacious path and rhythm, even if that means disappointing or disrupting others.

As you step forward and claim and name the space you need, there are a few things I need to share with you to set your expectations and set you up for success. One, expect to be met with both relief and resistance — from the system, from people, and even from yourself. Two, working with time and space to receive what you need and create sustainable success is a lifelong practice; embrace this superpower as something you utilize just like Wonder Woman uses hers. You practice by making more awake and empowered choices every day — what you say yes or no to, how you plan and focus, and how you interact with others in your agreements and expectations. Put the practice to practical use; experiment. And three, you will be most successful if you start with small acts that have a mighty impact.

Small but Mighty Acts for Liberating Your Time

What follows are some small but mighty acts of liberation — things to stop doing and to start doing — you can experiment with right away. As you read through them, choose one "stop" and one "start" to put into practice in your life now. Remember, you don't need to do anything *more*; this is about you doing what you are already doing, differently.

Stop...

1. Feeling guilty for taking the space or time you need. Unless you have stolen from, cheated, or intentionally harmed a person, guilt is a distorted reaction and a waste of your life force. Stop wasting your energy feeling guilty for things that don't warrant guilt.

2. Asking for the time and resources you need like a beggar or as if you need permission. You have a right to receive what you need to do the job, meet the demands, and keep yourself healthy and sustained. Be empowered and *state* what is needed. Stop asking for permission.

3. Being more loyal to others or the organization than you are to yourself. The cost you pay to put the organization or other people before your own health or needs is never worth it, ever. The system will survive without you; you will not. Other people, unless they are your non-adult child, will find their way. And even your children need you to be loyal to yourself; they learn by watching you. Stop being disloyal to yourself.

4. Acting from obligation. Giving from obligation comes from guilt and fear. Be willing to say no or "not now," or find the path in which you can give from an open heart, in a way that doesn't sacrifice you. Stop giving out of obligation, guilt, or fear.

5. Giving your time and space away like you have an endless supply. You have only so much mental space and physical and emotional energy available before you start to get overfull and overtaxed and then overwhelmed. Time is a resource of which you have a finite supply. Be aware of what you can afford to give, and give only that, out of generosity. Stop emptying your life-force reserves.

6. Acquiescing to time constraints to "make it work" and robbing yourself of what you need. When you are met with resistance and inflexibility from others or the organizations you work within, do not submit or comply silently. Do not consent to any agreement that does not support you. Set new expectations. Stop sucking it up.

7. Waiting for enough time or space to appear before you make changes. If you keep waiting for there to be time for what you need or what truly matters, you will be dead, retired, sick, or full of resentment before it arrives. Be honest about what needs to shift, and get support to take action. Stop waiting.

Start...

1. Staying true to yourself, even if that means disappointing another. Make this self-sustainability promise to yourself: "I will stay true to myself, even if that means disappointing another." It is one of the most loving acts you can take. You release obligation, guilt, resentment, and self-sacrifice, and usually the outcome is better for everyone.

2. Stating what you need and staying committed to finding a solution that works for you. If you stay clear and committed to what you need, and stay open and fluid as to the form, the Universe can work with you to create the space you need even if it doesn't look like your mental picture or ideal. This often takes more time on the front end, to find the wise and harmonious solution, but it will save you much time and life force on the back end.

3. Being honest – with yourself and with others – about what you have the space for and what you don't. Honestly share when you don't have the space, in a way that creates expansion versus contraction, and the Universe will work to rearrange resources so you and others feel more supported. For example, instead of saying, "No, I can't do that; I am too busy," or "Yes, I can take that on" (when your inner wisdom is screaming *No!*), you say, "Thank you for asking. I would love to, but right now I just don't have the space. Keep me in mind for next time" or "Here's another resource..." or "What I can do is..."

4. Creating space in small ways, and time and space will start to grow and expand. Because space works on a spiral pattern that naturally generates momentum, when you choose to create space in small ways, your experience of having the space you need and feeling spacious grows. As you feel more empowered and sustained, your inner conviction, courage, and commitment grow, and the reality around you shifts.

Each of the women who shared their stories and stands put at least one of these into practical action and received results. Kristin started creating space in small ways by reclaiming fifteen minutes of her morning for her connection-and-protection practice. The 7 AM start time constraint did not change. She didn't wake up at 4 AM. She just reset the rhythm of her bookends to create space. This created a momentum that led to her taking a stand to reclaim her weekends, which is now in progress and happening in small but mighty ways.

Jan took a new job after a year of overworking in her previous job. She asked for a month in between and was refused. She got clear on what she needed: space with herself, her family, and her sisterhood to regenerate. She stated to her new organization that she was depleted and needed to regenerate. She agreed to start in two weeks and created an agreement to take a two-week and a one-week vacation during her first three months of employment. True to need, open to form. Not optimal but not a total self-sacrifice, either.

These actions may seem small, which they are, but don't mistake their simplicity for lack of potency. If I have learned anything from living everything I am sharing with you, it is that the simple things we do in daily life — the practices, structures, choices — are what make the big differences. While you may make sweeping changes as you liberate yourself from the overculture and fishbowls, it will be the small but mighty shifts you take from this book and put into practice that will give you the clarity, confidence, and courage to do things differently.

Know Yourself
What momentum can I ignite to create space now?

- *How am I accepting a time constraint? Or acting from guilt, obligation, or overloyalty to others (or an organization) that is creating overwhelm and pressure?*
- *What one small but mighty shift can I make, right now, to create more space for what I need?*
- *What support do I need to make that shift and stay committed, no matter what?*

Harmonizing Practice
Shut Up and Slow Down Before You Say "Yes, I Can"

Rarely say yes to a request or invitation right away. Give yourself space to consider what a yes does to your space and time. Slow down. Breathe. Tune in and ask:

1. *Do I have this time to give?*
2. *What will this do to my space?*
3. *What do I want to give?*
4. *What is in harmony to give?*

   Choose the way that creates harmony.

Chapter 10

RELEASE: **Make It All Happen Now**

EMBRACE: **Focus on What Matters**

Time-based pressure can be healthy and helpful,
or unnecessary and toxic.
Wise women know how to tell the difference,
so they can live in and be supported by the flow.

If I asked you, "Would you like to be more focused? More productive? More efficient? Have superpowers that enabled you to easily meet all the deadlines and time pressures you face?" what would you reply? Your inner achiever and overwhelmed doer would likely say something like, "Heck yes! Show me, please!"

But what if I asked you, "Would you like your life to feel more fluid? How about possess the superpower to know what to focus on when, what to let go, and what to move to another time? The inner wisdom to see when a seemingly fixed deadline set by others, or yourself, could be moved to create more space? The inner conviction to speak up and take action to reprioritize the many things that feel like they all have to be done now into a harmonious, sustainable flow, where things happen in right timing?" Sound nice? Perhaps even make you exhale? Me, too!

But which do you honestly believe can help you deal with the real demands of your life? Achieve the goals and milestones that matter to you?

Well, the good news is, you don't have to choose. You can be a woman who is like a force of nature, intentionally focused on achieving her goals and getting what matters done, *and* a woman who is receptive and fluid, who knows how to create a flow to any project or goal that is supportive and sustainable, and creates space for what really matters. Do you remember our lesson on time and space? You are seeing it again right here in this equation:

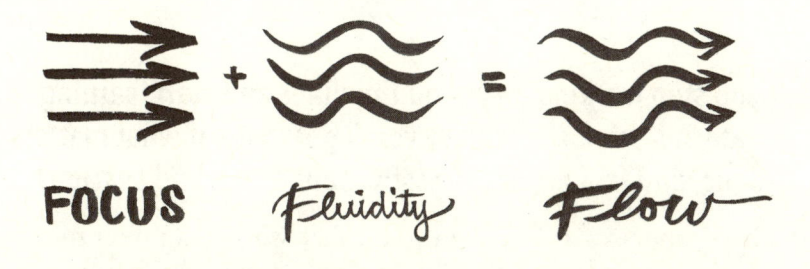

FOCUS + *Fluidity* = *Flow*

Focused Intention + Intuitive Fluidity = F.L.O.W.
F.L.O.W. means "**F**ocus **L**ife force **O**n **W**hat matters."

Focus + Fluidity = Flow. This is the elevated formula for how you can achieve, succeed, and get what needs doing done, in a sustainable flow. Take a good look at the glyph above. Focus is denoted with linear arrows, which, like time, are rooted in fixed structure. Fluidity looks like waves, which, like space, create open and flexible structure. Just like time and space work together to create more harmonious ways of operating and creating, so can focus and fluidity. They are like yin and yang. You need both the *structure* of focus and *spaciousness* of fluidity if you want your projects, goals, and desires to happen in a way that is supported, sustained, and successful. Focus sets you in a direction. Fluidity opens you up to receive guidance, wisdom, synchronicity, and opportunity.

This equation — as you learn to apply it — has the power to

liberate you from feeling like your only option is to drive to unrealistic and unhealthy time-based expectations set by others, or yourself. The invitation is to embrace *Focused Intention + Intuitive Fluidity = Flow* as a practice and a formula for approaching how you work, make choices, and set expectations. The application of this equation is part of how you stand as the empowered conductor (recall the Harmony Wheel) who stays focused on what matters, in right timing, working to expectations that are sustainable and provide enough space and healthy pressure. We'll spend the rest of this chapter making this practical and applicable. But first, let me share why you would even want to consider what I'm suggesting.

If you stop working on forced timelines and start learning to create and work in the flow, you'll get more of what matters done, and feel more successful, supported, and spacious.

You have more experience than you realize with your power to create and work in the flow, which means this is really about becoming more aware of and adept at something natural within you — like working an underused muscle. Have you ever worked on a project or toward a goal where things seemed to come together — the resources, people, opportunities — in ways you couldn't foresee? You had a mental idea about where you were headed. There were due dates you intended to drive to. But as you progressed, you sensed that trying to meet the original timelines were beginning to create pressure that felt stressful, and not in a healthy "eustress" way. One choice would have been to keep driving full throttle ahead to your destination like a speedboat. This is what people do when they work with only half their power — *focused intention* — completely ensconced in their mental faculty, fixed on the deadline.

But instead of driving relentlessly to the end goal, you and others were able to open up, slow down, get curious, and change course or shift the completion date. You became fluid instead of remaining fixed. And a more harmonious outcome occurred. Time seemed to expand, pressure released, and a previously unseen path emerged, which you followed to a more sustainable success, in better timing. You never conceived this path in your mind, but making the choice to alter the expectations felt good in your body and heart. This is what working in the flow looks and feels like. This is your intuitive feminine wisdom working for you.

Working this way — with *focused intention* plus *intuitive fluidity* — is like sailboating versus speedboating. You still have a focused destination in mind, but you work with the wind and tides to tack your way, pausing and receiving guidance as you progress, going with the natural forces and rhythms rather than pushing your way straight through, powering against the tide and wind.

Some people call this working in divine timing, right timing, or aligned timing. If you've ever experienced it, you know that instead of feeling like you are running a sprint or marathon that never ends, you feel supported, led, guided, held through the process. Even if there are times of challenge and intensity, just like a good sailing adventure, with both strong winds and calm waters, the whole of the journey is enlivening. You emerge stronger because of it, and you learn and receive from it. This is how wise women work with time and space to achieve our goals in a way that is supported and sustainable versus blindly driving to a fabricated, human-made deadline or trying to do too much at the same time, too fast.

The more you practice *Focus + Fluidity = Flow* in your daily choices, the more you learn to trust your intuition, work with the Universe, and use your powers of focus in a healthy, balanced way. And the more you see what really is negotiable and malleable within the systems you interact with, the projects you run, and the plans you set, and what's not. Over time, as you make more choices from the harmony of focus and fluidity, your life naturally starts to come into a rhythm that supports and sustains you to create real, whole-life success. Not always in your timing, but often with a much better flow and outcome than you can imagine in your head.

What I just shared might make total sense, or it may just be starting to spark open your awareness. In any case, take a breath. We just did some subtle but potent consciousness expanding. Much like Einstein's theory of relativity and $E = mc^2$ equation blew open the way people understand how this world works, seemingly simple equations such as these, when applied, open up our eyes and minds so we can access unseen possibility and the deeper wisdom of doing things differently. But the possibility gets activated only if you put the equation into practical application and experiment — which is what we are about to do.

Remember that this isn't about you doing more, or finding more time; it's about doing what you do differently — which can feel new, awkward, uncomfortable, or even challenging. That's transformation, liberation, and learning — you choosing to stretch yourself in healthy, empowering ways. So here's where we go from here — we put this potent equation to use to up-level how you go about focusing, prioritizing, and getting what truly matters done. We start by opening your wise-woman eyes to the difference between the two kinds of times pressure: the kind that can be healthy and helpful, and that which is unnecessary and toxic.

Time-based pressure can be healthy and helpful, or unnecessary and toxic. Wise women know how to tell the difference.

Take a look at the glyphs on the next page to get an idea of what healthy and helpful pressure looks like in you and what unnecessary, toxic pressure does to you. Healthy time-based pressure (on the right) creates a span of time for things to happen within that gives you the motivation and space to get them done. Setting a due date or intentional time for completion, as well as milestones and midpoint markers, is essential to the creative process — this creates focused space and motivates action.

Notice how the starting point and completion point form a *time span*, a shape that creates a space that holds the focus, like a bridge or rainbow. Without an intentional end point, things would be too fluid, people would lack focus, and the goal might never be achieved. But you don't sprint, push, or fight your way to the due date at any cost. Notice the milestone and midpoint markers. The pressure stays healthy when you keep the completion date in mind but stay focused on the smaller time spans, which feel more digestible and doable rather than overwhelming. You wisely pause as you progress to these points to reassess what's needed and possible, and you adjust whatever needs shifting — dates, life-force focus, resources. You use the time span — the shape and space it creates — to give yourself and others permission to respond and make choices with focus and flexibility. The result is flow — you and others stay focused on what matters; you create in a supportive, sustainable way that leads to success in aligned, divine timing.

Here's a real-life example. I had a due date to turn in my first draft of this book, which created healthy, helpful pressure. The expectation gave me a focused intentional completion point that created a span of time, which motivated and supported me to make choices that created the space I needed to write. These choices included saying no to doing other things, paring back my staffing expenses to alleviate financial pressure, and creating focused intervals of space over the span of several months. Without the pressure of the due date, I would have struggled to make space for writing within a full life and business. I would have tried to squeeze writing in versus given myself the focused space I needed (and deeply desired) to pull this book into form.

Now go back to the glyph and look at the woman on the left. Ever feel like her? That is you working to deadlines and expectations for growth and goals that go unquestioned and are often unnecessary and unrealistic — a.k.a. toxic time pressure. That is you trying to focus on too much at the same time. Working this way sends you and everyone else into overwhelm, eats up life force, and fragments your focus so you are less efficient and productive. You may look like you are getting more done when you work this way, because the swirl and intensity create a frenzy of activity, but rarely are you tending to and completing what really matters.

This is how many organizations, teams, projects, and businesses are run, blindly focused on driving to the deadline, putting people into spastic reactivity mode trying to make too many things happen too fast, all at the same time. You've likely had this experience more than one time, right? Was this pressure necessary? Yes, some of it. But not most.

Toxic time-based pressure is at the root of why you can find it impossible to stay focused and why you feel so much pressure to do so much, so fast, at the same time. But without language to name what's happening, it's hard to find the internal power to question whether the time-based expectations are necessary or healthy. You want to be able to tell the difference so you can lead the way to creating and operating in a sustainable flow — for yourself and others. Let's give you some language that will empower you to discern between healthy, valid time-based pressure and unnecessary, toxic time pressure — so you can start seeing what is real, needed, and in the flow.

Learn to spot pressure caused by fabricated deadlines and you'll become empowered to alleviate undue pressure, and find the flow.

Take a read below of three common types of *fabricated* time constraints that can seem imperative or set in stone in the moment but are really human created and dictated. When you have the wise eyes to see and the words to call out the undue pressure, and the courage to speak up, you'll often find there is more flexibility and space available. As you get good at this, when you feel the pressure in your body, instead of sucking it up, you speak up and do things differently. Notice which of these fabricated time pressures you've experienced before or are experiencing now.

3 Kinds of Fabricated Time Pressure

1. FALSE URGENCY – the conviction that things must happen now, and fast! The energy of urgency is put into the field to get people moving and reacting. Multiple priorities are all given the highest priority — everything has to be done right away. It's held like a red alert, when really it's a soft yellow. You can feel false urgency when it's unleashed — everything speeds up and people whirl in reaction. Different from moving swiftly through a project or responding quickly to a real immediate need, which feels intense but grounded, false urgency is rooted in fear, so it creates swirl. Because this urgency often stems from someone's unconscious anxiety or frustration, the same chaotic feelings get activated in the situation and within the people involved.

2. UNREALISTIC EXPECTATIONS – trying to do too much, too fast, without enough space or runway. When unrealistic expectations around *how much* can be done in a time span arise, you feel like you are trying to stuff one hundred pounds of potatoes into a ten-pound bag. When expectations for *how fast* something can be accomplished are unrealistic, you feel like an airplane that has been allotted a hundred-foot runway versus the six thousand feet needed for takeoff. Or like you are expected to run a marathon in half the human time. You feel the pressure of too much in too short a span. These impossibilities are not about stretching to excellence, although some will say so. Working like this pushes people in ways that do not create more value, just more stress and work.

3. FORCED DEADLINES – setting unmovable dates for when things must be complete by, when those things are not really fixed. A deadline is set that everyone holds like a line you cannot cross. You know more space is needed, you sense this due date is more of a command or desire than a necessity, and you can see how driving to it will create pressure that isn't necessary or healthy. Everyone pushes way too hard to meet this date. In reality, this timeline is based on a person's or organization's ideal or desire, which makes it much more flexible than people think or say. Moving the deadline may have an impact, but no one will perish. Forcing people to drive to this deadline versus being flexible is where the toxicity comes from.

Do you know where the word *deadline* comes from? Deadlines emerged in the 1800s during the US Civil War to describe the boundary around a military prison beyond which a prisoner could not venture without risk of being shot by the guards. Shot for going past a deadline. While we may not shoot people with real bullets for missing a time marker today, there are both stated and unstated implications and consequences for going beyond set deadlines. No wonder most of us feel visceral fear about not meeting a deadline!

Just the violent connection to war, prisons, and being shot was enough for me to stop using deadlines. One small but mighty act of liberation you can put into practice is to start noticing how often you speak the word *deadline* — notice both how the energy feels and how challenging it is to change your words. Replace *deadlines* with healthy pressure points. You have to use a few more words, but try choosing other language for completing a project — *completion date, milestone, due date, goal date to complete by*. Remember, new words equal creating new consciousness.

Know Yourself
Which fabricated time-based pressures are creating overwhelm for me?

- *Which one of the three fabricated pressures is or has been most present for me?*
- *If I look beyond the surface, what is at the root of the pressure? What's the real impetus driving the timing?*
- *If I felt empowered, what would I give voice to? If I felt empowered, what would I do differently?*

As you start to become aware and hip to these fabricated timelines — whether you are the one creating them or they are coming from someone else — you can make choices to alleviate the false urgency, unrealistic expectations, and forced deadlines. The key to liberation will be to *slow down* like the woman in the "Healthy Time Pressure" glyph, not speed up like the three-headed woman. You have to unhook yourself from the swirl, step outside the pressure, and see what is real and needed, and then, rooted in yourself, you can show up and speak up as a grounded presence that works wise to create a path of sustainable priorities and timing — flow. We will spend the rest of this section teaching you the how, focusing on the ways you have the internal power to do things differently.

But before we go there, let me be clear. As you start calling out toxic time pressure and being a voice for a more sustainable and focused path, I am not suggesting everyone will come to their senses and say, "Sure, we can change the timeline or due date!" Expect that people will resist. I *am* suggesting that you embrace your power to take a stand for speaking up from your fierce feminine wisdom, even if there's resistance. Be clear on what is in your control and what's not. Ask courageous and clarifying questions; make suggestions rooted in focused and fluid reality — keep being a voice for a different possibility even if the wisdom is not received at first.

And then, regardless of what others do or don't do, be stealth! Alter how you and those you influence work, to be more humane and sustained. Start small, with what is in your power to change, remembering you have eight realms of possibility within your harmonized, whole life. You have more power than you think.

Read on. What follows are three practical self-sustainability applications for creating more focus, more right timing and prioritizing, and more space. You can start experimenting with these now, without needing any permission or buy-in from anyone else.

Stop trying to make things fit into timing without enough space.
Start looking for and choosing what's in the flow.

Practical application #1: Invoke your power to "reflow."

When you feel yourself trying to make things fit into a time span without enough space, *reflow* meetings and due dates to create healthy time spans and pressure instead. You'll know you are trying to make too much happen in too little a space if things feel crunchy and tight, and you feel frenzied, fragmented, or frustrated. From this day forward I invite you to look for and choose what is in the flow, instead of cramming it in and embracing the overwhelm. Embrace the following self-sustainability stand to release the pressure to make it all happen now:

Instead of fitting or forcing things in, I flow things in.

Reread those words and just notice how they feel. Exhale. Now here's what I want you to try in your daily life. When you find yourself working on a project, making a decision about timelines or what to do when, or looking at how packed with meetings and to-dos your day or week is, and you feel the pressure-inducing energy start to swirl up or contract within you, hear my voice saying these words to you:

Slow down. Press the HARMONIZE *button. Find the flow!*

And then instead of trying to figure out how to make it all fit (from your mind), slow down and use your intuitive sense to find the flow (just like in the sustainable creation glyph you learned in chapter 7). Then take the courageous and wise act to *reflow*. Flow — move — to-dos, meetings, due dates, even things you really want to do, to another day, week, or month that is in better, more aligned timing. Choose a new time, date, and space for when you will reconnect to, revisit, or reengage with whatever you reflow. You can even put a space holder on your calendar so you know it won't get lost or not happen. Then focus your life force and resources only on what is "for now."

Flowing and reflowing meetings, to-dos, timelines, and due dates is a practice that takes experience and repetition to become adept at. The best way to get good at this is to learn to trust your physical sensations and your emotional feelings more than your mental thoughts. Your feelings — in your body and heart — always alert you to the danger zone of forcing timelines and expectations that create distress versus harmony. It's one way your feminine wisdom communicates with you. Take a read through the differences between how flow rooted in healthy time pressure feels versus forced, fabricated, and unhealthy time pressure.

Flow Rooted in Healthy Pressure Feels...	Forced, Fabricated Pressure Feels...
• Spacious, open, and expansive	• Constrictive and contracting
• Rooted and grounded	• Frenetic and grasping
• Enlivening and energizing	• Stuffed and stifling
• Harmonious and doable	• Chaotic and disruptive
• Challenging yet supportive	• Challenging and stressful
• Calm and centered, even if there's intensity	• Anxious or frustrating

Notice how these physical and emotional feelings may be showing up in your current situations at work, relationships, plans, and projects. Take this wisdom of discerning between healthy and fabricated pressure into your daily interactions so you become aware of your choices around timelines, priorities, focus, and urgency. As you start to see more, you will feel empowered more to create the space you need, which will liberate you from some, if not much, of the unnecessary time pressure you feel.

I would not ask you to try something that I myself have not embraced and tested. I make use of this practical application a lot, including in the writing of this book. Remember I told you about the due date of the book? Well, there's more. As I approached the date to hand in the manuscript, I knew I didn't have the space I needed. I had a choice: Drive myself hard, work fifteen-hour days, and do whatever it took to get the book done (and pay the price later). Or, instead, get clear on what I needed and then tell my publisher what I could do. Invoke my superpower to create space, using the "reflow."

Honestly, the thought of voicing what I needed in order to create in a sustainable flow brought up visceral fear — anxiety-producing emotions and thoughts like *What if they don't give it to me? What if my book will be delayed?* But I exhaled; rooted into my self-sustainability stand to never create or motivate myself by unnecessary, overwhelming, toxic pressure; and used the F.L.O.W. equation. I didn't *ask* for an extension. I *stated* what I needed (focused intentional action) and then let go (intuitive fluidity) to allow the Universe to work with the publisher to create a new flow that worked for us both. I used a harmonizing process I will share with you in just a bit. First, we have to talk about why it can be so hard to find and trust the flow.

Having the inner trust to reorganize, rearrange, and reflow meetings, priorities, and deadlines takes courage. Following a different trajectory than planned may disappoint another or seem impossible, which brings up fear in even the most confident woman. Expect that when time-based pressure shows up, you may find it challenging to get clear about what is forced and what is in the flow. Expect that you may resist stating what you need and then letting go to find a better flow, for two reasons:

1. **To find the flow – right, aligned, harmonious timing – you need a strong connection with your intuition.** You can't find flow with just your intellect — you have to sense into it, feel into it, step outside the pressure, to find the wise path and expanded possibility. If you don't have a strong connection yet to your intuition, that's okay. Just know that strengthening your intuitive connection and power is essential for getting out of overwhelm and making choices that lead to success that creates harmony. I have lots of resources and ways for you to strengthen this connection (listed in the book readers' kit).

2. **There are parts within you that don't believe you really can have the space you need.** Parts afraid if you let go to find the flow, everything will fall apart or not happen fast enough. Or that you'll disappoint others and create conflict. Parts that are used to the current reality and doubt that it can be any different. These parts of you may freak out when you start to work differently. They will create, add to, and even embrace the toxic time pressure. Expect self-sabotaging self-talk and emotional commotion to show up. Just don't let it run you.

Consider this: *If you learn to discern between the supportive time pressure and the toxic time pressure you put on yourself, you'll be happier — and more productive.* I will show you next how to become more aware of your specific sabotaging parts, but first, here's the harmonizing practice I use to find the flow and reflow. Use this in the moments you feel time pressure, can't find the flow, or are not sure if the time pressure is healthy or helpful.

Harmonizing Practice
Find the Flow Instead of Forcing Things to Fit

Slow down. Breathe. Tune in to yourself. Tune in to the situation. Say the words: "Find the flow." And ask your feminine wisdom these inquiries (write them, speak them, or ask another person to guide you through them):

1. *What is real?* (This helps you pierce through fabricated time expectation.)
2. *What is needed now?* (This tunes you in to focusing on what matters.)
3. *What do I need?* (This tunes you in to what you need to create a sustainable flow.)
4. What can I flow into another [day, week, month]? (This invokes fluidity to lead you to flow.)

Then take action. Physically move what can flow into another day, week, or month by marking it on your calendar, as a placeholder. This is important. The act of moving it and creating a space for it later settles down the parts of you that are afraid to trust the flow.

Practical application #2: Become aware of how you create unnecessary and toxic time pressure for yourself and others, and then start making different, more supportive, sustainable choices.

While it would be easier to blame the overculture and others for all the unnecessary pressure, the truth is that you and I are bigger contributors to the pressure we feel than anyone out there. We drive ourselves to schedules and expectations we've conceived in our minds, and as a result create overwhelm for ourselves and others. We pressure ourselves to meet personal and professional milestones that start out as meaningful desires but become like weights around our necks or whips at our backs. Ideals about what age we should get married, have a baby, or buy a house. Expectations for when we should reach a certain salary, revenue marker, or achievement.

We let ourselves believe that operating this way makes us more focused, more productive, more successful at achieving our goals. But if you and I were being truthful, we'd admit we've used these markers more to beat ourselves up or make ourselves feel like something is wrong with us than to support us to create professional and personal realities we feel successful within. Sadly, this self-induced pressure is starting younger and younger, and left unconscious, it doesn't seem to abate with age. Which is why you and I are going to dive in and give language to the toxic time pressures you've been using to set expectations to motivate and drive yourself (and likely others). Aware, you become empowered to choose differently.

Self-Induced Toxic Time Pressures

Read each of these eight common ways we put unhealthy and unnecessary time pressure on ourselves. As you read, many may ring true for you; that's normal. Find the ones that feel most active now. Circle those.

Are you...
1. A card-carrying member in the Impatience Club? You get frustrated because things take longer than you think they should. You often feel like you should "be" farther ahead, or like you should have reached X milestone by now.

2. Setting your expectations for personal and professional growth and goals based on the overculture's distorted images or other people's success? You set your expectations based on the images and ideals you've seen in the external world, or you compare yourself to what other's have accomplished, and then judge yourself for not measuring up. Because these are rooted in the consumption- and accumulation-driven overculture, not in the reality of a healthy human being, you never feel like you are doing or accomplishing enough.

3. Holding yourself to time milestones that should make you happy but stress you out? You set expectations and measures for success based on mental ideals about by what age or time you should reach certain personal or professional goals. Or by what other people achieve. If it doesn't happen, you feel bad or put more pressure on yourself.

4. Short-circuiting because you see the whole picture of all that needs doing and feel like you have to do it all now? You can see all that could, should, and needs to be done, so you feel like you have to do it all now or hold it all so it doesn't fall apart. You try to do it all and fragment your energy, or you freeze because you don't even know where to start.

5. Trying to do more than is humanly possible in one day, week, month, or year? You keep trying to stuff one hundred pounds of to-dos in a ten-pound bag, to squeeze too much into a time frame that cannot fit it in, and then feel bad you could not get it all done.

6. Making your choices from a broken "internal timing belt"? You push to make things happen faster or before they are really meant to. In the moment, internally, it feels right to push yourself and others, but upon reflection, you are ahead of yourself. Your internal timing belt tells you to act now, but actually waiting for later, or slowing down to create a longer span to gestate and grow the idea, project, or what have you, would have been a better choice.

7. Trying to bring all your ideas into form at the same time? You have a lot of good ideas and creative impulses, and you feel like you need to be acting on them, now. You feel bad if you are not making them all happen.

8. Trying to take care of too much? You really do have too much to keep track of and take care of, which makes you feel fragmented. So much stuff creating too much pressure.

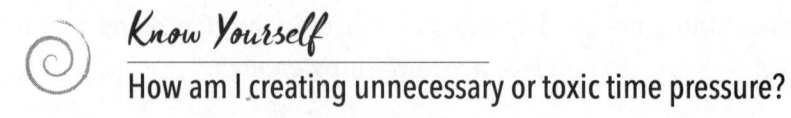

Know Yourself
How am I creating unnecessary or toxic time pressure?

Choose one of the self-induced toxic time pressures that most resonates now and then answer these questions:

1. *What is the impact of operating this way? On me? On others?*
    Operating this way is causing...
2. *What's the self-talk about why I must do things this way?*
    I have to...
3. *What is at the root? If I took the pressure off, what am I afraid would or wouldn't happen?*
    I am afraid that...
4. *If I were empowered, what one small but mighty action could I take to relieve pressure?*
    It would feel so good to...

I don't want you to feel bad or judge yourself for any of this; in fact, I want you to embrace this part of you — not to let it run you, but in such a way that you become more self-aware. What I can share with you is that these self-sabotaging ways of working and motivating ourselves never fully go away. Wise women just become more self-aware of theirs and put support and structures in place to make wiser choices.

For example, I am aware I am a lifelong card-carrying member of the Impatience Club — I joke that I've tried to tear the card up or give it back, but in times of stress or stretch, the impatience comes back. I also know my internal timing belt is usually ahead of the timing of when the world is ready for what I have to offer. I used to push, force, and spend my resources to make things happen faster than was in the flow, and I paid the price by exhausting my life force, resources, and team. So patience is now my practice. I surround myself with people who feel empowered to say to me, "Not now, Arylo." I proactively seek their counsel before setting dates for when to release or do things by asking them, "What is in the flow? What's aligned timing for this? Is this for now or later?" And I've put structures into place to help me set the rhythm for how I create and for the expectations I set, resulting in a much more natural way of growing my work, desires, and vision. It's at the foundation of sustainable success. It's a way of living. I'm excited to share a small part with you here.

Practical application #3: Stop interacting with your projects, goals, career, wealth, and dreams like a mountain to climb, a marathon to run, or something to manage or make happen. Start relating to what you are creating, growing, and influencing in more natural ways, supporting what matters to thrive and giving you space to savor the process.

Would you rather operate like a factory here to crank things out, in which you are the machine, whose value is based on how much it can produce in how short a time? Or instead, how about receiving some wisdom on how to *grow* what matters in the way things naturally grow best on the planet? In cycles. In cocreation with the Universe. Your role is to focus on tending, cultivating, and being in relationship with your creations and relations, like a garden or a field. This may sound a little metaphoric and esoteric, but stay with me.

Metaphor is one of our feminine-wisdom tools for liberating ourselves into new, elevated possibility. It opens up the imaginal realms and gives us permission to explore and eventually embrace a path, a threshold, that crosses us over into a new reality. Moving from the factory-race mentality to a field-garden reality is a subtle shift that has very real-world practical application. Not only for how you achieve your goals and complete your projects but for how you feel throughout a lifetime in which you will grow, create, cultivate, and tend many things, because you are in harmony — in sync and flow — with the natural cycles. Consider embracing this feminine wisdom:

Instead of focusing the same amount of attention and resources on everything at the same time, vary the energy and focus you apply over the cycles of how things naturally grow.

Before I started to wake up to this wisdom, I had never considered that I had a relationship to the earth and its cycles. Of course, I knew there were seasons and moon cycles, but how that related to my success, personal wellness, and ability to get things done in my life, I had no clue. Honestly, if you had started talking to me about growing my work like a garden, I would not have listened. I didn't know what I didn't know. I was moving so fast and had been so disconnected from my feminine wisdom, I wouldn't have had "time" for such things. Now, I cannot imagine living another way.

Once you step into the secrets of wisdom, and start exploring and experimenting in your daily life, you find there is a structure for creating a reality in which you can not only achieve your goals and complete your projects, but also grow your dreams, wealth, relationships, and mission — and sustain your health. You stop pressuring yourself to be more productive and efficient. You start living your life with focused intention and intuitive fluidity focused on what matters, and you feel creative, on purpose, stretched in good ways, with space to savor the process and breathe.

There is so much to share on this, and I don't want to overwhelm you. So to end this chapter, I thought we'd sit down and have an appetizer from this feminine-wisdom feast. What follows are a few self-sustainability principles to consider embracing and one of my favorite harmonizing practices for focusing your days, weeks, months, and years in right timing, on what matters, in the flow: the Power Pause. These actually have the power to give you that time and space you've been looking for.

Self-Sustainability Principles for Prioritizing and Productivity, the Way People and the Planet Work Best

Slow down so you can digest these feminine-wisdom appetizers for prioritizing and productivity. As you read each of these self-sustainability principles, let yourself take in what I'm suggesting through the lens of both the metaphor and how each could relate practically to your work, projects, goals, intentions, and desires currently.

You have a finite amount of time, life force, and resources. Make choices rooted in what really matters and what is in right timing.

You may *want* to give to everything or do many things, but then nothing gets the time, attention, and resources it needs. It's like planting a garden with more to take care of than you have the space or resources for, so nothing really thrives. Wise women embrace their time, life force, money, and support as *resources* to direct and spend. Stay connected to your feminine wisdom (which knows right timing) and the deeper desires of your heart (which knows what matters to you) so what you choose to give your life force to is supported by the flow, and creates a return and outcome (a harvest) that nourishes and sustains you.

You can't do and grow everything at the same time. Make conscious choices to focus and reflow each cycle – weekly, monthly, and quarterly.

You can only focus on growing four things max in any given cycle — a week, month, quarter. When you don't make conscious choices about what to focus on, you lack focused intention and structure, and you end up running around like the three-headed frenzied lady, so things may get done, but you end up fried and your resources depleted. Wise women pause at the start of a cycle — daily, weekly, monthly, and quarterly — to get clear on what to focus on, and what to reflow. This enables the equation *Focus + Fluidity = Flow* to do its magic. Pause to consciously choose your focus in the rhythm of the natural cycles.

You want to vary the life force and resources you give to projects and people over time. Make conscious choices to shift from growing things to maintaining them.

Early in their life cycle, things need more energy, time, money, and attention. Eventually, the amount of focus, energy, time, and resources from you should lessen, which opens up space for new things. Like plants and trees, which develop deeper roots as they grow, and like children, who grow more independent and self-sufficient, your projects, relationships, businesses, and offerings should become more self-sustaining, and need less from you, as they grow and mature. They will keep producing fruit and bounty if you just *maintain* them. Wise women make conscious shifts in how much they give to projects and people, over time, and free up energy and resources to tend to other things, including receiving more space for themselves. Move people and projects to maintenance mode, without guilt!

Not knowing about or not choosing to embrace these three self-sustainability principles is where I see many women sabotage themselves: they don't or won't make the shifts in the number of things they are trying to grow and focus on at one time. They don't or won't make a conscious shift in how much time, life force, or resources they direct to any given thing. So they keep trying to grow and tend — do, take care of, create — too much, so of course they are overwhelmed, depleted, and often discouraged.

As I said, this is just the appetizer to a world of wisdom. I'll share one more morsel with you — one of the foundational practices that I credit with keeping me out of burnout and overwhelm. It's the practice that ended the cycle I was stuck in, depleting my resources and life force by trying to do too much, too fast, in too short a time frame — fragmenting, versus potentizing, my life force and resources. It's called the Power Pause.

In the Feminine Wisdom Way we take Power Pauses quarterly, as personal-leadership retreats near the equinoxes and solstices, which are four natural shifting points during the year. Instead of setting goals at the start of the year, focused and driving hard to the end point, you pause to check in, reflect on what's happened, and refocus. Just like growing a crop in a field, you never know what is going to take root and grow and what might not bloom as expected. What you intend at the start in the goals and expectations you set will be affected by the world, just like a field is affected by the weather.

When you pause — which we will talk about more in the next chapter — you make wiser choices about how to refocus your life force, resources, and team; reset expectations; and choose consciously what to grow, maintain, let go, and seed for the next cycle.

You can also take mini Power Pauses at the start of a day, a week, or a month to help you gain clarity on what to focus on and what to reflow — which releases pressure and creates space to focus on what matters most, including your needs, during that time span. I call this harmonizing practice "Feel. Focus. Flow." (See the glyph below.) *Feel*: you give your heart a voice to state what you really desire to focus on — imagine that! — starting with your needs. *Focus*: then you get clear on what's best to focus on within the time span. *Flow*: this gives you the permission to flow things into different times rather than struggling to fit them in. The power comes by inviting your feminine wisdom to guide the way. She'll find the flow, then your intellect can help create the linear path.

Let's walk through this together, so you can have an embodied experience. First, choose a time span to work with — today, this week, or this month. Then grab some paper or your wisdom journal; press the PAUSE button; and let's create some space, focus, and flow for you! I love this practice so much that in the book readers' kit there's a harmonizing-practice video and card (like the glyph on the facing page) for you. Print out the card and keep experimenting with this mini Power Pause to start your day, week, or month.

Harmonizing Practice
Feel. Focus. Flow.

Choose the time span you want to bring focus to – today, this week, this month. Slow down. Breathe. Tune in to this time span by closing your eyes and taking a few deep breaths, imagining and visualizing it. Tune in to the aligned timing by choosing to let go of control. Tune in to your feminine wisdom by reading each inquiry out loud, and then write or speak what comes. Pause after each one.

1. *Where do I desire to focus my life* [insert time span]?
2. *What is needed* [insert time span]?
3. *What can I let go or flow to another time?*
4. *Where do I choose to focus my life force* [insert time span]?

Chapter 11

RELEASE: **Push. Force. Strive.**

EMBRACE: **Pause. Flow. Pace.**

Wise women choose to pace, not push.

I was recently speaking at a conference about how applying feminine presence to the way we lead our organizations, world, and lives has the power to create sustainable success. Where individuals and organizations can achieve a greater impact, receive what's needed, and focus resources to sustain long-term health and short-term sufficiency. After the talk, a woman who works as an executive coach approached me. She was using words like *feminine* and *women's empowerment*, so naturally I was excited to talk with her. But I about fell to the floor when she began explaining what she believed we women needed to do to make a greater impact: "I think we need to train our girls and women to be more Sisyphean to win and get into positions of power." If you don't remember who Sisyphus is and why this was so disturbing, but so affirming of why we need to do things differently, here are the CliffsNotes.

Sisyphus was the king in Greek mythology who was condemned to repeat forever the task of pushing the boulder up a mountain, only to have it roll back down again just as he neared the top. He eventually became aware of the absurdity of working this way, yet he never stopped pushing. Just like many of us, he kept striving, grinding, believing he had no other choice. What I said to the woman, and I want to share with you, is this:

You do not have to push so hard.
You are not a machine. You are a human being.
Wonder Woman would just leap over the boulder.
A wise woman would walk around the boulder.

And then they would keep walking their path, enjoying the process, pausing to savor their effort instead of striving or grinding away.

"Driving, striving, and grinding" is not the only way to succeed, achieve, or live.

There is another way.

Striving and grinding may have been necessary to reach the point we are at, but what is needed now is different. We could choose to keep trying to win at or survive in games rooted in competition, domination, and accumulation, and systems that treat humans as resources and put profit above people and the planet, in which we really do have to strive or grind to succeed. But it's not the only way to achieve our goals and have the impact we desire. Committed and devoted — yes! Grinding and striving — no! We need another elevated equation, and I have one:

Push. Force. Strive. ➡ Pause. Flow. Pace.

Read the words on the left side out loud to yourself — how do those feel as the way to approach your work, goals, and overall desires to succeed? *Push. Force. Strive.* Then read the words on the right, *sensing* what working this way would *feel* like, in your body, your life. I have to say, my body lets out a big, huge exhale when I read *Pause. Flow. Pace.* It's like a directive from my fierce feminine wisdom saying

"Love, this is how we wise women do it!" If you can't quite feel it yet, doesn't "pause, flow, pace" just sound better? Instead of pushing, you pause. Instead of forcing, find the flow. Instead of striving or grinding, pace yourself.

Choose the Rhythm of Your Reality

While in the past, you may indeed have needed to grind, strive, and push, from necessity and circumstances, what if today was a new day and opening into a new way? One in which you embraced your power to choose the rhythm of your life? You can keep grinding and striving, forcing things to happen, or you can open up to what it looks like to pace yourself and whatever and whomever you influence, love, and lead. Let me lay it out for you:

> **Choice #1: Strive** ➡ to fight; to exert yourself vigorously; to try hard, battle, and compete.
> > Root: Anglo-French *estriver*, to quarrel, from *estri*, *estrif*, strife.
> > My translation: to approach your career, life, and goals by competing, battling, and trying hard.
>
> **Choice #2: Pace** ➡ to establish a moderate or steady rate or style of proceeding at some activity.
> > Root: Latin *pāce*, in peace, by favor; or *pāx*, by grace.
> > My translation: to establish a rate or style of proceeding at some activity that creates peace, favor, and grace. Harmony!

Pace yourself. Pace your projects. Pace your team. Pace your expectations. Choose a rhythm that creates harmony — grace, favor, and peace — versus action that feels like a fight that creates strife. I know this looks like just a word change, but by this point in our

Liberate Your Time 247

journey, I hope you are seeing that by embracing these word changes as equations for approaching your life and reality differently, you open up possibilities for how to do and think about things that you just couldn't see before. In the case of this equation, keep reading for the wisdom offered us by *Push. Force. Strive.* ➡ *Pause. Flow. Pace.*

When you pace instead of push yourself, other people, and projects, you create a rhythm that creates sustainability and success instead of exhaustion and distress.

Let's use our power of visual thinking to give you a sense of what pushing and forcing does to you, and what pacing opens up for you. Look at the glyphs below.

The one on the left is the imprint that drives you to "push, force, strive" — a setup for you to spend your life locked into a reality in which you have to push and strive for everything. This keeps you moving, or grinding away like a machine that never rests. Imagine this instead: what if you chose to drop your arms, release the forcing, allow yourself to breathe, and let me get you a latte! Seriously, let's slow it down and consider the possibility of you making a move to the elevated equation of "pause, flow, pace" for working, creating, and achieving.

Move your attention over to the glyph on the right. See the woman with her nose to the grindstone? That is you next time you find yourself in a situation in which you think or feel like you might be forcing, striving, or grinding — instead of continuing to push, you can choose to pause. Remember what we talked about in the last chapter about the emotional and physical signs of toxic time pressure; those apply here, too — they are the signs you are forcing. When you feel yourself forcing, here's what I want you to start doing instead:

1. **PAUSE.** Realize the choice point you are at — you could push harder, or you could slow down to find the right pace — and ask your feminine wisdom, *Am I forcing this?* Asking questions like this is called a *pattern interrupter* — it stops messages to your mind that say you have to keep pushing and opens up the possibility that you could do things differently.
2. **Find the FLOW.** Then move to the position of the woman in the middle. Slow down, tune in, and ask, *What would be in flow?* This will lead you to right timing and pace.
3. **Choose the PACE that is in harmony.** Alter your pace, output, and intensity. Centered and clear — harmonized on the inside — you then have the power and wisdom to step and stretch toward your goals, at a *pace* that supports you and sustains your life force and resources.

Start experimenting with this equation in your life. When you feel yourself pushing or forcing — instead of ratcheting up your life force to produce faster and make it happen or putting your nose to the grindstone — *Pause. Flow. Pace.* You can find a harmonizing-practice card to help you in the book readers' kit. Exhale. I've got some more wisdom about this to share that I think you are going to love and find deeply supportive, if you choose to embrace experimenting with it.

A sustainable life that supports you to succeed includes varying levels of pace – daily, weekly, monthly, and yearly – not one continuous intense push.

I've stated many times that there is no magic pill or set of life hacks for getting out of overwhelm. Creating a sustainable life in which you are supported to really thrive is a practice, a path, and a choice. So I won't start suggesting now that you will never have to push to see something through to completion or take care of what needs doing. I won't lie and promise that you will never have to put in ten- or thirteen-hour days, work into the night, or have weeks of intense output where you feel stretched as thin as spaghetti. This will happen. Expect it. Just don't accept it as the "normal" *rhythm* and *pace* for how you live the majority of your days. And when you find yourself in these times of intense output or stretch, get *more* support, not less.

Remember the yogic wisdom: stress is a part of life; it's toxic stress that has become socially acceptable that we are saying a big *No more!* to. The same is true with the pace of your life. "Normal" is not working eighty hours a week for months on end. "Normal" is not pushing or driving yourself or others for weeks to meet a deadline, promising it's an exception, and then doing the same mad sprint again, like that rock-pushing man. There will be times you need to push, but just like in childbirth, you don't and can't push for weeks, and once you've given birth, you don't choose to run a marathon and push yourself more.

The Three Harmonic Rhythms: Intensity, Flow, and Replenishment

Earlier, I asked you to become aware of your life force daily, as a practice, to avoid burnout before it hits. Now I am asking you to become aware of the *pace* at which you are operating within your life, all parts. I am inviting you to embrace your power by refusing to accept an unhealthy, unsustainable pace as normal and instead purposefully choose the pace at which you work, create, and operate. As the conductor and choreographer of your life, you are at more choice than you think to establish a pace that creates harmony versus havoc and toxic pressure.

The glyph on the next page is what cultivating harmony looks like when the pace of your life — daily, weekly, monthly, yearly — is healthy and sustainable. There are always three rhythms present no matter what is happening at work; in the world; or with your relationships, health, home, and wealth: *intensity*, *flow*, and *replenishment*.

1. **INTENSITY: You are moving very swiftly, or experiencing high levels of productivity, creation, or stretch.** You give more life-force output, work more hours, or deal with challenges or many things at once. You may be going through a major life transition like moving or divorcing, or a transition like kids going back to school or an intense work project or situation. This rhythm can be invigorating or really taxing, is always extra stressful, and is never sustainable for long spans of time.

2. **FLOW: You are moving along at an active but sustainable pace.** It's like walking in a way that feels enlivening, even skipping or sprinting for a short time, and definitely also taking in the view. You meet challenges like you would a dance partner, and then move on to the next, with grace. This is the "normal" pace at which you are meant to operate, create, and work the majority of the time. Here giving and receiving are in harmony.

3. **REPLENISHMENT: You are slowing down to regenerate and fill your life-force reserves, which is necessary to sustain yourself.** You are receiving, allowing your body, mind, and nervous system to calm. This might be stillness or sleep, or an intentionally slower pace, where your mental processor, physical stamina, and "doer" is off duty. The root of *replenish* means "to fill." Filling your life force daily, weekly, monthly, and yearly is essential, especially during high periods of intensity. Not optional.

Consider these three rhythms and how this would play out if you were conducting an orchestra. If you only played at the pace and volume of intensity and never created space for people to breathe, you would blow out your wind section, the string players would quit due to bloody fingers, and the audience would head for the hills. Then think about your own life, and how you acclimate and accept living days and weeks in an intense pace or swirl, surrounded by drama, stretched too thin, moving too fast, until you crash.

Three Rhythms of a Sustainable Life

- INTENSITY
- flow
- replenishment

Then consider doing this instead: consciously structure your days, weeks, months, and years to contain all three of these rhythms. When you do, your life naturally comes into a more sustainable harmony, and you become more productive and successful at reaching your goals. You focus on what matters, and pace yourself, so your life force does not wane into the danger zones of burnout. And your overwhelm lessens.

Now don't get overwhelmed at the thought of trying to create structure! This isn't about trying to organize your life by some manufactured time-management system. Living this way is a practice of how you cultivate the inner harmonic state you need in order to meet the intensity and activity of the reality of your whole life, dancing with all realms within it, in such a way that you can stand centered, clear, and confident, and keep your life force sustained, even in the midst of pressure. For starters, just look back at the glyph and consider this:

Your life has a rhythm, created by the combination of the pace of your days, weeks, months, and years. To create a more sustainable pace for yourself, start becoming aware of these rhythms.

The world out there is not slowing down. Intensity is part of life. We could accomplish so much more of what matters and make a greater difference, without sacrificing our health, happiness, and well-being, if we shifted our relationship with intensity and reclaimed our power to set the pace and rhythm of our days, weeks, months, and years. What follows are three specific small but mighty acts of liberation I encourage you to experiment with, and embrace, when you are in a time of intensity.

Stop glorifying and victimizing being "busy" or "overwhelmed." Start realizing when you are in a time of intensity, and name and claim it as such.

Small but mighty act of liberation #1: Release being busy; embrace that you are experiencing intensity.

As in literally stop using the word *busy* at all. What I love about the word *intensity* instead is that it is empowering, whereas the words *busy* and *overwhelmed* sound as if you are not at choice as to how you are using your life force. But we are always at choice. There are times when your life will feel and be intense. One choice is to pull out your "badge of busyness" and call out your "burden of overwhelm." Have you ever asked someone how they are doing, and they reply, "Oh, I am soooo busy!" or "It's such a busy time." Or they exclaim, "Oh, I am just feeling so overwhelmed!" And then some part of you colludes with them, and says, "Oh, me too, so busy!" or "Yes, I get it" or "I am so sorry to hear that."

We have all done this. We glorify being busy, as if being busy makes us more valuable. We emphasize the word *busy*, because deep down we would like someone, anyone, to acknowledge and witness our overwhelm. So disempowering. It reminds me of two old ladies with nothing better to do than complain and commiserate, versus two wise women who choose to wield their power of Creating Space, conduct the pace of their lives, and support each other in times of stretch.

Consider what you are affirming next time you choose to state how *busy* you are. Next time you throw up your badge of busyness, notice your internal energy and also what happens between you and the person you are talking to. Look at the glyph below; this is what you look like.

Blurting out "busy" is like throwing up a badge that says, "Stay away! I don't have time for you. I am occupied, and your energy is meddlesome." Or "Come closer and pity me; commiserate with my victimhood." The busy badge pushes away connection and support when what you need more than anything in intense times is both. When someone says to you, "I am busy this week," do you feel any space to reach out or lean in? To offer energetic or emotional support? No.

What if instead of putting up your badge of busyness, you embrace that you are in a time of high *intensity*, and powerfully claim and name it as such? I can tell you what will happen, because I kicked *busy* out of my language library years ago. You will feel empowered, with freedom of choice, even if you are in a challenging situation. People will feel the space to support you — they will text you, leave you a voicemail, or send a short love boost via email. You will feel supported and connected, even if just for a moment, during an intense time. And you'll receive a deposit into your emotional life-force bank account, providing you with replenishment. And after the intensity settles, you'll have people to connect with.

Naming and claiming being in an intense time, without needing to make it good or bad, is so empowering. In times of intensity, you are going to stretch, with great energy, strength, and concentration, to meet your purpose or aim. Intensity and intention are like kissing cousins; we need a more intense energy and focus at times to help us reach our goal. Remember any time you stretched yourself, your team, or your resources to meet a goal, and it was intense. But intentional stretch that creates a period of intense output, concentration, and activity is different from chronic strain, where intensity is the norm.

Truthfully, my fierce feminine heart, who is here to create and cause an impact and design a life I love, loves the power of intensity. But she just doesn't want me — or you — to set up house in intensity and move in permanently. And in the past I have. Addiction to intensity is a real thing that doesn't just apply to people who play extreme sports.

Here's what's important for you and me to acknowledge. When we are in times of intensity, then great energy, strength, and concentration are required. We will feel this intensity in our physical, mental, and emotional bodies. A wise woman uses her practices and superpowers to breathe and move through intensity. She names the experience as intense without calling it good or bad. She chooses to give a greater amount of energy and concentration to an activity that has purpose for her, for a *limited* time span. Same for you. Imagine choosing to meet intensity like an intentional stretch as you navigate the course and changes of your life, versus a swirl that sucks you up or takes you down.

Start with this simple choice to elevate your language: remove the word *busy* from your language library and replace it with the word *intense*. When you are in a period of intensity — intense output, focus, or stretch — or going through an intense situation, say so. Say, "It's *intense* right now!" or "I have an *intense* week ahead" or "I'm in a period of *intense* output." When someone asks how you are or what your week is like, remember: Busyness isolates. Intensity invites connection. Share that it's intense and then open up your heart and connect with the person, with words like "Thank you for asking. Just you asking feels supportive," or "When the intensity slows down, I would love to connect more." Notice how naming the intensity opens up connection, compassion, and curiosity and leads to you feeling supported.

Small but mighty act of liberation #2: In times of intensity, replenish daily and weekly, no matter what.

Remember in part 2, "Liberate Your Life Force," we talked about your bookend practice, and downshifting daily? The same self-sustainability principle applies during times of intensity. To have the life force you need to meet the intensity without becoming overwhelmed by it or depleted after it, you have to downshift and replenish — daily and weekly — during the intensity, not wait for it to be over. Which means at the end of a day or week you consciously choose to shift and slow down your pace from a state of high intensity; through a flow state; and into the replenishment state, where your body, brain, heart, and spirit are relaxed enough to receive rest and fill up. Consider embracing this feminine wisdom:

> *Don't wait until the intensity is over to replenish.*
> *Choose to consciously downshift, daily and weekly.*

What I know without a doubt is that downshifting is just straight up one of the most powerful practices you have at your fingertips. You are doing it anyway at the end of every day and every week, just unconsciously and often to the detriment of your life force and long-term sustainability. You have to choose to downshift *consciously* from intensity to flow to replenishment or you will default to downshifting hard as a way to cope with the intensity, and crash into replenishment using some of those self-sabotaging downshifters we talked about in chapter 5.

Downshifting in healthy ways during intense times is challenging, even for those who have strong meditation practices, support, and a consistent self-care practice. We stop doing our morning practice and stop getting physical-body or emotional support. We numb out and tell ourselves we will get back to the yoga, meditation, morning space, massage, supportive relationships, and so forth when the intensity dies down. For short time spans, this can be okay, not ideal, but if you can at least stay conscious of your choices, you usually make it through and do return to balanced rhythm. But other times, the intensity doesn't die down, until you go crashing down. Whatever your coping strategies are to deal with and downshift from intensity, I offer the following to you instead.

Self-Sustainability Stands
for Times of Intensity

Etch these two self-sustainability stands into your internal operating system, and next time you find yourself in a period of high intensity use them to make the wise, sustainable choice.

1. **In times of intensity, I downshift and replenish at the end of every day and week.**
2. **In times of intensity, I ask for and receive more support and more connection.**

Hear my words, wise woman to wise woman: *downshifting daily and weekly and receiving more support and connection during times of intensity are not luxuries; these are essential.* When you find yourself in a high level of intensity, you will feel like you don't have the hours in the day, or the energy to replenish, or sometimes the money to spend. You will want to revert back to all your sabotaging ways of managing stress. Or pull back on investing in support. Expect that. Just don't choose to give in to the old programming that you "don't have time" or "can't spend the money." Which you likely could make a logical case for. Instead, use your superpower to create space by naming and claiming what you need. And remember, support has a way of showing up in a form that costs less money than you think when you choose to claim what you need.

Small but mighty act of liberation #3: Mindfully downshift in the period just as the intensity is coming to an end so you don't inadvertently make the high level of intensity you've been operating at your new normal flow state and pace of operating.

Many women make the mistake of crashing after an intense period, going with a hard downshift from high-gear intensity to low-gear replenishment — getting sick, overindulging, or whatever their go-to toxic habits are to manage stress. Others take only a short breath — a brief pause — before going back into intensity, versus downshifting to the flow state and creating enough space for replenishment. So instead of resetting their pace to a normal flow state, they raise the frequency of their lives an octave. Their new normal flow pace becomes what used to be their intensity pace, but they don't see it.

Consider how this may have happened to you in the past, or perhaps even now. You keep raising the intensity — hours worked, effort given, resources applied, responsibilities taken on, dramas dealt with — until you've fried your mind, depleted your body, or drained your resources. Think of increasing the pace of your life like moving up octaves on a piano keyboard. You start with middle C, playing at a frequency and pace that is strong, solid, and repeatable, your flow state. But then you move into a period of intensity and up an octave on the keyboard, which has a higher pitch. You play here for a while, working at this accelerated level, and your system — physical, mental, emotional, and energetic — acclimates to this frequency and rhythm.

This becomes your new normal. So instead of going back down to middle C as the need for intensity starts to wane, you stay here, and then another project, drama, situation, or opportunity comes along. Or a creative idea or organizational initiative pops up needing more life force and resources. Instead of downshifting, you upshift and go another octave higher, again and again. A faster vibration. Until one day you find yourself playing the keys all the way to the right on the keyboard, a frequency never meant to be played for hours, days, and weeks at a time. The frequency and pace cannot be sustained, and that's when you crash.

When you operate this way, you become addicted to the intensity and the activity. And you don't know how to come down. Like an addict, you just kept needing more intensity, more activity, more stimulation. So even though you want to slow down and find a more sustainable flow, your nervous system freaks out. It's wound so tight and is so used to being "on" that your physical and emotional body, energetic system, and mental processor can't come down. So, you either crash hard, distract yourself, or numb out to depress the intensity, and like most addicts, you go right back into the intense activity and then repeat it all over again. Even if the space appears, with a weekend free or a vacation taken, you cannot downshift to meet the slower pace, because your system is so revved up.

One of the common intensity coping strategies I've seen is what I call the "intensity-to-indulgence swing dance" — see if this resonates for you or for someone you know. You work, produce, and push like crazy for days and weeks — you live and breathe intensity. To release the stress or to counterbalance all the giving, to feel rewarded for all the self-sacrifice, you indulge, not just a little but a lot. Maybe for you it's food, TV, shopping, wine, a vacation, or _____ [insert the binge]. This feels good at the time, but ultimately the swing to overindulgence drains your life force and resources. The yo-yo continues, repeating the same intensity-to-indulgence pendulum swing, until at some point you burn out and your body or bank account makes you stop. I know this is not a sustainable or smart strategy because I used it myself for years. How about you — what are your common intensity coping strategies? And which are working for you, and against you? Answer the inquiries below, and then experiment with the harmonizing practice of consciously planning for and doing intensity downshifts — it's been a life-shifting practice for me. *Remember, mindfully downshift after periods of intensity, or the intense pace will become your new normal — the new flow state — and you'll burn yourself and others out.*

Know Yourself
How do I deal with intensity?

Recall a time of intensity in which you've been caught in the grind or the strive.

- *What things do I do to cope with the stress that ultimately drain me?*
- *What habits and support systems do I have in place that sustain me?*
- *What way of grinding and striving or operating at high intensity have I come to accept as normal?*
- *How is this supporting me? How is it sabotaging me?*

Harmonizing Practice
Do an Intensity Downshift

During periods of intensity, practice downshifting daily and weekly by choosing to slow down from intensity, into flow, into replenishment in supportive ways versus numbing or spinning out. And next time you know you are heading into a period of intensity, make a downshifting plan for how you are going to come out of the intensity that includes space – days and weeks – for resetting and reflowing your rhythm and receiving deeper replenishment. Name and receive the support needed to do so.

Beware of ascribing your self-worth to being busy, striving, and grinding. Find where the fear of slowing down your pace or pausing comes from within you, and you'll find freedom.

There's one last piece for us to explore. Do you know what is at the *root* of your pushing, forcing, striving, and grinding? Most women do not, and until you are aware, it's darn near impossible to break the imprints that make you fear slowing down and taking the space you need and crave. As crazy as it may sound, there are ways in which you have ascribed your self-worth and safety to being busy, striving, and grinding. Which is why even if you know working this way is not working, and even if you know your body, mind, heart, and spirit are being negatively affected, you still keep pushing, forcing, grinding, and striving.

Because I've been taking such a stand for finding new ways to succeed and achieve that don't sacrifice our health, deeper hearts' desires, and human needs, many women feel safe being honest with me about how they really feel inside. When they drop the invincible-superwoman mask, many of my dear friends and the women I advise, whom you would consider strong and accomplished if you met them, share the following with me:

"I just cannot keep up this pace anymore."
"If I keep working this way, I am going to get sick."
"This is just not sustainable."
"I am going to die if I keep working this way."
"I cannot do it again."

I myself have said similar words. Perhaps you have felt this way yourself? Or know someone who has? What I say to these women, have said to myself, and now share with you is this: You must go deeper. Go deeper and look within at what is driving you to accept this reality that makes you keep driving, striving, and grinding. Are you holding on to some distorted belief that if you just have more of something, such as money, staff, or time, or reach some marker of success or milestone — a title, number on a paycheck, or revenue total — you'll have enough to slow down, stop killing yourself for your work or mission, take care of your body, and have a full life that you actually have the space to savor and enjoy?

Too often, after these cries of exasperation and overwhelm, we put our noses back to the grindstone; set our minds on the next milestone; and keep producing, creating, moving up, and taking on projects, trying to succeed in systems built for burnout — including ones we create. We may hit our marker for success, but rarely does the reality of having to strive, drive, and push change. In fact, just the opposite; now there is only more to take care of and do. I am asking you to choose to do it differently this time. To go deeper. Will you?

The simple truth is this: We cannot give ourselves the space to pause or replenish, nor can we create a reality in which we can be *both* successful and sustained, in part because we've been imprinted to value ourselves based on how busy we are; how much we've achieved; or how hard we have to push, strive, and grind. Or we've been so laden down with the reality of just having to survive, we haven't had space to even consider the pace we'd prefer, because we are drowning, barely keeping our heads above the water. This is true, for so many of the reasons we have stated about the way this world is currently structured; what society values; and the increasing pace and demands on us financially, physically, mentally, and emotionally to just keep up. As we've said since the start, "It's not our fault. And…you and I, and all the other women on this planet, are the ones with the power to change it, together."

The way forward is this: We bravely look underneath all the push and grind to see the lies, fear, lack, feelings of "not enough," and distorted ways we value ourselves, and heal and free ourselves from them. We re-root ourselves into the truth of our inherent value and a real, felt sense that we are held and guided by something greater, of which we are a part. To start us moving in this direction, I have a few inquiries for you. Just read these for now and take them in to start opening a deeper level of self-awareness.

1. How might you be ascribing your self-worth to how busy you are or how hard you strive, grind, and sacrifice yourself?
2. What might you fear about slowing down, pulling back, or making a significant change?
3. What familial, peer, or societal imprints or past experiences may be driving you to keep pushing or putting up with the intensity, as if it's normal or the only way?

I'd like to share a short story with you about the first time I allowed myself to go this deep and wake up to my fear of slowing down and stopping the push. Then I'll take you through a series of inquiries that can help you do the same, if you choose.

I had no idea that a striving imprint was driving me so hard and causing so much of my overwhelm until I did my first forty-day receiving practice. I created and put myself on this practice for the first time over a decade ago to unearth the imprints causing me to work so hard, effort too much, and burn myself out. Forty-day practices are among the most powerful I've found to reveal and break sabotaging, limiting imprints, which is why I still do them every spring, summer, fall, and winter, teach them, and create them for others. Yogic science teaches that if you focus on anything for forty days and put a practice and structure around it, you can reveal and break a pattern, habit, belief, or emotional trigger that is unconsciously running you. Aware, you can make change. Scientists say your brain starts to see things differently around days twenty-eight to thirty of repeating the same activity.

My breakthrough came on day thirty-six. I was hanging out in Canada on an island for a week with a friend — still working, of course, but also creating space to just be and focus on some creative projects that mattered to me. I had walked out to a set of large stones in the water to do my morning practice, which included chanting the same mantra daily for the full forty days.

There I sat, head to toe in white yoga clothes, chanting away, when like lightning, this wisdom bolt dropped in. And — shazam! — I became awakened to an imprint I had been blind to:

"If I am not driving or striving, then I am not surviving."

Whoa. I think I stopped breathing for a moment as I felt this penetrate my heart and mind, and I saw what unconscious internal imprint I had been blind to. If I was not driving and striving — pushing — to make things happen or to reach my goals and vision, I was not going to survive. I saw it all so clearly, how the achieving, the drive to the goals, the inability to slow down without twitching or feeling guilty, was rooted in this underlying fear, causing me to push, effort, and struggle way harder than I needed to. I also saw how I had unconsciously created the reality of never feeling truly supported and always feeling pressured to do it all. Of course, if I was always driving and striving, there was no space to be supported, no space for the Universe to lend a hand, and no space for others to lift me up.

After blindly operating this way for thirty years, I finally got it at a visceral, embodied level. I had connected my literal survival to striving and driving. This opened up a portal to my liberation. Like most old programming, it needed to be upgraded. The truth was, working this way — striving and pushing — was not sustainable and wasn't going to give me what I needed to achieve what I truly desired.

You have your own version of deeply ingrained imprints that drive you to burn yourself out. The question is, do you want to reveal the root sources of the overwhelm, burnout, and struggle you experience that are tied to your self-worth and basic needs to survive? Yep, this is deep, but that is what I promised you. There is nothing to fear here. Only freedom. I will lead you through this next step, to open the door for you and point you where to look. It's your choice whether you want to step through the portal to more fully embrace your power to create a more sustainable reality for yourself.

The inquiries below will get you started in exposing the roots of the driving, striving, and grinding that likely no longer work for you. Do them. The harmonizing practice that follows is for you to use in your daily life when you feel yourself pushing. It will help you reveal what's under the surface driving your thoughts, feelings, and actions. After you complete these inquiries, take an exhale, go for a walk, just let this all marinate. Pause. Then when you feel fresh, come back and we'll take the daring act of liberation, in which you get to use your feminine superpower to create the space you crave, and need.

Know Yourself
How am I pushing, forcing, grinding, and striving in ways that are sabotaging me?

- Where in my life do I feel the push, grind, or strive happening?
- How do I know? How does it feel emotionally? Mentally? Physically? (Answer for all three.)
- What action is the "push, force, strive" compelling me to take?
- What does my self-talk say about why I must operate this way?
- What benefit am I receiving from operating this way?
- If I stopped pushing, what am I afraid would happen? Or would not happen?
- What does my feminine wisdom know is true?

Harmonizing Practice
Go Deeper: Why Are You Pushing So Hard?

When you find yourself in the push, grind, or strive, pause and go deeper. Get curious about what is really going on within you. Set down what you are doing and hold a "self-honesty hearing" with the intention of getting real with yourself. Use these two inquiries to reveal what's happening inside your internal operating system: *Why am I pushing? What am I afraid will happen if I slow down?*

DARING ACT of LIBERATION #4

Reset Your Weekly Rhythm: Create Focused Space and a Fluid Pace

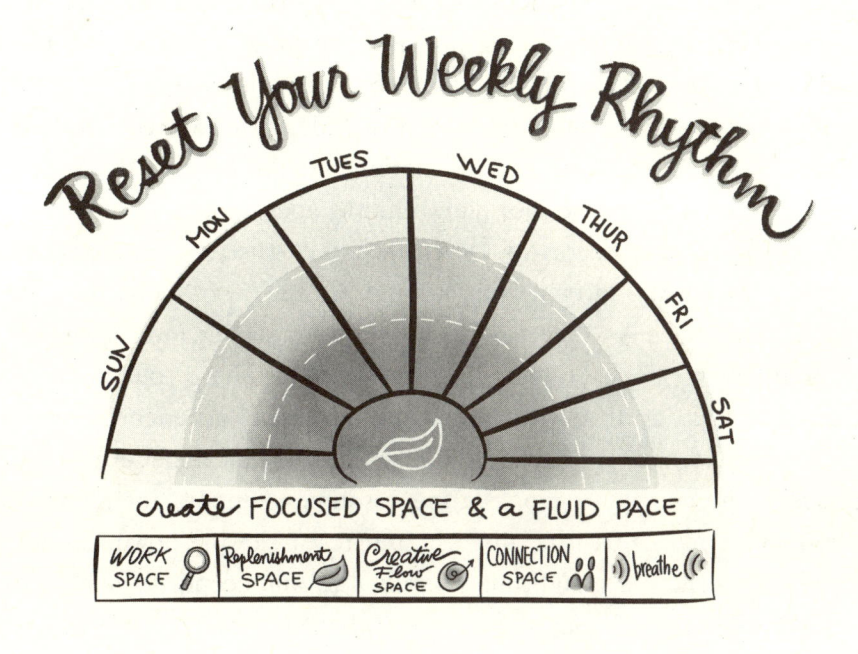

Embrace that like the ocean, you need to ebb and flow. As a human, you need to rest. And as a woman who has things she desires to achieve, you need focused space to work.

I wrote this book almost entirely looking out at the Puget Sound, while living on an island off the coast of Seattle. As I gazed out my window from my writing desk, I watched the tide go in and out twice a day. As the tide ebbs, you can see the ocean floor, as if the sea is emptying itself. Just when you think the water may never return, it flows back in, and the Sound appears full again. I sometimes think that the Universe moved me here so I could feel and see the natural rhythms of our planet. So I could trust this natural flow and pace in myself, and then share it with you.

Have you ever considered that your body and psyche are built to flow with the natural cycles of how the earth and the Universe actually work? This is what makes you a human being versus a machine or a cyborg. But unlike the ocean, who trusts the ebb and flow, most of us do not, and for valid reasons. For one thing, we've been conditioned to value forward-pushing action and productivity over the cyclical pattern of natural creation that includes space for regeneration (like the end of the winter, in which plants go dormant, or the end of a day, when the sun goes down and the sky goes dark).

And at an even deeper root level, most of us have experienced times of scarcity when we weren't sure when or if the flow of money or support, or the means to meet our basic need for shelter, love, and food, would return. We've experienced foundational parts of our material world of safety and security dropping out. All these experiences create imprints within us that make us doubt that the flow might ever come back if the energy — money, time, resources, support, intensity — ebbs. This makes us fear, mistrust, and resist slowing down, resting, and taking the space and time we truly *need* and deeply *desire*. Which is why when the space appears, or even when we create it ourselves, we can't relax into it. We feel compelled to fill it, or do something.

The path to transforming these imprints is to have embodied experiences, over time, in which you embrace a rhythm that allows you to exhale and inhale, where your activity and output ebb and flow, where your resources wane and wax. And things work out just fine. This is the way the natural world has sustained itself for millennia. All life inhales and exhales. If you don't breathe, you die. The ocean waters ebb and flow, and always come back. The moon waxes and wanes, just like your energy is meant to. The pace you work at and life force you give are meant to ebb and flow in these same cycles. As you start harmonizing your rhythm with the natural rhythm, you begin experiencing sustainable success, because you come into sync with your natural rhythm. Which is your next daring act of liberation.

Your Mission

Start creating a more sustainable rhythm to your week by proactively creating the space you need to get work done, replenish yourself, and tend to what matters to you. And stick with it, without apology and with fluidity.

STEP 1: Embrace That You Need Both *Focused Space to Work and Create* AND *Fluid Space to Breathe* Built into the Rhythm of Your Week

You are the happiest, healthiest, and most productive and efficient when both focused space to work and create and expansive space to breathe are part of the flow of your weekly rhythm. Yet you are likely not getting enough of either. Your first step is to embrace and name this need. Read the following two self-sustainability stands and consider what embracing them for yourself would give you:

1. **I need focused space to work and create, to replenish, and to tend to what matters to me.** What a woman can get done and how much she can tend to, if she has "focused space," is kind of spectacular and mind-blowing. Focused space is dedicated time/space with a clear intention and purpose that is so strong within you that what doesn't belong to that intention is not allowed to infiltrate. Stuff and people may try, but because you are rooted in your focused intention and commitment, you flow whatever it is into a different time/space. Without focused space built into your rhythm, you spend your days reacting to other people's needs, participating in meetings/sessions all day, or just taking care of immediate demands and alarms. So your needs never get met. You don't have time to do the work that comes from all the interactions. The projects and relationships you care about never get life force or resources because all of them are sucked up in dealing with your day-to-day.

2. **I need fluid space in my week to "breathe."** To create a sustainable pace for your life, you must have space to "breathe" throughout the week, not just at the end of it. A wise woman puts intentional spacers in her week; she doesn't expect them to magically appear or wait until Saturday to breathe. Just like a symphony player needs to take multiple breaths throughout a performance to continue to play their instrument, so do you. These spacers can vary in length. By design, using them to structure your week creates a variety of rhythms that feels much more like a strong heartbeat flowing through a series of yoga poses than a ticktock routine or stressful sprint.

What follows is how we make this actionable in your daily life. But before we go there, I'm going to ask you to embrace that these needs you have are real by using our practice of taking a stand. You've got to *give voice* to what you need — name it — before you can receive it. Write these two self-sustainability stands out in your handwriting, or say them out loud, as your intentional act to create the space you need and crave.

> *"I need focused space to work and create, to replenish, and to tend to what matters to me."*
> *"I need to put space in my week to 'breathe.'"*

STEP 2: Name and Claim What You Need and Desire Space For

There are many things you likely would love space for, but let's not overwhelm you. Let's focus on what matters and name and claim four needs and four desires, for now. Using the sentence starters below, write out one need and one desire in each of the four realms. Note: You ask about both what you *need* and what you *desire* because you will often receive different responses. "I desire" is like giving your heart and soul the microphone to state what matters to you personally. "I need" is like putting your wise-woman foot down and clearly stating what she requires in order to do what's being asked.

Realm	I NEED more space for...	I DESIRE more space for...
1. My work		
2. My personal wellness		
3. My self-expression or creativity		
4. My relationships		

STEP 3: Create and Claim Space in Your Week Using Space Creators

Each of the four space creators listed below relates to the needs and desires you just named.

1. **Work space:** Solo space just for working, not going to meetings or talking to others. This could be for a specific project or task that never has enough space. Or a project that needs more space now than it's getting.
2. **Replenishment space:** Space just for your personal wellness: filling up your life force, resting, and doing things that nourish you. No work. No technology. No thinking or planning. Just being, savoring, and receiving.
3. **Creative-flow space:** Space for your self-expression or creativity: the projects or experiences you really care about but that never get enough life force, resources, or attention. Space for expressing yourself, not having to be productive. Space for creatively imagining new possibilities. Or open space for doing whatever comes up, no plans, just going with the flow.
4. **Connection space:** Space for your relationships: to connect with the people who matter to you or for connection with

those you want to get to know. Or for groups and communities that feel supportive and sustaining.

This is where the nice idea becomes your daring act of liberation! Now we create the space in your actual linear calendar. Looking back at what you identified in the last step, create space to focus on what you need and desire for each of the four realms, every week, for one month. Put these four spaces into your calendar as an intentional stand for what matters to you now. Mark it to claim it!

Work with your intuition to find the natural flow — feel and sense, instead of trying to figure out or block out. I encourage you to claim an hour or two, or more, for each realm each week. Remember, you are going against the grain of an established routine or the chaos from a lack of pattern. Treat this like an exercise that moves your brain and body in new ways. Experiment for one month and see what happens. Remember you start in small ways to create significant shift.

Harmonizing Practice
Put a Slow Start into Your Weekly Flow

Choose one day a week over the next month to change the pace of how you start your day. Instead of hitting the ground running on Monday or pushing past hump day on Wednesday, create a flow that feels slower and spacious. I call this a "slow start" or a "space morning." Choose the same day each week, or experiment. The goal is spaciousness; the "how" can look different from week to week. Sometimes for me it's a bath to start the morning (yep, I said that) or journaling, going for a languid walk, doing a longer yoga set, having a meaningful conversation with my partner, or lying in bed listening to meditation music and just breathing.

STEP 4: Get Support to Stay True to Yourself So You Don't Screw Yourself Out of the Space

Even after a decade of living this way, I can resist taking the space I both need and crave. Our time imprints and fear are that deeply ingrained. At the end of a long week in which I just gave or created a lot, my Inner Mean Girl can still rear up and demand to know "Why are you tired?" Seriously, those are the words I hear in my head. Followed by the judgment "Why are you tired, Christine? What have you really done?" She makes me feel like I have to justify receiving Saturday as a full day of replenishment, even though a Saturday Sabbath has been part of my weekly rhythm for over three years.

You, too, should expect resistance. The remedy? Proactively put support structures into place that you can lean into to reassure the parts of you that don't believe it's possible, wise, or safe to take space, slow down, pause, or shift your pace. What follows are two structures I use — "program interrupters" and "permission lines." In the moments when you waver or you feel the pressure to keep going, pushing, or forcing, or to give away your sacred time and space, use these. The key is to proactively set up the structure so it's there when you need it. This is your final step before living this into reality. Imagine a world in which *sacred rest* — devoted space for replenishing — was just as normal and valued a part of our days and weeks as working.

Program Interrupters

"Program interrupters" are like station turners that shift you out of self-sabotaging imprints into self-compassion and self-empowerment. Like small but mighty self-sustainability stands, they interrupt the old programming so you can make different choices.

Read through the list and choose one or two that resonate for you. Or make up your own by asking, *What do I need to hear to take the time and receive the space I need?* Write these in your journal. When you sense you are denying yourself the space you need, walk away from the situation and *repeat* the program interrupter until you feel the shift and gain the power to take the space.

1. I am not a machine. I am a human being.
2. Replenishing and resting are doing something. I am replenishing and resting!
3. Slowing down makes me more productive.
4. [Insert your first name], don't mistake peace for boredom.
5. I give myself permission to savor the process.
6. I don't need to justify why I am tired. I can just be tired.
7. I work in divine timing, not my timing.
8. I trust the rhythm the Universe sets.
9. I promise to give generously to myself.
10. I am choosing to do things differently.

Bonus: Make your own HARMONIZE button! Write your chosen program interrupter on a small piece of paper. Put it on or near your bedside table, put it where you do your morning practice, or take a picture and save it as your phone's wallpaper screen so you can "press" it and give yourself permission to receive the space you need.

Permission Lines

Ask an ally to give you permission to take the space when you waver. Succeeding in this daring act of liberation is all about giving yourself *permission* to take the space. When you can't give *yourself* permission, you need to call in reinforcements to give it to you. Here's how.

Ask a person you trust to be your space-creating permission partner. Explain that you are experimenting with receiving the space you need, and ask if they can be available for a "permission line" — where you reach out via phone or text when you are about to deny yourself the space you need and desire. You tell them what you need ("I need...") and what you desire to reflow ("What I desire to move to another day is..."). They ask you "What's real?" You reply. And then they give you permission to do whatever you need, with those words: "I give you permission to..." Find an ally. Share the permission line. Then use it.

Harmonizing Practice
Drop the Obligation, Guilt, and Questioning and Give Yourself What You Need

If you feel like you should be working, doing something, or pushing forward but are tired, know that you need to replenish. Or if you just want to chill out, don't judge yourself. Rather than asking *Why am I tired?* or pressuring yourself, take a stand for yourself. You don't need a reason to be tired or to take space; you need to receive what it is you need. Press HARMONIZE and do this instead:

1. Tune in. Ask yourself: *What do I need?*
2. Give that to yourself no matter what.
3. Call in reinforcements to support you to stay true to yourself.

PART FIVE

Liberate Your Power

*Women hold the power to birth
new realities through the choices we make
in how we live and lead our lives,
and who we choose to be within them.*

Chapter 12

RELEASE: **Take It All On**

EMBRACE: **Stay Focused on My Part**

Wise women know they make the greatest impact when they focus their life force and resources on what they have the power to change and bring into harmony, and the wisdom to release the rest.

You and I have the power and potential to make a great difference in this world by how we choose to live, lead, and succeed in our own lives. I believe that every woman is a leader, if she chooses to be. When I use the word *leadership*, I notice that many women go right to, "Well, I'm not a leader," because they don't hold this or that position or title, have this or that job, or influence lots of people. But there's a more accurate and empowering way to think about and embrace your influence as a leader.

Leadership is not a position given to you or a title you attain. It is a presence and way of being you choose to embrace and embody. Among your family and friends you can choose to lead by inspiration or suggestion. You can choose to lead within any organization, community, or group by how you show up, speak up, and make choices. You become the leader of your life when you embrace your innate power.

Our last program upgrade is an invitation for you to more fully embrace and embody your power to be the leader in *your* life first. To take a stand for sustainability in your own life and every system you influence, from your family to the organizations and communities you live and interact with. To consciously choose to seek and cultivate harmony in how you work, create, relate, and live, even if that means slowing things down, asking challenging questions, and challenging the status quo of how things have always been. To find the courage within you to do things differently, to do what is right for you and the people you love and lead. To follow and trust that deep feminine wisdom within you to guide the way. And then, centered and sustained within, to be a guide for others. This is how we change the world, one heart at a time.

One of the things we've explored throughout this book is our power as women to birth new realities and create new ways of being, succeeding, and working. Many wisdom traditions refer to women as the weavers of the new dream for humanity and the planet. I love the image of women around the world each holding a thread that is specifically hers to weave into the fabric of her life, organization, family, and relationships. Every thread is needed to create new realities in this world, but because we are in this together, none of us has to hold or have all the threads, just our own. This is how we eradicate the overwhelm, burnout, and disease caused by taking overresponsibility.

You have a part; I have a part. We are most powerful and have the potential to make the greatest impact when we focus our life force and resources on what we have the ability to change and bring into harmony, and wisely release the rest. You have more power than you likely know. And the way your authentic power expresses itself is likely different from the distorted images and models of power the overculture heralds. By the end of this section my intention is for you to more freely direct your feminine power and more clearly hear your own wisdom on how to create more harmony, wholeness, sustainability, and wellness — *true* success — for yourself and all that truly matters to you. Let's start with another superpower, which is one of my favorites, and one you and I need at this time more than ever.

**You have the power to make shift happen,
just by the choices you make.**

Making changes. Making a difference. Making the world a better place. Of course you and I want these things for ourselves, our children, and the planet. But honestly, when you think about making changes, making a difference, and making the world a better place, doesn't it sound somewhat daunting and overwhelming? Like more to do, in a reality in which you have taken on enough. Or like *Where the heck do I even start in a world that is so off-kilter?* If we approach change from the base level of consciousness we started this journey on — without our superpowers and feminine wisdom — yes, it would be a hard, exhausting, and defeating endeavor. Good thing you just went through a major upgrade in consciousness — eleven of them, to be exact, with one more to go!

We've been preparing for this moment, to connect you more deeply with your power to influence change and create new realities. In ways that don't require you to push, rage, or convince but instead support you to do things differently. In ways that are right and in harmony for you and the people, systems, and parts of the planet you can have an impact on. Allow me to share with you a superpower that makes this possible.

The Feminine Superpower of Harmonic Defiance Is...

Choosing to defy the systems and realities that do not work for you, not by ranting and raging but by doing things differently, in wise ways that cultivate harmony.

Choosing to proactively create new realities by how you design your life; lead within your organization, community, and family; and show up in your relationships.

You don't ask for permission. You just *choose* what is in harmony. And do it.

Read that definition again, slowly, and consider what it's suggesting. Speak the superpower out loud — "Harmonic Defiance." I just love speaking the words *Harmonic Defiance*; it gets my fierce feminine heart all energized! *Harmonic Defiance*. You defy the systems and ways of working, living, leading, succeeding, relating, and doing business that don't create sustainability, wholeness, wellness, and connection, by choosing to do things differently. In big and small ways. In the big choices in how you design and show up in your life, organization, team, and family. And in small ways that may seem insignificant but are more significant than you know.

What follows are three self-sustainability principles for wielding your power to make change happen through Harmonic Defiance, with some specific examples of big and small acts that all had significant impact. Take a read through each and consider it in light of your current circumstances. Then we'll go straight into a daring act of liberation to reveal where you have the power right now to make significant shifts in your life to release some of the pressure and overwhelm, so you have the energy, clarity, and resources to focus on what truly matters to you, and what's your part to do.

Don't waste your life force and voice fighting, ranting, and raging. Focus on what you can influence and go where the flow guides you.

With so much in our world today to be outraged by; so many things that need attention, fixing, saving, and righting just in our local communities; and a plethora of imbalances to speak out about, a woman could very easily exhaust herself fighting, raging, and working to change people and systems that don't want to budge. Or she could get so overwhelmed or short-circuited that she just goes mute and fades into the background. Neither is going to work.

Wise women do not waste their life force and resources screaming into the wind, adding to the frenzy and fear, pushing against forces that don't want to change, or trying to convince those who don't and won't open their minds. We also don't sit back and accept the things happening in our lives, around us, and in this world as okay.

So what do you do? You keep your wise-woman eyes wide open to observe all that is happening at a personal and systemic level, and you act, respond, and speak, wisely. You choose to direct and focus your life force, resources, and voice in two-step, with the Universe at your back, in right timing. You change how you respond to situations that do not work for you. Instead of fighting them; reacting to them; and adding to the fear, frenzy, frustration, and separation, you stand grounded and rooted in your center and speak wisdom from your fierce feminine heart. You choose to do things differently in the spaces and places you can influence, in ways that create harmony for yourself, other people, and the planet.

I have ten words that sum this all up, which I invite you to embrace and keep with you at all times, like a superpower in your back pocket. One of my students, the daughter-in-law of Ann Richards, former governor of Texas, shared with me how Governor Richards dealt with the good-old-boy Texas politics in the early 1990s. You can imagine it had to be infuriating, exhausting, and really challenging. And lonely at times. How was she able to make changes and not get completely exhausted by the overall cultural reality of the time? One of Ann's mottoes was the following, which has now become one of my go-to self-sustainability stands, my mantra to power up my Harmonic Defiance:

I am not going to waste my chi on that.

Just say those words out loud here with me and think about a situation in your life that you wish would change but, frankly, is like a vortex that sucks up your life force. Take a stand by stating: "I am not going to waste my chi on that." Empowering. Choosing not to waste your life force fighting whatever or whoever doesn't want to change.

And instead using your power to focus on what *you* can change. Be a big *yes* to showing up fiercely when you need to. And an even bigger *Yes!* to going about your life doing things differently — stealth-like — creating new realities for yourself and others, without asking for permission.

To start experimenting with your power of Harmonic Defiance, use this simple but mighty harmonizing practice next time you feel yourself speaking into the void — pushing, forcing, fighting, trying to convince others who don't or won't open their minds — or trying to control something you can't really influence.

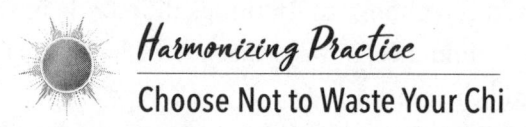

Harmonizing Practice
Choose Not to Waste Your Chi

Slow down. Breathe. Tune in to body and heart. Notice how you are wasting your chi, pouring out your life force. Feel the drain in your body. Notice the emotions being triggered within you depleting life force that could be used in more impactful ways. Tune in to the field – the people, place, or situation – that you are pouring your energy into. Take a deep inhale and exhale, and then take a stand by saying to yourself, "I am not going to waste my chi on that." Release. Refocus.

Don't ask for permission. Be stealth and do what's right for you.

A woman embodied in her power is like a stealth wise woman, not an arm-twisting evangelist or righteous zealot. She's also not playing the "see-me, see-me" game, which turns you into a person who needs to be seen and recognized by the external world to validate your worth (social media thrives on this). She's also no wallflower waiting for the world to invite her to dance. Power is about doing what feels right and true for you, with care and consciousness, without needing external validation or recognition. You choose to believe that who you are, and your part to play, matters, makes a difference. You take action with fierce compassion in a way that creates a powerful impact without having to tell the world you are doing it, and you don't wait for permission to do it. You just do it.

This is why I call this being *stealth*. Not as in being sneaky but as in having no need to draw attention to ourselves or point out what we are doing. It's not about hiding; stealth is about moving into swift and graceful action unfettered. Ranting and incessantly talking about what you want to do or could do, versus just doing what feels right to you, invites resistance, yours and others', into your field. Plus, it's a waste of chi. When you act from that clear centered place within guided by your feminine wisdom, people often see your act of Harmonic Defiance after you've taken it. But instead of resisting or adding in a bunch of fear or chaotic energy, they usually are inspired and want to know how you did it.

You likely have been using your Harmonic Defiance in this way already; it's what many of us do naturally. But without language to articulate it, you can't access or direct the full potential of the power. Naming the presence of Harmonic Defiance in the choices you make is how we start opening up the full flow of power within you. I didn't have the term *Harmonic Defiance* to articulate the Crazy Wisdom choices I'd been making for decades, until I read the words in a book by Barbara Marciniak (thank you, wise-woman sister!). Now that Harmonic Defiance is part of my language library, I use it intentionally and I share it with every woman I can.

Recently, I was having lunch with a new friend who had no idea she possessed this superpower of Harmonic Defiance. She shared a story about how her eleven-year-old daughter joined the local lacrosse team. The boys' league had a helmet rule; to play you had to wear a helmet. Wise, given the ball is hard and dense and doesn't soften under pressure. But the girls are not required to wear a helmet, even though they play with the same kind of ball. Alli told her daughter, "If the hard ball hits you in the head, it's going to be bad. The boys wear helmets; so should the girls. I don't care what others do or if it's not a requirement. If you want to play, you wear a helmet."

At the next game, with her daughter geared up with a helmet, mother after mother came over to Alli, saying things like "I wish my daughter would wear a helmet" or "I wish the league would make a regulation that mandated helmets for the girls, too." The women were waiting for a regulation to be instated by the governing force versus embracing their power of Harmonic Defiance to do what felt right for them and their daughters. When I told Alli she had embraced and embodied her superpower of Harmonic Defiance, first she looked at me quizzically; then she smiled. She had never considered her choice to do things differently, in the way that felt in harmony for her and her daughter, to be a superpower that was influencing others to embrace their own power. She didn't do it to be recognized or heralded as a leader; she just led. Wise-woman superpower activated. Now, your turn.

Know Yourself
How have I embraced and embodied my Harmonic Defiance?

Recall a situation in any part of your life where you chose to do what felt right — in harmony — for you, the people you love or lead, or your organization or team, without asking for permission or needing to share and talk about it with tons of people.

- What is one act of Harmonic Defiance I have taken in the past? (Name it.)
- How did I feel when I was taking this action? (Recall what you felt like emotionally, physically, and mentally.)
- What was true about me or the situation that supported me to take focused action?
- If I could direct my Harmonic Defiance now, choosing to defy a way of working or doing things that isn't working for me, what would I do differently?

How I wish all of us learned Harmonic Defiance earlier. But here we are now, and wow, do we need this superpower! The times we live in are too ripe for distraction and the dissipation of life force. Too much swirl going on out there to dump your chi into or get so overwhelmed by that you don't know what to do. Thank you to women like Barbara and Ann, who gave us these words to articulate and access this superpower. There's more; keep reading. As wise women living in intense times, we must choose to stay focused on our part.

Don't take it all on. Stay focused on your part.

One of the ways we diminish our power as women is that we see all that needs doing — in our lives, with others, in our organizations, and in the world — and we get completely overwhelmed or we try to take it all on. We are taking too much personal responsibility for the issues and problems around us and in the world. And it's too much pressure! Additionally, our fierce feminine hearts, while courageous, are also deeply compassionate, so at times it's almost like we can feel the grief, injustice, and suffering of the whole world, which short-circuits our system. We must do this differently.

You don't want to turn off your ability to see the entire picture of what is needed, and you don't want to turn off your empathy and compassion for people and the planet. Your capacity to see what's really happening, to see how things are interconnected, and to feel from the heart is a foundational part of your power. But you cannot channel all that needs doing through you. You cannot let the injustice, grief, and harmful happenings in the world short-circuit you. Empowered wise women practice this self-sustainability stand:

I stay focused on my part.

Give this stand some voice; say it out loud: "I stay focused on *my* part." This applies to every relationship you have, to your sacred work and career, to the projects you work on, to what truly matters to you;

your part to play in this world is to restore it to a place of harmony, just in how you choose to live. Your power comes from knowing what your part is, embracing your part as more than enough, and then making the choice to stay focused on that part. Embracing and embodying your power of Harmonic Defiance will support you to do this.

Remember the glyph on page 96, of the woman standing in her harmonized field, with her magnetic field strong, where she is rooted in the earth, connected to a universal source, supported and therefore radiating her full presence and power? When you stay focused on your part, rather than trying to do it all, take it all on, or make change where it's not wanted, you become her. You become an instrument for harmony that, through your very presence and what you create from that rooted core, makes a difference.

That difference may look like something we would call "big," in which you easily see the large number of people you affect. But measuring your impact based on numbers reached is like valuing yourself based on the size of your social-media following or your bank accounts, or how many degrees or external accolades you've amassed. The wrong measures.

Part of reclaiming our power as women has to be changing how we value our "part." Some of the most powerful women are not running companies or organizations; they are mothering future generations, planting gardens in impoverished cities, talking to battered women on helplines, and making the art that people need to sustain hope in our intense world. Impact and power should not be measured based on *big* and *small* (another duality reality) or on how much money or what volume of results is generated, because (1) the truth is, none of us really know what our impact is; and (2) the value systems of this current world are distorted.

What's more relevant and empowering for you, me, and women everywhere is to get clear on our parts and to embrace those parts as valuable, no matter what the overculture says. What's needed is for women to stand together with other women who hold different threads and parts, so we can see how collectively all the parts are taken care of. And we can reflect for each other how valuable and needed our parts are, give each other permission to embrace the power in that, and stay focused and feeling like we are enough. And that we are doing enough. We lose so much power and waste so much chi because we are focused on too many parts, or focused on the wrong parts, usually because of one of the five power leaks below.

The 5 Kinds of Power Leaks

1. **We don't value our part** – we don't believe what we are doing is enough.
2. **We don't know what our part is** – we are like a windsock with no pole, without clear direction and intention, or we have never taken the conscious act to explore, articulate, and embrace our part.
3. **We know our part, but we are scared to step into it** – we focus on, and stay stuck in, the wrong places.
4. **We've decided to be the master controller of the Universe** – we do *all* or *too many* of the parts.
5. **We don't know how to connect with other wise women whose parts support ours, and vice versa** – we isolate, compete, compare ourselves, or operate like a lone wolf.

If we could just embrace and value our parts, stay focused on our threads, trust others to do their parts, and work and weave together, we'd stop fragmenting our power, and we'd all have a lot more space, life force, and resources to sustain ourselves, the planet, and the people we love and lead. Let's press PAUSE for a moment. Take in the glyph on the next page to see what we are talking about here.

Recognize the overwhelmed three-headed woman? Taking it all on, you will spread yourself way too thin by letting the concerns and pressures of the world, organizations, and others infiltrate and set up camp in your energetic, emotional, and mental fields. No wonder you can feel like you have no space; look how crowded your personal field can get! Living this way, you fragment and dissipate your focus and life force, leak your power, and lessen your impact. There is a different way.

Take It All On

I HAVE to do something about this!!

...and this... and this... and this...

OR

Focus on My Part

*I KNOW my part.
I VALUE my part.*

My PART is ENOUGH

Imagine moving yourself over to the reality on the right — where you just stay focused on your part, I stay focused on mine, and every woman does the same. And then together, we weave — create — the new way, world, organizations, systems, reality. We each know our part, value our part, and embrace that our part is *enough*.

Some of us have clarity on our part now, others are in the discovery process, and others still are redefining their part. For all of us, what's essential to embrace is that we cannot make the difference we desire — for ourselves, others, or the world — if we are overwhelmed, trying to do too much and take care of too much; focused in the wrong places; depleted; or just barely surviving. Before you can stand strong and clear in your part, you need to know how to stay centered and sustained in this chaotic, changing world so you can tune in to your deeper wisdom and cultivate the vitality you need. That's what you and I have been doing together through this book. Congratulations on arriving here, now.

We have a few pieces left to really root in the wisdom you've gained, and to open the portal to possibility. What follows are a few short but mighty inquiries to spark some awareness about your power leaks and your part to play. Read them, answer them, and illuminate some wisdom for yourself — you may even surprise yourself!

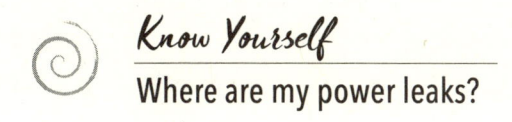

Know Yourself
Where are my power leaks?

- *Looking at the five kinds of power leaks, which are present for me now?*
- *How might I be wasting my chi on parts that are not mine to play?*
- *How might I be dismissing my power or devaluing my part because I am comparing it to other people's?*
- *How might I be overcontrolling (doing too many parts), taking overresponsibility (holding too much), or underconnecting (doing too much on my own)?*
- *What's the impact on me? Personally? Professionally?*

Here's an example of just how hard power leaks can be to see within yourself unless you are looking for them. You remember my student who shared Ann Richards's no-wasting-chi words with us? Well, her name is Sharon and she is a powerful woman in her own right: a talented artist, trained psychotherapist, and creativity teacher, with a gift for invoking feminine presence and wisdom through her painting and poetry — imagery with depth and feeling. But because she was surrounded by women who expressed their power in more traditional ways — politicians, doctors, CEOs, and lawyers — she devalued her part and fragmented her power. In her head, she spent more time comparing herself to her accomplished friends and family than acknowledging or wielding the potency of her art. She wasted a lot of chi on social media, raging against whatever smelled of injustice and misogyny, instead of focusing her power where she could make a difference — using her images and words to create a different reality for people to see and consider, one that valued the feminine. Sharon's return to her power took root as she committed to a bookend practice, opened up to receiving support from a sisterhood, and embraced in her heart that her part was more than enough. The unproductive anger stopped, and her power was free and focused to show up fiercely through her voice and art when and where it counted.

Embrace the truth that your part matters, that it is, and you are, more than enough.

Next, I have a few words to share from my fierce feminine heart to yours, for the times when you may doubt that your part is enough or that you are doing enough. Slow down, and as you read these words, I encourage you to also really *receive* what I am sharing with you.

Whatever your part is, we need you to do it, because only you can. Focus your life force and resources on your part with all your heart, while also making sure you get what you need.

Surround yourself with a wise sisterhood and conscious communities of others who are daring to do it differently.

Imagine us all like weavers standing in a big interconnected web, each of us with our threads, our strings, our part to play in the bigger universal tapestry. Trust that others will stay focused on their part, so you can focus on yours.

Remember that while change and creating new realities unfold one step at a time, you also work in the realm of space, so great shift can happen in ways you have yet to imagine.

Trust your heart wisdom. And stay true to your soul path.

*It's not your job to figure out how to make the change happen.
Be honest about where the shift is needed and stay committed.
Then receive the support you need so you can navigate the inner work
to meet the challenge and the possibility, so you can harmonize and rise.*

*And remember, pace yourself and savor the process!
This is not a sprint; this is the gift of your life.*

If you know your part, outstanding. Stay focused. If you are exploring your part or it's shifting — outstanding, too! This is the self-awareness and self-empowerment journey; our part is always unfolding and evolving. This is also the realm of feminine leadership. I've included more possibilities to go deeper from here in the conclusion. But for our purposes right now, read and reflect on the inquiries below. You can pause to answer them, or just consider them sparks for future exploration. To complete this section, we have our last daring act of liberation and a sweet Power Pause to savor our journey and your commitment to your sustainable success.

Know Yourself
What might be my part to play?

- *What parts am I playing that are not mine and are adding to my overwhelm and burnout? Personally? Professionally?*
- *What is my part to play in the primary relationships in my life right now?*
- *What is my part to play in making a difference in this world through my sacred work, career, and self-expression?*
- *In what ways am I already playing my part and making an impact?*
- *What parts have I been playing that it may be time to release or redesign?*

DARING ACT OF LIBERATION #5

Embrace Your Power to Release the Pressure

Pinpoint the source of pressure you are feeling within you, and you'll become empowered to take focused action to release or redesign it.

The last daring act of liberation I am about to share with you has been a life-changer and life-challenger for me ever since I conceived it and started teaching it to individuals and teams. A life-changer, in that it has the power to illuminate exactly what's causing pressure for you in ways that are unnecessary, unhealthy, and frankly no longer going to work for you. A life-challenger, in that it makes you get real about what you have the power to change and what you don't, and in either case calls you forth to take action. I call it the "Pressure-Point Release," because just like your body has specific energetic and muscular points you can massage, put an acupuncture needle in, or apply heat to in order to release the pressure, if you can pinpoint the source of the stress you are feeling within you, you can then take focused action to release the pressure, receive support, and create space so your life force, clarity, and power can flow through.

Your Mission

Identify all the self-created and systemically generated stressors you are under. Use your power of Harmonic Defiance to change what you can.

To get started, grab two sheets of paper and make three columns per page. The first column should have the most space, as you will write sentences here. Title this PRESSURE POINT. Columns two and three can be smaller, as you'll make a yes/no choice. Title column two INFLUENCE and column three REDESIGN/RELEASE.

STEP 1: Reveal All Your Current Pressure Points and Release the First Layer of Pressure

Write all the things that are creating pressure or stress currently for you in the first column. Do this for all parts of your life, professional and personal. Write as much as you can, so you can see the pressure you are feeling. Consider all the realms of your whole life (refer to the Harmony Wheel on page 49) and include the following:

- Things that are creating stress because they are currently happening or because they are not happening (these can be small, mundane things or big, life things).
- Responsibilities and roles that are too much for you to hold or handle. Or ones you no longer want or just don't feel in alignment with.

- Things that feel dissonant or like they don't change, no matter how hard you try to change them. Or things that are lingering desires that aren't coming true.
- Time-based expectations or constraints that are creating pressure on you — from yourself or others.

No one but you is looking, so be honest and specific — it's okay to include people here. Shame, guilt, or self-judgment may arise; do your best to breathe through it (this is part of the process). State what is or what feels true for you. Self-honesty is your portal to freedom.

Once you feel like all the pressure points are on paper, pause. Read through what you have written, and breathe. Don't skip this step, or the rest of this process will be a mental exercise versus an embodied experience that can lead to transformation. Read each pressure point, one by one, and literally exhale out the pressure it is causing you. This is the first layer of pressure release.

STEP 2: Identify Your Power of Influence

Now, ask yourself if you have influence over each pressure point one by one. *Influence* just means *influence*. You don't need to know *how* to change something or someone in order to have influence over a situation. Influence is not control; it is a form of inner power, and you have more than you think. To *influence* means to align yourself with a higher universal power to create flow and harmony in any situation. It's not about exerting your will or getting others to change; it's about working with the Universe to guide you to what you can, with its support, affect and change to create more flow and harmony for yourself, others, and the world. Move through this swiftly and intuitively. *Don't* try to figure out what you can change; *do* ask your feminine wisdom, *Do I have influence over this — yes or no?* Then put a *Y* for "yes" or *N* for "no" in the column. Pressure-release layer two — you have more power than you think! Exhale.

STEP 3: Empower Yourself to Release or Redesign

Next, for those pressure points you do have influence over, inquire: *Do I release? Or do I redesign?* For those best to *let go*, write "release." For those best to *transform*, write "redesign." We use "redesign" versus "change" because truthfully change feels like a lot of heavy lifting. "Redesign" is about you choosing to shift your *relationship* to this situation, person, or thing from one that creates dissonance or drain to one that is in harmony, and moves you toward a more sustaining reality. Here's how this works: You choose to redesign or release what's not working, *even if* you don't know the how. Then the Universe can work with you — it will work on your behalf to bring you the support you need to make this shift. You embrace this as a *catalyst you choose* versus a circumstance *happening to you*. Tremendously empowering. Expect what emerges to be both challenging and liberating. Trust that you will be supported. Pressure-release layer three — you don't have to do this or figure this out on your own.

STEP 4: Choose to Release the Pressure

Next we use our tool of visual thinking to begin to release the pressure. First, choose one or two pressure points you have influence over that you are willing and ready to transform. Circle these. These are the ones you will go into your life and work with as a catalyst for your liberation and sustainability. Choose ones that feel good in your body — a stretch, but possible and important to you. Don't choose what feels like pushing a rock up a hill or an unwinnable battle. Also don't chicken out and avoid what your Crazy Wisdom is calling you to act on. This will stretch you, and healthy stretch releases pressure. Choose a pressure point to work with that feels doable in the short or medium term and one that is a bigger, longer-term shift. You can also choose just one to work with; one is enough. Here are some of my real examples:

Toxic Pressure Points to Release or Redesign

Bigger: $65,000 of credit-card debt created to start business
Medium: Toxic relationship with longtime friend
Small: Not getting good rest because I fall asleep watching TV

Then get a clean unlined sheet of paper and draw the "I feel the pressure" glyph below, with no words for now. This will be the only thing on this side of the page; we'll use the other side later. (Note: there's also a template in the book readers' kit.)

Draw the circle, with four lines crossing to make a box in the center — this symbolizes the pressure you feel boxed in by. Write the toxic pressure point you choose to release and transform in the center. Then prepare to feel uncomfortable. We are going to tap into the emotion and self-judgment that's under the pressure — you have to feel and be with it before you can release it. Slow down. Tune in. Use the sentence starters below to speak your wisdom (you know the process — eyes closed, hand on heart, take a breath, and make the inquiry). Then write your responses in the glyph as shown.

1. **Feeling:** *How does the pressure feel?*
   The pressure feels like...
2. **Impact:** *What is the impact on me?*
   The impact is that I am...
3. **Consequence:** *What's the consequence of not making a different choice?*
   I'll never be able to...

4. **Judgment:** *What's the judgment I have against myself about this? I judge that I should…*

Once these are written out, write the words *I Feel the Pressure* outside the circle. Then pause. Look at your current reality. Let yourself feel this, emotionally in your heart and energetically in your body. And breathe, exhaling the pressure you have been experiencing and also putting on yourself. It has been there already; you're just letting yourself feel and release it now.

Then here's how we start the release: you choose to let go or at least lessen the self-judgment and feelings of disempowerment you've be holding on to — because this is what keeps you stuck. Choosing to release yourself from these internal pressure creators — which you have control over — is the first step toward shift. Just as you would put a warm compress on a physical pressure point, give yourself some emotional and mental relief by applying self-compassion and self-empowerment. Say these words to yourself, slowly — as an act of personal liberation:

> *"I was doing the best I could at the time.*
> *I have done nothing 'wrong.'*
> *And now it's time to do something different."*

Exhale.

> *"I don't have to know how to change this or have all the answers.*
> *I just need to be willing to shift my relationship to this pressure,*
> *take small but mighty steps, and open to receive support."*

Exhale again. Move your body to move the energy. Most people avoid being with *what is*, which is why lasting change doesn't happen. Kudos to you for having the courage to feel and see what's there. Powerful. And wise. With some internal pressure released, you can start taking steps to release the toxic pressure by (1) being *willing* to change your *relationship* to the pressure, (2) making small but significant shifts, and (3) receiving support.

STEP 5: Choose to Harmonize Your Reality

Flip your paper over to side two. We are going to re-vision this pressure point — turn it from toxic pressure that binds you to healthy pressure you can use as a catalyst to create a more sustainable, supportive, aligned reality for yourself. Over time, as the pressure releases and you start to receive what you need, you begin experiencing less toxic pressure and overwhelm and a more sustainable reality, one that feels in harmony for you.

Take a look at the glyph to the left. This is us choosing to twist the toxic pressure point one quarter turn, like loosening up a tight lid on a jar or a tight screw. The lines that once boxed you in expand (thank you, self-compassion and self-empowerment!) and the square becomes a diamond — which is a symbol for initiating self-empowered change, and moving yourself into expanded possibilities. Draw this diamond on the other side of the paper, without the words.

Our last step is where we move into empowered, inspired action, which will stretch you. Sometimes, this is where your Inner Mean Girl, full of rational objections, mental limiting beliefs, doubt, and confusion, will want to shut you down. That's okay, I know all about her, and I came prepared. She's just trying to protect you from feeling all those deeper fears and emotions — but you've already unearthed these through our last twelve chapters! Which is why I saved this daring act of liberation for last. If you have an emotional or mental reaction that makes you feel disempowered, discouraged, shut down, or even overwhelmed, remember your power of Harmonic Defiance and use it. You have the power to change the systems and your reality by doing things differently, through the choices you make, fueled by your fierce feminine heart, led by your deep feminine wisdom.

Using the inquiries below, here's what we are going to do: First, reveal the support that could help you start making this shift. Second, explore the possibilities of what you could do, until we find what feels good and doable to start. Third, tap into the juice that's going to fuel you going forward — the new possibility you will create and experience by taking this daring act of liberation. Fourth, choose to work with and release this pressure in a healthy way to create a new harmonized reality. For each of the inquiries, it can be helpful to speak aloud or write out a bunch of possibilities, ideas, and thoughts. Then home in on the supports and actions that feel in harmony. Let's do this!

1. **What support would I love to receive?** Consider both (a) practical support that provides know-how and physical support that meets a material need; and (b) emotional/spiritual support that deepens your self-awareness, expands your wisdom, and helps you navigate this change.
    a. *I would love to receive…*(Describe potential practical or physical support.)
    b. *I would love to receive…*(Describe potential emotional or spiritual support.)

    Choose two supports to start with, and write them in the bottom part of the diamond.

2. **What actions can I take to release this pressure?** Name potential actions you could take, without having to know the "how." Then choose one step you can take and one thing you give yourself permission to do.

    a. *I could...* (Let your intellect and imagination speak the possibilities.)
    b. *I can take a small but mighty step and...* (Describe action.)
    c. *I can give myself permission to...* (Describe action.)

    Choose two actions to start with, and write them in the upper part of the diamond.
3. **What becomes possible if I take action and receive this support?**
    a. *I would feel...* (Describe feelings.)
    b. *I could...* (Describe possibility.)
    c. *It could be...* (Describe possibility.)

    Write two feelings and two possibilities on the outside of the diamond.
4. **What is the healthy pressure you choose to release or redesign?**

    Write the pressure point you choose to harmonize in the center shape using these words:

    I choose to release/redesign...

To seal the deal with yourself, write this self-sustainability stand outside the diamond:

> *"I embrace my power to release the pressure.*
> *I open to receive the support I need."*

Work with this pressure point consciously for a full quarter or a full six months. Create a time span involving the natural cycles — like equinox to equinox or solstice to equinox — and use it like an incubator or a catalyzer for you to make this shift with grace, ease, and courage, feeling supported! Really experience your Harmonic Defiance and stand for self-sustainability in action. Be aware of your body, heart, mind, and spirit stretching and transforming. And remember, work with the Universe to cultivate this new harmony — take actions, ask for and receive support, and know that this will shift over time.

Conclusion

Welcome to the Sisterhood of Wise Women Choosing to Do It Differently

Deep exhale. Before we go one step further, I want to tap into our feminine superpower of receiving and one of your new harmonizing practices, the Power Pause — by choosing to reflect on what has just occurred before moving on to the next thing, to acknowledge all the effort, commitment, and courage you have just given. While I do have some next steps to share about how to keep this momentum we created together going and growing, first we pause to reflect, and receive. One of the reasons we feel so burned-out and overwhelmed as women, like we are never doing enough, is because we don't create the space to reflect.

If you don't stop to reflect and acknowledge what's happened, you don't fully receive the energy and benefit that come with the realization that these things have occurred.

Your brain doesn't register these things as real, so it's like nothing happened. You suffer from what I call *achievers' amnesia,* so you keep feeling like you have to do more, more, more — which we just spent twelve chapters liberating you from! On the other hand, when you pause to reflect and receive, you slow down to really *feel* in your body and heart that things are different because you chose to focus on and commit to exploring and doing them differently; your body embraces it, your mind registers it, and you feel the goodness. You breathe. And then from a place of enoughness you make choices about what's next.

Take this short but mighty Power Pause here with me now. Looking back over our adventure in liberating your success, life force, heart, time, and power, answer these inquiries using the sentence starters:

1. What three changes have you made that you are proud of?
    I am proud that I...
    I acknowledge that I released...
    I acknowledge that I have embraced...
2. What have you learned about yourself and how you operate and what you need?
    I am aware that I...
3. What do you see about the systems that you were blind to or didn't have words to describe before?
    I can now see that...
4. What wisdom do you want to remember and keep living by?
    I know that...

Write out the answers, really. Acknowledge how you have grown, shifted, and awakened. Let yourself *feel* and receive the wisdom and self-awareness so you can keep using them.

Then for our final ritual here together, I'd like to officially welcome you to the sisterhood of women who are choosing to do it differently and, as a result, changing the world, through their presence, voices, and choices. We will be successful only if we do this together, each focused on our part, supported, sustained, and in sync with the Universe.

My part to play is to create the structures and experiences for women like you who have the courage and commitment to do things differently. Women who embrace both their intellect and intuition and expand their minds and open their hearts so they can create possibilities beyond what is known, ones they are empowered to make manifest in this world at this time. My part is to create places where you can come to tune in to your own inner knowing, that deep well of feminine wisdom and sisterhood where you can be real about your human needs and fears and also be held and supported in your outstanding power to be a force of change and wisdom.

The sisterhood of wise women choosing to do it differently is open to anyone who is willing to embody her power of Harmonic Defiance and make choices in which wellness, wholeness, sustainability, and harmony are at the core. We don't have membership cards; we notice each other, though, by what we do and how we do it. We are the women who take a stand for redefining success and creating new systems and structures based on everything we just explored together, which looks something like this:

> *"I achieve the impact and influence I desire.*
> *I receive the sustainability and support I need.*
> *I stay connected to those I love, including myself.*
> *I stay focused on what truly matters to me.*
> *I create space to savor my life."*

We run our lives, families, organizations, and communities and influence our culture and society by choosing to slow down; speak up; and find ways of working, living, succeeding, creating, and relating that don't sacrifice people and planet but support the whole of life to thrive.

We don't try to tackle it all. We don't feel responsible for it all. We do our parts and embrace that they are enough. Instead of striving to do more, make more, consume more, accumulate more, blindly following the unsustainable race and pace, we pause and seek out new realities where we really can do less, receive more, and make a greater impact. And we embrace that any change we want to see out there in the world or in the people around us starts with the shifts we make within ourselves.

We embrace that self-awareness and self-honesty is a superpower, and we continually seek to know and understand how we work within so we can be the most powerful presence for harmony in all realms of our lives, and the world. There's more on how to connect with the communities of women and the feminine-wisdom and leadership trainings I lead in the pages that follow — I invite you to connect in.

But first, as you prepare to take what you learned and apply it in your life, it's good to be aware of where you might get wobbly and need support. Take a moment and answer these inquiries. Then write your answers in your wisdom journal. Make these your focal points and practices for the next quarter, half year, or full year — you choose the time span.

1. *What do I know will continue to be my struggles and challenges in staying centered and sustained? What support can I put in place or start to cultivate?* (Choose up to three.)
2. *What promises — self-sustainability stands — could I take for myself and promise to keep and practice?* (Choose up to three. I made a list for you in appendix 1.)

Last, your power of Harmonic Defiance and your trust in your feminine heart will continue to grow in your daily life, relationships, organizations, and life-design choices when you use the superpowers, harmonizing practices, and wisdom you've gained. As wise women choosing to do it differently, we embrace that we are here to shake things up, not follow the status quo. We trust that the "how" is already embedded within our fierce feminine hearts. We move into creative action and step into the unknown and uncertainty, because we now have the power to weave new realities and create new ways of living, working, leading, and succeeding. Here are a few of the ways we "do" this.

I invite you to...

1. Embody your power of Harmonic Defiance. Be a force of change in the world by how you choose to live and lead in all parts of your life.

Make courageous choices to step out of conventional wisdom and your comfort zone, to lead from your wise-woman heart wisdom and fierce sacred-rebel Crazy Wisdom. Cultivate the support and sisterhood you need to do so.

2. Gather women together for real conversations about the challenges – within themselves and the systemic overculture – that lead to expanded possibility and empowering, sustaining choices. Create the space for women to drop the invincible-superwoman masks and speak plainly and truthfully about what's not working. Create the space to do more than complain or create Band-Aid solutions. Create space for conversation that leads to connection and transformation, personal and collective. For more on how to gather women in this way, check out the "Gather Your People" part of the book readers' kit; gathering people is one of my superpowers and what I teach others to do.

3. Run your own teams and organizations as a woman who honors the feminine way of working and operating, and who proves we can be productive and profitable, and also sustainable. Don't ask for permission; show through example how there is another way. Be the change you wish to see.

Remember, your presence is enough to change this world when you are rooted in your power center, your fierce feminine heart; sustained in the ways you need to feel cared for; and clear and focused on your part, speaking your feminine wisdom, without apology or holding back. Never wasting your chi. Always receiving the support and sisterhood surrounding you.

You are that powerful.

Welcome to the sisterhood of women choosing to do it differently.

I am grateful we are now connected.

Appendix 1

Self-Sustainability Stand Summary

Throughout this book I have shared with you self-sustainability stands and principles that guide you to design a *whole* life, in which you are supported to express yourself fully, make a meaningful impact, be financially sustained, feel healthy and vibrant, show up for those you love and lead, go for and achieve your dreams, *and* breathe. I've summarized them all here for you for easy access. Use these self-sustainability stands like stakes you put in the ground to hold you true to your commitment to doing what is right, sustainable, and in alignment for you and those you love, lead, and influence. In times of stress and stretch, choose one or two and write them out where you can see them daily, to keep you centered. Use them when you feel off-center or find yourself in situations or habitual patterns that are draining you. Use these as reharmonizers, saying them to yourself like a mantra or promise to encourage you to start making a change toward more supportive, empowering choices.

For Liberating Your Success
- I refuse to just keep doing more.
- I release trying to do, be, and have it all.

- I can do and be anything, and I have to make choices.
- I embrace my power to make choices that are right for me.
- I trust and follow my feminine wisdom, even if listening to it challenges me.
- Work/life balance is b.s. I am finding a new way.
- I am the conductor of my life.
- I choose to stay in relationship to all parts of my life.
- I release responsibility for keeping it all going.
- It's okay for me to focus on just a few parts of my life instead of trying to focus on all parts at the same time.
- I choose to create a whole life and refuse to accept anything less.
- I cultivate the inner strength to stand centered and balanced within my life.
- I promise to design a life I love.

For Liberating Your Life Force

- I choose to retain, not drain, my life force.
- I never serve from my reserves.
- I regenerate and refuel before I crash.
- I refuse to make myself sick in order to rest.
- I refuse to get sick, burn out, or sacrifice myself for my work, my mission, or another person.
- I promise to replenish my life force, daily.
- I set my field for harmony every morning.
- I connect with myself before connecting with the outside world.
- I protect my energetic and emotional fields.
- I set. I connect. I protect.
- I release stress every day in ways that support me instead of sabotage me.
- I choose to downshift daily in ways that support me to rest and replenish.

For Liberating Your Heart

- I stay conscious about how much I give to my work and my relationships.
- I refuse to give or work from self-sacrifice.
- I stop equating my strength with my ability to do it all.
- I stop equating my self-worth with how much I give.
- I am at my best when I am receiving what I need.
- I make choices that create harmony between what I give and receive.
- I am honest about what resources — time, money, energy — I can give.
- I give myself permission to give less if I start to feel depleted.
- I model giving and receiving in harmony for those I love and lead.
- I receive, versus refuse, support.
- I receive support without feeling guilty or like I have to give in return.
- I know what I need, and I name it, without apology.
- I make choices based on the resources actually available.
- I cultivate support and sisterhood so it's there when I need it.
- When I set goals for what I desire to *achieve*, I also name the support I need to *receive*.
- I promise to give generously to myself.

For Liberating Your Time

- I need more space.
- I choose to create the space I need.
- I choose to create space for what matters to me.
- I choose to take the space I need, without guilt or apology.
- If the system or people won't give me the space I need, I reset expectations.
- When I claim the space I need, the Universe supports me to create harmony.

- I stay true to myself, even if that means disappointing another.
- I am honest about what I have the space for, and what I don't.
- Instead of fitting or forcing things in, I flow things in.
- I refuse to create or motivate myself or others by unnecessary, overwhelming pressure.
- I refuse to accept an unhealthy, unsustainable pace.
- I choose to focus my life force on what matters.
- I set a sustainable rhythm with space for intensity, active flow, and replenishment.
- In times of high intensity, I consciously downshift and replenish daily and weekly.
- In times of intensity, I ask for and receive more support and connection.
- Replenishing and resting are doing something. I am replenishing and resting!
- I don't need to justify why I am tired. I can just be tired.
- I am not a machine. I am a human being.

For Liberating Your Power

- I don't waste my life force and voice on fighting, ranting, and raging.
- I focus on what I can influence and release what I can't.
- I am not going to waste my chi on that.
- I don't ask for permission. I am stealth and do what's right for me.
- I don't have to take it all on.
- I stay focused on my part.
- I value my part. My part is enough.
- I embrace my power to make a difference just by the choices I make.
- I am choosing to do things differently.

Appendix 2

Gather Your People

Use This Book to Create Real Connection, Conversation, and Change

I have always envisioned this book held and passed around by the hands of many women — women who feel inspired to use it to create deeper levels of conversation, connection, and courage among the women they love, influence, and lead.

We gather our power in sisterhood, in meaningful dialogue where we feel safe to drop the masks and be real. Not to bitch or complain. But to tap into our deeper wells of wisdom and vast storehouses of fierce courage. To share our stories, our realities, our dreams, and our true desires, without fear of being judged. To speak truth about what's no longer working for us and what our Crazy Wisdom is guiding us to do instead. Every time I gather women in this way, what I witness is this:

> *When women come together in sisterhood,*
> *with intention, shift happens.*

A woman who feels supported and seen in sisterhood is more likely to speak up, stand up, and do what's right for her and those around her — even when, *especially* when, it stretches her. It is in connection with other conscious, open women that we gain more clarity and conjure up the confidence within ourselves.

Any woman, including you, can choose to gather women together, personally or professionally, and use what's in this book to create connection, conversation, and transformation. I put together a "Gather Your People" guide in the book readers' kit, which includes conversation points to create meaningful connection and processes for tapping into each other's feminine wisdom to take supportive, self-empowered action, such as:

Part 1: Liberate Your Success

Connection: Share your Crazy Wisdom stories. Share a time you followed your intuitive feminine wisdom in making a personal or professional choice. Share:

1. About the situation
2. What you felt emotionally, mentally, and physically
3. What your Inner Mean Girl or negative self-talk was saying
4. What your inner wisdom was saying, and how and why you trusted it

The women listening then state what this story tells them about the other woman, by reflecting: "What I see in you is..."

Transformation: Tune in to your feminine wisdom to support each other to get clear on the right path for you now. In groups of two or three, use the harmonizing practice "Embrace What You Know and What's Still in the Mystery" from chapter 1. One woman shares a current situation or choice and speaks: (1) "What I know is..." (2) "What's still in the mystery..." The other women reflect back from their intuition, "What I heard was..." and then ask, "What is one simple but mighty step you can take this week?"

That's just one example of simple, powerful, and fun ways to create meaningful connection and inspired, supportive action using the five parts of this book. I created templates, a video, and more. Go to the book readers' kit at www.OverwhelmedAndOverIt.com to learn more.

Acknowledgments

*I*n sisterhood this book was conceived, nurtured, stretched, held, guided, and born into what you are holding in your hands today. As this is my fourth book, I can truly say that every book has taken a village, but *Overwhelmed & Over It* specifically required a web of support, each thread offering a special part, without which my three-year journey to write this book would have been much harder, and less full of joy. I exhale as I reflect on just how supported I have been and am — which was not always how I felt within my inner landscape or outer reality for most of my life. But today, and going forward, supported and sustained is the only way. It is from this place I say thank you to all of those who held, supported, sustained, and guided me. I will do my best to name all, but for any I miss, know you have made a difference to me.

First, gratitude to the women who over the past decade-plus have given me the great gift of witnessing their awakening, transformation, and elevation — whether that was through personal mentorship; a retreat, workshop, or training; my feminine-wisdom school; my podcast; or a friendship. Your willingness to drop the masks and be real, to share with me from your heart, opened the doors to the practical wisdom and heart that's here in this book. Thank you; you know who you are. And an extra gratitude hug to the women who said yes to including their stories in this book, almost all using their real names, as an offering of sisterhood.

Second, to the circles of women who blessed this book, who blessed and held me through it — including each of the women within the Starseed Sisterhood, the Sacred Rebel Sisterhood, and the Feminine Wisdom Way. Thank you for standing for this work and for me. Your energy, reflection, and deep generosity opened up my heart to receive pure sister love in profound new ways.

Third, to those who supported me on the material plane to bring the daunting task of writing a book that really could lead women out of overwhelm, without overwhelming them! To Georgia Hughes, my editor, who for the third time used her superpowers to take a good book and make it great. Thank you for stretching me and this work. Deep gratitude. To Shannon Kaiser, Tracy Cunningham, and Sharon Zeugin, for standing with me through the creative process to find our cover — we did it! And I love it! To Karen Faber and Laurie Jacobsen Jones, for the generous gift of using their mountain and seaside homes during the first phases of trying to find the structure for this book — thank you for sharing your sanctuaries before I found mine. To my agent, Michele Martin, thank you for being a wise-woman adviser to me throughout the entire process; your counsel and passion for this project has meant a lot. To all the beautiful souls at New World Library, including Kim, Alex, Kristen, Tona, Munro, Ami, and Marc, thank you for creating good books that stand the test of time. I am grateful to be one of the authors in your wisdom library. To the fifteen women book readers who generously gave their time, energy, and thoughts to help me find the subtle shifts that were needed to make this book as accessible as possible, your insights made a significant difference. And to Katherine Torrini, who has been so much more than the illustrator of the wisdom glyphs in this book. A deep bow of gratitude for the many, many hours you spent with me creating, concepting, and refining — your generosity, brilliance, intuitive superpowers, and spirit of play are woven into the fabric of this offering to the world. Know that.

Fourth, to my teachers, who opened the doors to wisdom for me, especially Ariel Spilsbury and Pele Rouge Chadima. Thank you for being there for me as I walked through my many initiations to make courageous choices that, while on paper may have looked like a sacrifice, never sacrificed my heart and soul. Eternal gratitude for helping me remember who I am, why I am here, and what is really real.

Fifth, to all the women and people — known and unknown — who have walked the path for freedom, sisterhood, equality, love, planet, and people throughout time. My words and teachings at this time would not be possible without the courage it took for you to rise to play your part. Thank you for speaking up, standing up, and being a stand for something greater.

Lastly, to the beloveds who have held space for me for the entire journey this book has taken me on — which *has* been a journey. The saying "Be aware of what you write about" is straight-up wisdom. To Mary McCrystal, for always being there to remind me that I had to truly be in harmony within myself and live in harmony through my choices in order to write a book that could guide others to find harmony for themselves. Thank you for the many wise-woman morning councils, the deep reflection, and the love given when what was being asked of me challenged my own comfort zones, imprints, and fears. To Lea Guthrie, your kindness, generosity of spirit, and deep, simple profound knowing has been a stabilizing force in my life and in the communities and schools you have helped me create — thank you for your presence, which is always so much more than enough. To Shasta Nelson, who was writing and birthing her own book at the same time. Our monthly femma-minds, where we could just be real with both the frustrations and the elations, made this journey so much more fun. I'm forever grateful for your commitment to sisterhood, especially ours! To Noah Martin, my soul partner in love and life, none of this is possible without you. You kept me fed and nourished, literally;

otherwise I would have subsisted on brownies and coffee alone while writing, LOL. But more than that, thank you for the hours when you sat and let me read to you, for the wise insight you provided, and for the patience of being in partnership with someone who has been writing hours and hours, days and days, for three years. I love you every day. To Sahaji, our border-collie soul dog, thank you for keeping Noah company while I wrote, and thank you for being a bundle of love in my life. *Sahaji* means "to live in a state of grace," which is my practice for myself, and my prayer for the world. Which leads me to the final acknowledgment — profound gratitude to Grace, the divine mother, the deep unwavering feminine spirit, the Presence that is beyond mental understanding but that I felt with me every step of the way. Whatever this force of love is, it is strong and real. Thank you for leading the way. May I and we continue to trust the deep internal wisdom that guides us.

Notes

Preface

p. xvi   *"to free (a group or individual)..."*: Dictionary.com Unabridged, s.v. "liberate," accessed March 1, 2020, https://www.dictionary.com/browse/liberate?s=t.

Introduction

p. 3   *collective systems as the* overculture: Clarissa Pinkola Estés, PhD, "Clarissa Pinkola Estés, Author of *Women Who Run with the Wolves*," "Features," Penguin Random House, March 13, 2017, https://www.penguin.co.uk/articles/2017/clarissa-pinkola-estes.

p. 3   *"the dominant and often power-mad culture..."*: Dr. Clarissa Pinkola Estés, "Dear Brave Souls. On the word I've coined called — The Overculture," Facebook, March 4, 2015, https://www.facebook.com/29996683634/photos/dear-brave-souls-on-the-word-ive-coined-called-the-overculture-q-a-soul-asks-i-a/10152805542223635.

p. 4   *For doctors in residence*: Accreditation Council for Graduate Medical Education, *ACGME Common Program Requirements (Residency)* (Chicago: Accreditation Council for Graduate Medical Education, 2018), 33, 45.

p. 4   *Forty-one percent of teachers*: Jenny Grant Rankin, PhD, "The Teacher Burnout Epidemic, Part 1 of 2," *Psychology Today*, November 22, 2016,

p. 4   *Seventy-two percent of entrepreneurs*: Sherry Walling, "Are You Dealing with Founder Depression? Some Signs to Look For," Zen Founder, March 5, 2018, https://zenfounder.com/managing-stress/are-you-dealing-with-founder-depression-some-signs-to-look-for.

p. 5   *Employees in packing and shipping facilities*: Chris Pollard, "Workers Pee into Bottles to Save Time: Investigator," *New York Post*, April 16, 2018, https://nypost.com/2018/04/16/amazon-warehouse-workers-pee-into-bottles-to-avoid-wasting-time-undercover-investigator.

p. 5   *185 have national paid-leave laws*: "Is Paid Leave Available to Mothers and Fathers of Infants?," WORLD Policy Analysis Center, accessed March 1, 2020, https://www.worldpolicycenter.org/policies/is-paid-leave-available-to-mothers-and-fathers-of-infants/is-paid-leave-available-for-mothers-of-infants.

p. 8   *"This new pressure on the mind…"*: Harbhajan Singh Khalsa Yogiji, PhD, "Quantum Technology of the Shabd Guru" (lecture, Española, NM, March 1, 1995), compiled by Mukhia Singh Sahib and Gurucharan Singh Khalsa, PhD (April 1995), Yogi Bhajan Lecture Archive, http://fateh.sikhnet.com/sikhnet/articles.nsf/7a1578096f5ebe0987256671004e06c4/3fef23cc095608c487256671004e4676!OpenDocument.

Chapter 1

p. 27   *The number of people on antidepressants*: E. J. Mundell, "Antidepressant Use Jumps 65 Percent in 15 Years," HealthDay News, WebMD, August 15, 2017, https://www.webmd.com/depression/news/20170815/us-antidepressant-use-jumps-65-percent-in-15-years#1.

p. 27   *describing incoming freshmen as "crispies"*: Nancy Sokoler Steiner, "SAT, Grades Not Enough Anymore," *Jewish Journal*, November 18, 2004, https://jewishjournal.com/news/los_angeles/community_briefs/10563.

Chapter 2

p. 53   *"to run or move rapidly along"*: Dictionary.com Unabridged, s.v. "career," accessed March 1, 2020, https://www.dictionary.com/browse/career?s=t.

p. 53   *"greatly loved; dear to the heart"*: Dictionary.com Unabridged, s.v. "beloved," accessed March 1, 2020, https://www.dictionary.com/browse/beloved?s=t).

p. 55   *And the person who holds that world record*: "Most balls juggled," Guinness World Records, accessed March 1, 2020, http://www.guinnessworldrecords.com/world-records/most-balls-juggled.

Chapter 3

p. 70   *The Sanskrit term* prana: *Encyclopædia Britannica Online*, s.v. "Sanskrit language," November 15, 2019, https://www.britannica.com/topic/Sanskrit-language.

Chapter 4

p. 93   *"inharmonious or harsh sound"*: Dictionary.com Unabridged, s.v. "dissonance," accessed March 1, 2020, https://www.dictionary.com/browse/dissonance?s=t.

p. 95   *Modern science teaches that the magnetic field*: Fraser Cain, "What Is Earth's Magnetic Field?," Universe Today, March 12, 2009, https://www.universetoday.com/27005/earths-magnetic-field.

p. 96   *helps make life on the planet possible*: Charles Q. Choi, "'Magnetic' Discovery May Reveal Why Earth Supports Life and Mars Doesn't," Live Science, July 30, 2015, https://www.livescience.com/51703-earth-magnetic-field-age.html.

Chapter 5

p. 108   *borrowed the term* stress: "History of Stress," Centre for Studies on Human Stress, accessed March 1, 2020, https://humanstress.ca/stress/what-is-stress/history-of-stress.

p. 109   *it's called* eustress: Mark Le Fevre, Gregory S. Kolt, and Jonathan Matheny, "Eustress, Distress and Their Interpretation in Primary and Secondary Occupational Stress Management Interventions: Which Way First?," *Journal of Managerial Psychology* 21, no. 6 (August 1, 2006), 547–65.

p. 110   *my study of yogic*: Kundalini Research Institute, *Vitality and Stress Teacher Training Manual* (Santa Cruz, NM: Kundalini Research Institute, n.d.), 21.

p. 110   *and modern science*: Bruce McEwen with Elizabeth Norton Lasley, *The End of Stress as We Know It* (New York: Dana Press, 2002).

p. 113　*Allostatic load is the cumulative wear and tear*: Bruce McEwen and Eliot Stellar, "Stress and the Individual: Mechanisms Leading to Disease," *Archives of Internal Medicine* 153, no. 18 (September 27, 1993), 2093–101, https://doi.org/10.1001/archinte.1993.00410180039004.

Chapter 7

p. 145　*One in three women*: "Facts about Heart Disease in Women," Go Red for Women, American Heart Association, accessed May 4, 2020, https://www.goredforwomen.org/en/about-heart-disease-in-women/facts.

p. 148　*with great exertion; strenuously*: Dictionary.com Unabridged, s.v. "hard," accessed March 1, 2020, https://www.dictionary.com/browse/hard?s=ts.

p. 148　*difficult to bear or endure*: Merriam-Webster, s.v. "hard," accessed March 1, 2020, https://www.merriam-webster.com/dictionary/hard.

p. 148　*To feel, cause, or be a source of*: Dictionary.com Unabridged, s.v. "smart," accessed March 1, 2020, https://www.dictionary.com/browse/smart.

p. 148　*To possess discernment*: Dictionary.com Unabridged, s.v. "wise," accessed March 1, 2020, https://www.dictionary.com/browse/wise?s=t.

Chapter 9

p. 200　*time is an illusion*: Alice Calaprice, ed., *The Ultimate Quotable Einstein* (Princeton, NJ: Princeton University Press, 2011), 113.

p. 201　*Yogic wisdom teaches*: Yogi Bhajan, April 5, 1978, "Yogi Bhajan Quotes on the 3rd Sutra (Time and Space)," 3HO, https://www.3ho.org/3ho-lifestyle/5-sutras-aquarian-age/3rd-sutra/yogi-bhajan-quotes-3rd-sutra-time-and-space.

p. 203　*as early as 600 BCE*: Nancy Atkinson, "Who Discovered Electricity?" *Universe Today*, March 3, 2014, https://www.universetoday.com/82402/who-discovered-electricity.

p. 203　*no word for it until 1640 CE*: Online Etymology Dictionary, s.v. "electric," accessed March 1, 2020, https://www.etymonline.com/word/electric.

p. 204　*unvarying, habitual, unimaginative, or rote procedure*: Dictionary.com Unabridged, s.v. "routine," accessed March 1, 2020, https://www.dictionary.com/browse/routine?s=t.

p. 204　*movement or variation*: *The American Heritage Stedman's Medical Dictionary*, s.v. "rhythm," accessed March 1, 2020, https://www.dictionary.com/browse.

p. 212　*Feminine wisdom teaches*: Sarah Drew, *Gaia Codex* (Mill Valley, CA: Metamuse Media, 2013), 96.

Chapter 10

p. 228 *Deadlines emerged in the 1800s*: "Your 'Deadline' Won't Kill You," "Word History," *Merriam-Webster*, accessed March 1, 2020, https://www.merriam-webster.com/words-at-play/your-deadline-wont-kill-you.

Chapter 11

p. 246 *rate or style of proceeding at some activity*: Dictionary.com Unabridged, s.v. "pace," accessed March 1, 2020, https://www.dictionary.com/browse/pace?s=t.

p. 250 *The root of* replenish *means "to fill"*: Dictionary.com Unabridged, s.v. "replenish," accessed March 1, 2020, https://www.dictionary.com/browse/replenish?s=t.

p. 262 *Yogic science teaches*: "Rewiring Your Habits: 40/90/120/1000 Day Sadhanas," 3HO, accessed July 9, 2020, https://www.3ho.org/kundalini-yoga/sadhana-daily-spiritual-practice/rewiring-your-habits-40901201000-day-sadhanas.

Chapter 12

p. 283 *I read the words in a book*: Barbara Marciniak, *Bringers of the Dawn* (Rochester, VT: Bear & Company, 1992), 52.

About the Author

Christine Arylo, MBA, is a transformational leadership adviser, teacher, speaker, and three-time bestselling author who works with women to make shift happen — in the lives they lead, the work they do, and the impact they desire to make in the world. Marrying twenty-five years of business experience with twenty years of extensive wisdom training, she is known for bringing new perspectives, profound insight, and practical tools that empower people to lead within their lives, organizations, communities, and relationships differently.

Arylo's work is dedicated to creating lasting personal, generational, systemic, and social transformation. She is committed to creating spaces for deeper conversations, creative collaboration, and real connections that break through to new ways of being in relationship with ourselves, each other, and the planet.

As the founder of the Feminine Wisdom Way, an online wisdom school for women, and Expanding Possibility, a feminine leadership consultancy, she offers teachings, mentoring, retreats, and trainings that have touched over 35,000 people on six continents. She loves hosting her internationally acclaimed podcast, *Feminine Power Time*, to elevate listeners' consciousness, liberate their hearts, and give them permission to follow their soul truth and embrace their power as leaders in their lives and the world.

Her other joys include morning talks over coffee or evening dinners over wine with soul sisters, getting her hands in clay with no purpose or need to be productive, and exploring the world with her partner in life and love, Noah, and their border collie, Sahaji. Visit her websites to learn more.

Ways to Connect and Go Deeper

To learn more about Christine, her personal and professional trainings, speaking, leadership advising and mentoring, other books, or podcast, visit:

Websites
www.ChristineArylo.com
www.ExpandingPossibility.org

Podcast
www.FemininePowerPodcast.com
(or your podcast app)

Newsletter
www.ChristineArylo.com/WisdomLetter

LinkedIn
www.LinkedIn.com/In/ChristineArylo

Instagram
@christinearylo

Contact Christine
Email: expandingpossibility@arylo.com

Resources and Tools from Christine

Overwhelmed and Over It *Book Readers' Kit*
www.OverwhelmedAndOverIt.com

Gather Your People Kit
www.Gather.OverwhelmedAndOverIt.com

Other Books by Christine
www.ChristineArylo.com/Books

The Feminine Wisdom Way
www.FeminineWisdomWay.com

NEW WORLD LIBRARY is dedicated to publishing books and other media that inspire and challenge us to improve the quality of our lives and the world.

We are a socially and environmentally aware company. We recognize that we have an ethical responsibility to our readers, our authors, our staff members, and our planet.

We serve our readers by creating the finest publications possible on personal growth, creativity, spirituality, wellness, and other areas of emerging importance. We serve our authors by working with them to produce and promote quality books that reach a wide audience. We serve New World Library employees with generous benefits, significant profit sharing, and constant encouragement to pursue their most expansive dreams.

Whenever possible, we print our books with soy-based ink on 100 percent postconsumer-waste recycled paper. We power our offices with solar energy and contribute to nonprofit organizations working to make the world a better place for us all.

Our products are available wherever books are sold. Visit our website to download our catalog, subscribe to our e-newsletter, read our blog, and link to authors' websites, videos, and podcasts.

customerservice@newworldlibrary.com
Phone: 415-884-2100 or 800-972-6657
Orders: Ext. 110 • Catalog requests: Ext. 110
Fax: 415-884-2199

www.newworldlibrary.com